D0387680

DATE DUE

OCT 1 2 2001			
NO	Newer	3/2012	

Communication and Society
Editor: Jeremy Tunstall

Children in front
of the small screen

In the same series

Journalists at work
Jeremy Tunstall

The making of a TV series
Philip Elliott
(available in the United States from Hastings House)

The political impact of mass media
Colin Seymour-Ure

The manufacture of news
Stan Cohen and Jock Young (editors)

*This book is the fifth volume in a series
edited by Jeremy Tunstall and devoted to
explorations of the interrelationships between
society and all forms of communication media.*

GRANT NOBLE

Children in front of the small screen

CONSTABLE
London

SAGE Publications
Beverly Hills, California

Published in Great Britain 1975
by Constable and Company Ltd
10 Orange Street London WC2H 7EG
Hardback ISBN 0 09 460250 6
Paperback ISBN 0 09 460770 2

Published in the United States of America 1975
by Sage Publications Inc
275 South Beverly Drive
Beverly Hills California 90212
ISBN 0–8039–0566–1
Library of Congress Catalog Card No. 75–15432

Printed in Great Britain
by The Anchor Press Ltd
and bound by Wm Brendon & Son Ltd
both of Tiptree, Essex

Contents

Foreword

I have served time at the Centre for Mass Communication Research, Leicester University, and Trinity College, Dublin, where this book came to mind and found expression. Between the two institutions, however, for twelve months I travelled overland to India and back where I observed peoples whose lives were complete without mass media and without even literacy. What I observed is given shape in Chapter 1 where I attempt to answer the question 'Why do we in developed societies watch so much television?' I consider myself fortunate that I can begin to ask this question from the viewpoint of a person who has never seen a developed society and am thus not hamstrung by the idea that ours is the best society nor the only way we may choose to live our lives. I found myself when I returned to 'civilisation' baffled at the seeming futility of the discipline of psychology, astounded at its research methods, frightened by its inability to quest for the truth of the matter, and puzzled by its all too ready assumption that our culture is given rather than evaluated relative to other cultural standpoints.

While I have tried to throw off the yoke of my psychological training, I am conscious when re-reading the book that I have periodically failed and have been forced to present data, especially if it has not been presented elsewhere, in a manner which might satisfy a psychological critic. At Trinity College psychology is located in both the faculties of art and science, neither loved nor neglected by either. The text somewhat schizophrenically balances between the two approaches.

Over the years too many individuals to mention have exerted influence on my ideas and thinking. I would like to single out James Halloran, the students at Sir George Williams University summer school in education 1972, and my competent editors, Jeremy Tunstall and Elfreda Powell of Constable. The publication of this book will afford as much relief to Miss Mary Fitzgerald who has typed and retyped so much of it as it will to my wife who has so ably commented on drafts of the manuscript and provided the moral support without which the book would never have materialised.

1

Why is television so popular?

The instant and virtually total popularity of television requires some explanation. 'Overnight a new box appears in the home and thereafter all leisure is organised around it', wrote Schramm *et al.* in 1961. The average American will spend 3,000 entire days – nearly nine years of his life – simply watching television. The fact that more time is spent televiewing than virtually any other activity suggests that television is meeting some fairly fundamental needs in modern industrial societies; needs, moreover, that were not satisfied by the mass media which preceded television. Regrettably social scientists tend to disregard televiewing as a research area, which leaves the fundamental question, 'Why is television so popular?', in large part unanswered.

Consider the medium it supplants: cinema films. For many social scientists films and television are synonymous. Yet film is viewed in darkness, in unfamiliar surroundings, the screen is large, the same characters rarely appear twice in films (until the advent of television) and film relies on the star to portray different roles. Viewers are said to identify with the star by putting themselves into his shoes while viewing and thus share his experience. The viewer has to lose his identity. Now consider television: it is viewed in the home with the light on, family members are present, the screen is only large enough to portray the talking head, and the same set of characters appears week in week out in series programmes accompanied by the same newsreaders. The viewer is not encouraged to forget who he is or where he is; televiewing is not an identity loss situation. Children report that they answer the talking head when it simulates face to face interaction. Children thus play opposite the screen characters. Up to 40 per cent of them, as will be seen in Chapter 3, take answering roles and their sense of identity remains intact.

When we talk of television, therefore, we are talking of a new medium, unlike others insofar as it simulates face to face interaction. It is as though the child were meeting people in small social groups. It is possible therefore that television may bolster individuality. Nor should it be forgotten that television is primarily a woman's medium since women tend to buy the advertised products and are heavier viewers than men. It would seem that television simulates conversation over the garden wall when the washing is put out. We have found in experiments that women more frequently than men answer television characters back. We have not, however, answered the question, 'Why is television so popular?', but we can rephrase it. 'Why should there be a need for simulated face to face interaction with a small group of regularly appearing television personalities?' It is a better question of which the answer demands that we look both historically and anthropologically at the way man lives in cultures beyond the reach of the mass media. I hope in this respect to be scientific. I take Einstein's definition of science: 'to explain the maximum amount of empirical variation by logical deduction from the smallest number of hypotheses or axioms'.

My first axiom is that the self may be viewed as looking-glass, that it is via the reactions of others to ourselves that we establish identity. My second axiom is that to live a harmonious life a person must come to know himself, must become realistically aware of both the faults and possibilities of his identity. Another person's reaction enables us to see the self as an object, quite literally as the 'me'. The 'mes' we view in the mirror reactions of others must be harmoniously integrated into the reflective and conscious 'I'. Historically speaking, what were the means by which the self became known and integrated? I shall argue that the structure of two prime institutions served this function: namely, the family and the community composed of extended kin with whom traditionally the child would have lived his whole life-span.

In the analysis to follow I shall rely in part on etymology and proverbs since it was by studying these that the theory developed herein took shape, and I further wish to point out that many of these ideas are as old as time and not merely confined to the seventy-year-old discipline of social science. The 'family' is above all an economic unit – derived from the Latin *famulus*-servant, and our word 'boy' from the male servant who looked after cows (*bovus*). The structure of the family is one of mutual service providing an integrated division of labour. Industrialisation and progress have considerably eroded this traditional function which may partly explain our media behaviour.

Kin, on the other hand, is essentially a social rather than an economic unit, in de Tocqueville's words: 'Kings and monarchies are made by men, but the community comes from the hand of God.' What were the functions of the extended kin in the evolutionary sense? A 'king' is merely 'kin' with a terminal 'g'; it is a unit of people bound together by marriage and alliance, where 'alliance' quite literally means to increase binding. But how does binding work? We find etymologically that it is related to the concept 'bend and reflect'. It seems possible that an important function of kin is social – to reflect the image of each individual member. Our relatives provide reference points by which the individual child brings himself into connection and comparison with a stable group of people. We find this idea in Aristotle's proverb 'A friend is another self', in Cotgrave's proverb 'A sound friend is a second kinsman' (1611), in Pythagoras' lesser known statement 'Among friends all things are common', and in Nuñez's proverb 'The best mirror is an old friend' (1555). Each proverb reiterates a most important function for the kin or community group; they provide a hall of mirrors so that each individual comes to see himself accurately through the eyes of the kin community. Since 'I cannot be your friend and flatterer too' (Crowley, 1550) it seems likely that individual identity is accurately established and anchored within the kin community.

Moreover, the structure of the extended kin unit traditionally ensured that each child in the community saw himself from the standpoint of a variety of members in that society, that the kin group represented society in microcosm – we find kin grouping of equal importance in primate social behaviour. The child is thus able to see himself from the point of view of the whole age-span of the community, from male and female standpoints, from that of blood relations and those who have married into the community. Mirrored by this variety of standpoints the child comes to see himself from several different, yet balanced perspectives and thus with some degree of accuracy. In other words the structure of the kin group which is representative of the wider society, fulfils a most important function; it anchors the child's identity via the mirror process to the larger society. That structure fulfils function – just how representative the community grouping is – may be judged from the proverb of 1566, 'It is a poor kin that has neither a whore nor a thief in it'. To see himself from the varied standpoints of a variety of members of society rounds out the child's self-concept and ensures that he will fit in with the larger social grouping.

If we understand this viewpoint, we shall perhaps understand the importance of television to our children, possibly be able to comment on the social functions of television (which means quite literally 'viewed from afar'), and understand McLuhan's famous phrase 'the global village'. The real question is whether industrial man still has the same needs as his pre-industrial counterpart, or whether 5,000 years of history were successfully eliminated by the industrial revolution. Nor should the following analysis be taken as a cry to return to the 'good old days', but rather to isolate those character-istics of the good old days that made them good – which provided individuals with harmonious self-concepts – and see whether a course can be plotted in which they are reconciled with the 'devel-oped' societies in which we live. If this appears too speculative it is a small price to pay after half a century of experimental social science whose relevance to the age in which we live is also questionable, as we shall see in the next chapter. My concern throughout is, however, that of the psychologist, concerned in the final analysis with the effects of social organisation on the individual. Viewed from this standpoint we shall hopefully be better able to understand the very important part that television plays for children in mass societies.

What follows is a comparison in terms of opposites between social life as it was organised in this country less than two centuries ago. Lest the reader should think what I call the village style is idealistic, it is worth mentioning that prior to the industrial revolution there were no less than 111 saint's days in each year, for the greater part of the population a four-day working week was an actuality.

I must however make it clear that the following analysis refers to both village and industrial societies in general, rather than in specific terms. Endless variation can be found in both types of society and my concern here is to abstract those essential characteristics which in large part are relatively universal in both types of society. Exceptions will abound and no one society will entirely fit

VILLAGE	INDUSTRIAL CITY
In terms of social organisation	
1. Few specialisations	Many specialisations
2. Each man an artisan or artist	Artisan and art skills the prerogative of the specialised few
3. Leadership rotates as community group concentrates on different tasks	Leadership fixed formally, but informally still rotates
4. Rhythm of life ever changing	Rhythm of life invariable
5. Little awareness of time and space as consumable commodities	Consumption of time and space as commodities
6. Tolerance for eccentricity	Eccentricity viewed as abnormal
7. Virtually no privacy possible	Privacy much valued
8. Communication within the family between different ages	Communication outside the family from like to like
9. Premium on wisdom	Premium on education
10. For the most part news immediately relevant since the individual must act upon it	For the most part news is removed from the province of the individual since he cannot act upon it
11. Whole of social organisation visible and can be learnt	Whole cannot be seen and learnt first hand
12. Organic in small scale; interdependence seen and felt	Organic only in large scale; interdependence taught but not experienced

into the following typology, but I have in mind on the one hand the distinct community of the Welsh village in the last century encapsulated in the account by Rees (1950) and on the other hand life as we know it in a suburban housing estate in a regional city. Both descriptions in large degree are 'ideal' types and the analysis can be accused of romanticising the village style and blackening the industrial style of life. Yet to live without ideals, merely to academically catalogue differences between societies, leads inevitably to both cynicism and to an anatomical list of village societies ignoring the heart.

It is hoped that the comparison between the two life styles makes evident the fact that in the village life is a cohesive integrated whole – no doubt too intimate and too constraining for modern man – whereas life in the industrial city can be fragmentary and discontinuous. The thesis presented here is that television, by exposing disparate individuals to the same familiar content, which is remarkably repetitive, does in part restore a village type of community. A better example is perhaps local radio which was conceived as a village pump from which local news could be disseminated. As far as consequences to the individual are concerned it is likely that he will become alienated, that is, made to feel an alien or outsider, when he can no longer see himself as a part of an organic whole. Individuals are no longer forced to engage in the types of self-analysis which constant contact with the same set of people is likely to force upon them, and which, it is argued, results in an integrated self-concept. It is possible in the industrial city environment to avoid this painful process, but to avoid this type of analysis is merely to escape from it, and this results in a fragmented and disparate self-concept.

In the paragraphs that follow I shall try briefly to elaborate each of the points listed and relate them to television.

1. It is important to understand just how specialisation affects the individual in relation to the community of people in which his identity is anchored. A community can support a small number of task specialists when its members are engaged in the same activities; but a community of specialists has no basis in common, has few areas of shared experience. Specialisation requires initiation by trade guilds, once indeed called mysteries, into skills generally kept trade secrets from other members of the community, often by means of inventing a language unintelligible to outsiders. Other members of the community are encouraged to rely on specialists and this can have harmful consequences for the individual, since he no longer pays attention to his own health when doctors are available, to the health of his animals when veterinary surgeons are available, to the welfare of his grandparents when social workers are available, and to the education of his children when teachers are available. The law would

appear to be that the more specialisation there is, the less people are encouraged to be responsible themselves, with the consequent result that they cease to pay attention outside their own area of speciality. In many village societies you find many people able to perform a large number of skills which we today delegate to the specialist. Each man must therefore extend himself in each activity, pay close attention to what he is doing, with the likely result that the self is used to the full and is rounded out.

Yet television can lay bare the mysteries of the specialist. To see the politician, the university lecturer, the policeman, the doctor or the plumber's mate on the screen is to immediately reveal the human animal which has been concealed behind the press release, the printed word, the single guise of the uniform, the white coat and the blue overall. The disguise of the specialism is all the more penetrated when the televiewer apparently meets these individuals in the illusion of intimacy, where the specialist is met as though in a face to face conversation with the self-conscious viewer. Viewers will discover, particularly in dramatic serials, the human side of the specialist and rediscover that they face exactly the same problems as does the viewer; for example, the wayward spouse, the disgruntled son and financial problems. Indeed many live specialists will be seen as unrounded individuals by means of pseudo-social interaction with them when they appear on the television screen. Hence perhaps the booming industry of public relations which attempts to create the desired image by means of a carefully trained spokesman.

2. While an ideal type, in village societies each man is an artist or artisan, in the true sense of the word 'art', 'to fit or join together'. In marked contrast individuals in modern industrial societies are excluded from art and artisan activities because they are now the prerogative of the professional few. A general rule might be that once a skill is professionalised, those excluded from that activity no longer have the self-confidence necessary to engage in that activity especially when they can compare themselves with the professionals on view nightly. In less well developed societies parents take pride in preparing (etymologically akin to parent) their children in the cultural traditions of story, music and song. For specialised individuals in developed societies, unaware that they can express themselves via the medium of art – a most important means of self-expression – the result can be further alienation from the self which becomes a bottleneck of inexpressible feelings.

Each successive mass medium has provided for greater and greater audience response from self-conscious individuals – from total immersion and identity loss in book and film to television where viewers with their sense of identity intact play opposite recognised characters (a theme developed in Chapter 3), to local radio and local television which demand community involvement. Viewed in this way one can understand how the mass media have developed, or almost returned to theatre where characters frequently address their audience directly. But there are still major shortcomings to be overcome. Increased public access to the mass media should erode the damaging ethos that art is the prerogative of the specialised few.

3. In village societies leadership is far from fixed and far from a position of dominance. The data from anthropology tells us that leaders often serve their followers and that it is not a position particularly sought after. Within village communities leadership rotates as different tasks demand different leaders. While most people will be capable of performing the same range of skills, one person is likely to be better than the others at a particular skill; thus the leader during ploughing is not necessarily the same man as the leader during house building. The repetitive life-style of industrial societies has led to leadership being fixed and associated with status. The boss expects deference on all social occasions; although inevitably one finds an informal set of statuses in any group which has a formally organised structure. The consequences of formalised leadership on the individuals who make up the group are that they learn only subservience roles and are unable to command respect as individuals, with a consequent increase in alienation. Moreover, should individuals find themselves in a position where they are unable to make their own laws; where laws are made by those of high status, it would seem likely to lead to anomie, if I correctly understand that term. In contrast, rotating leadership within the village is likely to lead to a situation where each man is in part responsible for the formal or informal laws which will govern the community. Almost inevitably, the individual who finds himself unable to command respect is likely to be motivated to escape from an alienating environment and perhaps watch television. As a friend once expressed it: 'After a day of zombie work, I feel like a zombie evening'.

4. In the village the rhythm of life is constantly changing, whereas in industrial cities the rhythms are fixed and invariant. This is a most important difference between the two life-styles, for it means that for the mass of the world there is in the villages, no work *per se*, and no leisure *per se*, but rather time when things must be done and times when there is less to do. Concepts such as work time, leisure time and overtime and the various ways we are accustomed to divide up time are non-existent in village communities, where there is a stream-like flow in the rhythm of life. Developed man, having completed his hours of work, feels that he is entitled to be entertained. Television may perhaps satisfy this need above all others; the feeling with the day's work over we are entitled to sit back and be amused. And, of

course, specialisation encourages a search for being amused by the professional rather than seeking to amuse oneself.

5. In essence, therefore, time becomes for developed man something to be consumed – that is, destructively used up. In village societies neither time nor space are thought of as compartmentalised entities. Internal space is shelter, its function undefined, and consequently is most divergently used unlike the bedrooms, sitting-rooms, offices and kitchens of developed man. While obvious, it is worth stressing what the consequences of such conceptions are likely to be for individual thought. Different 'times' and different 'spaces' become associated with differing mental poises; periods and places of activity and passivity. Work time and work space become a stage on which the individual must act in a different way from his acts in home time and home space. Moreover because he acts, as it were, on different stages he is likely to be guided by past conditioning as applied to each stage, rather than by detailed scrutiny or awareness of each situation. It may be guessed that the media provide a relatively constant backdrop in lives of increasing compartmentalisation.

6. People in village societies are prepared to tolerate and accommodate eccentricity and other unusual behaviour. Within the village there is a place for the idiot and his family assume responsibility for him. Deviancy and abnormality are not hidden away from public view as tends to happen when such people are institutionalised in industrial societies. Deprived of the sight of abnormality in the city, people are unduly frightened of it, possibly because it tends to remind them of their own frailty. Television, however, does provide sight of second-hand deviancy and abnormality, reassuringly distant in drama and relentlessly tracked down, cured or otherwise dealt with by the televised police and medical forces.

7. In the village practically all events are public knowledge, a situation which modern man might find intolerable. Clearly when the whole is visible it is difficult for any individual to have secrets, which is presumably why crime cannot escape detection in intimate communities. The unhappy connotation of the original meaning of the word 'private' – deprived – has been reversed in modern usage. This century has, in many ways, been the age of the individual in retreat from his fellows, perhaps epitomised in the concept of the semi-detached house. Paradoxically we find television and other mass media playing their part here. From the shelter of our hard earned privacy, the media provide us with the public lives of the screen community. Is it a disturbing research finding that in a recent survey in Canada people could list more television characters known to them than personal acquaintances? It is a characteristic of televiewers to gossip about the occurrences of fictional characters in television serials, for teenagers to gossip about the antics of pop

stars as did the Hollywood generation gossip about the private lives of film stars made noisily public. But with television the intimacy is increased; the feeling is that these persons are really known to the viewer and it is their activities on the screen which are the talking points, not their lives off the screen – in direct contrast to Hollywood. The gossip is now as though the screen events were taking place down the road. In this unique way television affords us privacy while at the same time providing our public gossip. Nor should it be forgotten that two viewers who have seen the same programme can at least talk about those characters, which provides a basis for discussion in both university common-room and factory floor alike.

8. In less well developed societies the family is of critical importance, and within the family there is a great deal of communication between the different ages. In modern developed societies family members are increasingly unable to bridge generation gaps, that is, communicate across ages. Rather they choose to communicate with equals from outside the family grouping. In village societies a member identifies himself by his kinship relations and by his family. In modern societies a person identifies himself by his occupation and his education; seemingly a small difference but one which indicates the erosion of the family grouping. Learning to communicate is of critical importance for individual development, since communication is a give-and-take process whereby two individuals come to understand the viewpoint of the other. Within the village and extended kin group each individual communicates and hence comes to understand the viewpoint of the old, the young, the parent and the middle-aged. Moreover, he can see the total life experience encapsulated within the kin group, and can see the roles he is likely to play in the future. If the world is a stage, the member of the extended kin group observes all the parts he is likely to play in later life.

Obviously in industrial societies, mobility tends to break up the extended kin grouping. Housing estates become nappy rows where young parents are virtually separated from the outside world. Small wonder the erring Doctor Spock is relied upon for child care and small wonder these parents are unsure as to how to bring up their children. The old in industrial societies can become equally segregated, often living alone and apart, the wisdom they have culled from life experience of little use. In village societies the experience of the old is available to the young.

9. The erosion of the organic extended kin grouping, perhaps the earliest and most efficient form of social security, throws new emphasis on education. Education is not only the spring-board to mobility but mobility also requires education to sustain the isolated nuclear family in its new location. The reasons for this tendency are complex, but the young today learn what their elders have never

heard of, the rate of change is so fast that parental experience is no longer thought relevant to new situations. Yet it should not be forgotten that to 'educate' is to 'lead out' the best potentialities of the individual. We tend perhaps to educate so that people may find employment, but tend to neglect the education of such basic skills as managing a family and bringing up children. Nor should it be forgotten that television can afford an opportunity to view organic, if idealistic communities, and for many it will provide their only chance to see both young and old in action. Television can act as a window on to the larger range of social relationships from the limited perspective of the isolated nuclear family. The one programme which Schramm *et al.* report disturbed delinquent boys was family serials. Similarly as we shall see in Chapter 4, many well educated viewers take advice concerning child-rearing and other domestic problems from the mass media.

10. In village societies talking is a most important activity, concerned with what people see and hear, the harvest, the traditional stories which transmit cultural values, and the people that one knows. For the main part what news there is will be immediately relevant to the individual concerned. The word 'gossip' having as its etymological root the sense 'God sib' or 'related to each other under God'. For the individual in mass societies, news is unlikely to be relevant in the sense that he can do anything about the event, quite the reverse of the village. News is thus removed from the province of the individual and it can be argued that it becomes of an escapist nature, so that it is no longer relevant to everyday life. News has to be out of the ordinary, and attract attention, and yet it is also ephemeral and transient, often no more than the journalists' conception (hotel fires in Korea and Howard Hughes). It seems likely that the individual with access to news beyond his effective sphere of influence will perhaps be alienated from the society which generates the news. But perhaps more worrying is the notion that whereas in the past the individual in the village necessarily paid attention to his environment because he was concerned to know what was going on, because events actually concerned the group of which he was a member, urbanised man is likely to use fundamentally distanced news as background, not worthy of full attention, which might explain the somewhat opiate quantity of news that we attend to.

Yet the fact remains that while the news is forgotten, the newsreaders are not. Almost by dint of their frequency of occurrence the newsreaders become celebrities (literally occurring frequently), and the public demand to see them in other guises. In a very real sense the newsreaders become gossip agents akin to the village postmen before them.

11 & 12. Finally with regard to social organisation it is repeatedly

apparent that in the 'single' stage village community the total social organisation is visible, and it is easy to see how social roles are interrelated. Any individual can see the models of likely future social behaviour, can see all the roles he is likely to occupy in the future and he has ample time to practise these roles by means of play. He knows he is a part of the social organisation and can see how he is going to fit in the future. Moreover his contact with fellow actors is lifelong, which will force frequent self-appraisal during interaction. In marked contrast a member of a developed society can shift from stage to stage, can avoid those actors likely to force painful self-analysis and can use the personality as a mask for stage management without having to integrate the self behind the mask. His concern is with the presentation of self, rather than the self-analysis forced in 'primitive' communities. Moreover industrial societies are not totally visible, and it is not clear how the parts interrelate. The individual in developed societies learns specific behaviours for each stage with a consequent identity confusion. The assumption here is that for a person to live a full and complete life he must to a large degree know himself.

We may perhaps understand that people attend to television for two seemingly paradoxical reasons. First, via television they can get away from the alienating society – to escape by being entertained, amused and thus reduce their alienation. Yet secondly, they can use television to take part in society in the familiar and neo-realistic society of the television serials, which often portray roles not visible in the real society in which they live.

A society totally visible with nothing to hide is whole, that is, not divided and healthy. The individual is therefore not divided – the literal meaning. 'All human life is there', quotes the *News of the World*. The mass media of television could be, and is, a powerful tool to render society visible. Its eyes can probe where individuals fear to tread and the likely result could be a decrease in the mystique with which institutions surround themselves. As Tolstoy said when film was introduced, 'What a powerful tool for showing how the peoples of the world live, but it will be prostituted like everything else.' The novel took centuries to perfect, television in its short life has hardly begun to develop. Properly used television could make us world citizens, if it were used to the full. Properly used television could show models of each social role such as are seen in the village community. But as a mass medium television cannot force self-evaluation, although it can bolster individual identity. Televiewing is not an identity loss situation, but neither does it provide the viewer with a mirror image of self – that essential feedback necessary for rounded development. Television as a personal medium, or community medium could, however, also serve this latter function.

We now turn to the consequences for the individual of living in an industrial as contrasted with a village society. The comparison is between the way we live contrasted with the way our grandparents lived and the way our world neighbours live.

VILLAGE SOCIETY	INDUSTRIAL SOCIETY
In terms of consequences to the individual	
1. Part of a visible community, interdependence clearly visible	Interdependence not clearly visible
2. Young learn by watching and doing. Stages of development marked by ritual. Young have well defined reciprocal relationships within the family	Schools teach skills in abstract stages marked by educational attainments. Young learn primarily subservient roles, suddenly expected to be adult
3. Self-concept fixed and stable in relation to the same group in the same place	Self-concept not stable or fixed since a member of many groups in different places
4. Every social role acted on a single stage, roles defined by specific conduct	Social roles enacted on different stages – fewer opportunity for reconciliation between roles
5. Communality of experience within the community greater for each individual than his separate experience	Individuals' separate experience thought of as greater than the communality of experience
6. Optimal use of resources, including the self	Far from optimal use of resources, including the self
7. Great need for empathy became interdependence known and felt	Less need for empathy, since individuals are more isolated

1. As already intimated the individual born into a recognisable community is immediately aware of his part in the social order and his work is recognised as valuable and rewarded. He is aware that his position is interdependent with the others. In most village societies both the old and young contribute to the total community by their labour and wisdom. In modern societies the position of the old and young is ambiguous. Children play little part in community affairs. With no role other than school child – a position of dependency – the child plays little part even in the family. Consequently there is little need for parents to establish reciprocal relationships with their children since there is little reciprocity between the two roles. This is most unfortunate since in other cultures the parents listen to their children because the interdependence is known and perceived. In many societies children and grandparents enjoy a close and reciprocal relationship, whereby the wisdom of old age and the freshness of the child is interwoven. In our society there is a great danger that these

two groups live in different places in isolation, with the mass media providing the only sight of the other. Grandparents and grand-children so much a part of the family serials viewed on television have become isolated in such ways as are unthinkable in primitive communities.

2. The child born into a recognisable community observes the social roles he will occupy in the future. He observes that social roles are marked off by manners, etiquette and ritual. Each pro-gression in the child's identity development is marked off by ritual to emphasise the transition and to demonstrate to him that he now occupies a new place in the pattern of social relationships. By way of contrast, prior to television, the greater part of industrial societies remained invisible, especially to children attending schools during the larger part of the day. Many children do not know what their fathers do since they have never seen them at work. Instead, children are taught in 'abstract' for skills as yet invisible to them. They are unable for sixteen years to practise what they learn as wage-earners. Unlike the village the progression to adult roles is abrupt – from school to work. Progress is marked off by educational attainment with little change in status outside school – for which they often will wear the same uniform. It is, therefore, not surprising to learn that theorists have argued that there are two mutually exclusive points of teenage reference: the school, where instrumental – that is, taught – roles are learnt; and the mass media dominated culture of the adolescent peer group which allows for self-expression. It is not surprising that so many children opt for the latter. The mass media show the adolescent what to do to be a recognisably visible teenager, how to dress and dance and how to treat his parents. Deprived of the rituals that mark adolescence in older communities, teenagers in large degree attempt to create their own. It is almost as though they give a licence to their 'stars', in the shape of unlimited finance, to show them what a teenager should do. I think now of the Beatles, whose image was projected as the perfect teenagers. It was their private lives which interested the fans as much as their music, and the fact remains that it is the way their stars live which interests teenagers. The teenagers in their school uniforms need to be able to express growth and change in the ways their village predecessors once did. The mass media provide a very important source of refer-ence in this respect, particularly for those who cannot, or do not wish to attain the identity and prospects afforded by attained educational status.

In the village the child assumed increasing responsibility matched to their resourcefulness, the conditioning was continuous, and the work roles contributed to the families' subsistence. Child labour need not necessarily be the horror described by Dickens. Those urban parents who do not allow for their children's self-expression must expect their children to look outside the family and to want to score over them by emphasising their superior differences to them. In industrial societies the identity crisis is inflicted upon the adolescent, and significantly it is the mass media, most particularly popular music, that the adolescent turns to.

3. We have developed from a society where the individual typically lived his whole life as child, parent, worker and grandparent in the context of the same group of people. It is perhaps apparent why the word 'identity' derives from the Latin *idem* – same, or over and over again. The stage was set, interaction consisted of repeated exchanges with the same group of people whose different social roles were marked off by means of etiquette and manners. The central and distinguishing fact about social behaviour in modern industrial societies is that the different social positions occupied by man are acted out in the company of different actors in different geographic locations. Identity is no longer over and over again but becomes face management with opportunity for concealment. It is almost as though a fine balance must be struck between isolated interaction only with two contradictory parents (akin to the double bind) and interaction with a kin grouping which is in some way representative of a larger social grouping. The context of an extended kin grouping provides an identity harnessed by repeated interaction with people well known to the individual, an identity moreover which is essentially honest insofar as the others on a fixed stage will permit few faults to remain unnoticed – in the words of the proverb, 'I cannot be your friend and flatterer too'.

Perhaps the most acute crisis of modern industrial man is the lack of a fixed audience on which to peg identity. Our young learn at least two modes of behaviour, often with differing vocabularies for home and school. These behaviours are often mutually antagonistic, appropriate for one place only, with consequent embarrassment when an actor appears on the wrong stage. The individual finds no repeatable core to his identity, which is not rounded out. Let us assume for one moment that the analysis is correct; what is the synthesis? The answer lies in the meaning of the word 'self'. It means 'the same throughout'. The solution is to find an identity which is consistent regardless of stage, and the same means of discovering this self must be employed as in the village. That is, by relationship, we must become self-aware. By relationship, by mirror image, we should come to know ourselves better; that is we must sharpen our concept of relationship so that it is used to promote self-awareness. The disturbing fact of increasing divorce rates suggests that we are increasingly unable to use relationship in this way. Moreover television does play an important role in modern industrial society. To use the analogy developed above, television provides a stage with a large number of stable characters with whom the viewer can interact without the danger that painful self-analysis will be forced upon him because the interaction is not dynamic. Nevertheless the same faces which appear frequently, the 'link' men, appear to interact with the viewer at home. Consequently the viewer feels he knows these people well enough, for example, to say 'hello' to them in the street. These screen personages provide a stable stage which makes no demands on the viewer – perhaps an important reason for television's popularity.

4. Barker (1968) estimates that the child in small-town communities in the USA acts upon seventeen separate stages, and the child in a northern UK city acts upon five separate stages. Perhaps we are not fully aware of the amount of social learning required before an actor can appear fully rehearsed on seventeen separate stages. He must learn his 'role' or script, for each stage. How does he learn the behaviours appropriate for each stage in the first instance? In the village all the 'how to behave' models are visible, the stage is known, the actor's role is not needed since the parts to be played have been committed to memory and have been practised in play before the show goes on. Urban man has to move from undefined situation to undefined situation until he comes to know how to behave in each new situation. Each part has to be learnt and it seems likely that he will look for familiar cues in unfamiliar settings in order to reduce the uncertainty associated with an undefined situation. It seems likely that he will make reference to the mass media, especially television, in order to recognise familiar cues in unfamiliar surroundings. We have data from interviews that seven-year-old children know how to order drinks in pubs at least eleven years before they can put this skill into practice. In Ireland telephone conversations sound like those in American movies, and Turkish police are exactly like Hollywood police replete with gum-chewing detail. We can predict, therefore, that television's neo 'reality' materials will provide many of the clues which enable individuals to recognise something familiar in an unfamiliar setting. We can predict that newsreel violence will provide more clues for subsequent imitation than *Tom and Jerry*. The stone throwing protester launching missiles at uniforms are worldwide as are the highjackers. Each exposure teaches a 'how to behave' model and defines the target of aggression – as we shall see in Chapter 7. Moreover, television plays a major part in helping to define those stereotypes we attach to various occupational and national stereotypes, especially those with which we have had no first-hand contact.

5. In increasingly specialised industrial societies the individual is encouraged to think that his specialised experience is shared with

only like specialists. Our mode of identification reveals this tendency, we say that we are of such a profession, it is the index to our identity. Children are encouraged to specialise at earlier and earlier ages and learn information which other children do not. This tendency reduces the perceived communality of experience which results from being human. In village societies with minimal specialisation the communality of experience is perceived as greater than the individual's separate experience, and that communality of experience results both from like work and from a recognition of being human. The fact remains that we are human, we have to confront the same problems and joys no matter what the specialisation. For this writer the appeal of television can largely be explained in terms that television 'when art' explores the human condition, drawing from the daily drama of life, to provide a culture common to the disparate specialists.

Coronation Street depicts the events of a single street or village and is popular because the producers have discovered that the interactions between a closed group of people are the most complex and dramatic events – as we social scientists are discovering to our cost. In the words of a television playwright Chayefsky (1955), 'You can dig into the most humble, ordinary relationships, of bourgeois children to their mother, of middle-class husband to his wife, of white-collar worker to his secretary – in short the relationships of the people. People relate to each other in an incredibly complicated manner. There is far more exciting drama in the reasons why a man gets married than in why he murders somebody.'

6. Closely related to what has been said above, and the remarks previously made concerning the effects of specialisation, is the concept that in village societies the self is stable throughout and used to the full, whereas in industrial societies the self is unstable and not fully exploited. Confront a village man with a problem and he will attempt to answer it because he is not dependent on specialists. He expects to be the master of several skills, is self-reliant and resourceful. Individuals in village societies are stretched and challenged because they are so often under threat from famine, invasion and illness. By way of contrast, developed man, unless a do-it-yourself specialist, comes to rely on the expert. He no longer repairs damage but replaces it. His way of thought has become specialised and habitual, and thus loses flexibility of approach. The self is not the same throughout, but most unevenly developed, and rarely challenged or stretched – except in times of national emergency. Moreover, the proliferation of stages means that the individual must learn the behaviour appropriate for each stage while at the same time having lost flexibility of thought. Television will provide for many their first contact with undefined situations. Simply put, television has the

capacity to make society visible and as a tool for transmitting reality from afar it has no peer.

Advertisers realised this fact long ago. Pictorial advertising works because pictures help to define unfamiliar situations. Advertisements are essentially learning experiences for situations where there is little first-hand contact. When a novel situation is encountered, past associative learning springs to mind rather than an objective definition of the situation. Advertisers are concerned to show people consuming their products, once again a refined form of visual learning. Moreover their basic product has a relatively flexible function, such as soap; advertisers are concerned to stress the unique and particular function of their product, for example, soap to wash hair. Clearly there is something ridiculous about some advertisements. Food, for example, is advertised with the specific function of slimming. It is a credit to television's power that these absurdities are not immediately apparent when we view people actually consuming these products. I should perhaps add that skinhead girls in Dublin were in no way bemused by such television advertisements. Their mothers chose soap for most cleaning functions and the girls seen using shampoos were seen not as factory girls but as secretaries for whom they held an intrinsic distaste. Viewed in this way, however, it can be argued many television programmes in fact advertise styles and ways of life. The urban child knows the sort of kitchen that represents high status, she has seen it in the *Lucy Show*. She knows how to demonstrate the status aspired for in the achieving society, alienation can only result from failure.

7. In order to cope with the multiplicity of roles and stages we have argued that the self has become increasingly fragmented, that the possibility of harmonious integration of the sub-systems of the psyche is less today even than in the time when Freud postulated his model of man as one of basic inner conflict. We have argued, that in 'primitive' one-stage communities the self is the same throughout since the actor cannot withold from public gaze, and hence cannot help but see himself in the mirror eyes of the constantly assembled actors. It has been suggested that relationship forces each participant individual to more clearly see himself, that is, to see himself from the point of view of the other. It has been suggested that this is a painful, yet necessary experience for the development of a harmoniously integrated personality. The tool by which integration is achieved is the taking of the role of the other, by seeing the self from the other's standpoint, by the development of empathetic abilities. As we shall see in Chapter 5, these skills develop but slowly during childhood. We are talking here of the role of the extended kin network in forcing the individual to evaluate himself from a set of balanced viewpoints representing the whole spectrum

of the likely life span of the individual. The individual actor must therefore come to see himself as he is seen by others, he must become sympathetic to the stance of the other and imagine how it feels to be the other person. Locked within a stable and recognisable community he knows what it feels like, for example, to be old, to be adolescent, to be married, to be a parent. He gains experience of these roles by empathising with others in these positions; he is initiated into each role via ritual, and the community provides for learning of social roles while ensuring that these roles are accommodated within the personality of the individual.

It is suggested that the community by its structure had the function which we currently ascribe to encounter and therapy groups. In modern developed industrial societies the individual learns the vast number of behaviours appropriate for each stage, but these behaviours are not integrated within the personality, the individual learns the mechanics of situation management but is not forced to see himself from the standpoint of others. Indeed he is often able to retreat to the authority of his role position (for example, teacher), precisely to avoid the painful necessity of evaluating himself from the standpoint of the other. It is also likely that the sheer amount of social learning required for the many stages he will manage constitutes something of a cognitive overload, the very pressure of which reduces the likelihood that he make the effort to see himself from the standpoint of the other – a tendency which culminates in the marriage guidance councillor who tries to make the partners see the other's point of view. In a village community where the interdependence of individuals one on the other for the very agricultural means of existence such as the harvest, or the rice planting is clearly visible, and where individuals share a similar life experience, each person does perceive the point of view of the other and knows how the others will feel if he lets them down. We find a very similar community developing within units of soldiers in wartime, where the individual soldier knows the others are dependent upon him. Child audiences readily perceive that it is in aggressive films that comradeship is most clearly visible.

Yet the individual child in a mass society cannot easily perceive the way in which his future labour will interrelate with the labour of others in the same factory, leave alone the way it interrelates with the wider society. Of necessity he becomes self-interested and is less able to perceive the points of view of the others in that society – be he manager or worker. For the most part he has little idea of how the others spend their lives, and even less idea of how people the other side of the world live. Television can make such life-styles visible, television could act as an eye in near and far away places, but it would have to show reality. At present reality is often so filtered as to present only sensational reality and fictitious exploits which properly belong to the novel.

Yet for this writer the defining characteristic of television's output is the frequency with which its better dramatic productions are concerned to depict events as realistically as possible, to demonstrate to the viewer what it feels like to be a real criminal or policeman in *Task Force* and to be really unemployed in *Coronation Street,* a tendency less evident in imported USA productions which have merely borrowed Hollywood styles and production techniques for the new medium of television. The regrettable result of which is to enable the viewer to put aside his real-life problems while not coming to appreciate how it feels to be a real life member of a modern industrial society.

2
Television research methods

Much has been written and said of late about the use of scientific
method in the sphere of social science. A wholly justified attack on
the traditional method of psychological enquiry has resulted in a
search for alternative methods of discovering and evaluating the
subject-matter of psychology – namely the way people think and
behave. In part the traditional method of experimental manipula-
tion within a laboratory setting with its accompanying statistical
analysis and emphasis on measurement has come under fire from
those psychologists anxious to make statements concerning real-
life situations. Those of us concerned to discover, for example, the
effects that televised aggression has on child audiences have found it
impossible to make general statements on the basis of the studies
already published. The nature of the evidence available is so limited
and curtailed that we face ridicule from a mature audience should
we dare generalise from research findings to predict what is likely to
happen to your child when he watches television on the basis of
research conducted within the laboratory.

Ironically enough students of psychology are in my experience
less able than their parents to engage in such wholesome criticism.
They seem to accept whatever they are told, and come to hold it in
almost scriptural regard, until confronted by systematic criticism.
Of course those of us with little to say will find the most elaborate
way of saying it so as to ensure our academic respectability and to
drag a smokescreen of words and jargon over the relative emptiness
of our research tradition. Where else other than in the social sciences
would one discover that a conflict situation refers to a child being
told his bicycle (regardless of whether or not he has one) has been
stolen and being asked whether he would (a) fight the thief, (b) let
the thief keep the bicycle, or (c) ask his mother for help. Clearly
conflict does not bear much relationship to the thing measured. It
goes without saying that where such language is used the thing
measured bears even less relationship to the real world. To make
statements as to effects of televised aggression, in the light of children's answers after watching westerns concerning the conflict
situation, as does Linne (1971), is clearly a most suspect procedure,
inviting ridicule.

Yet in that strange cyclical way that fashions in method in social science oscillate we find that the rejection of the scientific methods which produce such self-evidently nonsense results in favour of lengthy and pedantic introspection shows an equal lack of discrimination. The best of anything is good, the best of scientific method is good, the best of introspection is good. I should like here to criticise scientific method constructively, that is to point out its weaknesses and strengths so that we may employ this most powerful technique in a meaningful way to the problems of how television affects our children. This critique will fall under four relatively distinct headings: Why is the research done? Where is the research done? How is the research done? And, How are the results presented?

WHY IS THE RESEARCH DONE?

The somewhat glib aping of pure science amongst social scientists ensures in the first instance that research is rarely problem orientated. Not that problem orientation is the best approach for the scientist but the selection of the subject-matter of the discipline has clearly to be delineated. Too often the subject-matter of a discipline is but an historical accident, the only justification being that of the legal precedent. It is too easy to forget that the founding fathers of science were not without their critics, and whereas the founding fathers' delineation of the subject-matter of science is today accepted with almost the same certainty as the Jews accepted Moses' tablets of stone, their critics remain unread. 'True science investigates and brings to human perception such truths and such knowledge as the people of a given time and society consider most important. Art transmits these truths from the region of perception to the region of emotions.' Such was Count Leo Tolstoy's definition in 1898, a definition we should do well to keep in mind. I am more than a little concerned that thousands of psychologists devote their lives to tracking down the illusive number of nonsense syllables that can be remembered backwards or forwards, sideways and upwards when probably only hundreds of psychologists try to find out what effects television and other mass media have on our children. And our children spend as much time watching television as they do in school, and televiewing is second only to sleep in the amount of time we each of us devote to it during our lifetime. To quote Tolstoy once more: 'And scientists are really convinced that to be occupied with trifles, while neglecting what is more essential and important, is a characteristic not of themselves but of science.' Yet in spite of public concern regarding televiewing, the nonsense syllables win out.

Of course there is a reason for this state of affairs. Tolstoy once more: 'And as always occurs, the lower a human activity descends – the more widely it diverges from what it should be – the more its self-confidence increases. That is just what has happened with the science of today. True science is never appreciated by its contemporaries, but on the contrary is usually persecuted. Nor can this be otherwise. True science shows men their mistakes and points to new, unaccustomed ways of life.' To study the effects of television is to invite persecution, for a truly scientific study of the media cannot but show men their mistakes, not least the subjection of our children to the very worst form of propaganda during the whole of their formative years – the propaganda of advertising, the creation of false demands and neuroses. Yet to measure these effects is to invite financial suicide, is to kill the goose that lays the golden egg which funds research into the recall of nonsense syllables. Not of course that the picture is all black. Television, as we have suggested, could be a tool for social good, it could act as a mirror to a healthy community, but to postulate a use of this kind would involve a reorganisation of the institutions which control the mass media, hardly likely to prove a popular suggestion.

THE VALUE POSITION OF THE SOCIAL SCIENTIST

Moreover, the social scientist almost unwittingly adopts the prevailing values of his time. It is a regrettable fact that only now are social scientists becoming slowly aware that it is impossible to conduct research in a value-free vacuum. However tacit, assumptions must always be made. We do not have to look very far in mass communication research to find examples of these tacit acceptances of prevailing values. In their authoritative survey concerning the effects of the introduction of television in North America, Schramm *et al.* draw a key distinction between reality and fantasy materials on television. Reality materials are those which constantly refer the viewer to the problems of the real world, invite alertness, effort and activity; those which encourage thinking, offer information and so on. Predictably reality programmes are defined as news, documentary, interviews and educational programmes. Fantasy materials, on the other hand, invite the viewer to take leave of his problems in the real world, invite surrender, relaxation and passivity, offer wish-fulfilment, reliefs from threat and anxiety and annul the rules of the real world. In other words, those programmes which resemble the school curriculum are reality, and those which are not like the school curriculum are fantasy. Consequently the effects of television are assessed in terms of the vocabulary increases, and the ability to name statesmen. Yet Schramm *et al.*'s distinction on closer analysis appears somewhat arbitrary. In Chapter 1 we stressed the important function that television has in demonstrating social skills, the sorts of skills valued by children and not amenable to paper and pencil tests. Skills of the type such as making friends, manipulating bureau-cratic processes, coping with parental demands, knowing what to wear and how to dance. The sorts of skills often portrayed in what Schramm labels fantasy programmes, namely westerns, crime, drama, variety and popular music shows. Schramm *et al.* seem too concerned with a model of television directly affecting children and too little concerned with the uses a viewer makes of television.

Nor should it be forgotten that no society can exist without its myths – and our myths are most often found in fantasy programmes. Myths according to Malinowski, are 'charters for social action', or metaphoric expressions of values. Children who attend to fantasy programmes at least become familiar with the prevailing values of the society – just as children in village societies learnt their myths from the traditional stories.

WHERE IS THE RESEARCH DONE?

A psychologist will show you his laboratory with great pride. You will be encouraged to play with the many expensive toys with which it is equipped. Strange as it might seem, people, including themselves, watch television in their own homes. Television affects people as they sit at home and view. There is no need to simulate this activity in a laboratory as though the laboratory were consecrated ground. Some person in practically every family watches television, its effects can be assayed in the first instance by asking them about it in their own home, even while they are watching. One exercise I ask my students to conduct is to talk about television with their younger brothers and sisters. The students are first of all surprised that television is so potent in their siblings' lives, and even find the exercise revealing as regards the fact that television does not just affect children 'out there' but their own kin.

One mother, a devout devotee of *Sesame Street* sat down for a week to watch with her three-year-old daughter. She discovered as the child grew familiar with the fact that they were to watch together, rather than using the box as a baby-sitter, that her daughter had many questions to ask. Questions, moreover, which indicated the child's almost complete lack of comprehension of the programme. After one long piece of film which showed the garbage collection, we were left to watch the garbage floating out to sea in a barge. The child very sensibly asked, 'Where are they taking it, Mummy? Not to the sea?' Another father watched war films with his nine-year-old son. Not only did it give the father a chance to get close to his boy, but he discovered that, 'In war films people help each other, they

are kind to one another'. We have here, I suspect, the reason why
both the western and the war film are so popular; they are among the
few programmes which show kindly co-operation as well as aggression. It has been the aggression which has concerned the social
scientist, who has disregarded the fact that the war film is a vehicle
for the portrayal of kindness and co-operation.

Another student set out to discover whether her five-year-old
sister was in the least confused about the reality-fantasy of her
favourite television programmes. '*Tom and Jerry*', the child replied,
'are real', they lived lives both on and off the television screen.
Dixon of Dock Green was a real policeman. When the set was
switched off he was still a policeman. After four days of questioning
the child began to ask the mother, 'Is he real, Mummy?' Mummy
then had to explain how the films were made and how the actors
were used. The questioning itself activated the child's curiosity.
The strange thing is that whereas the parent will explain a story read
from a book, they rarely explain to the child how television works.
That parents can be surprised by what they can find out for themselves, if they but try, is depressing. No one can blame television
per se, unless they are sure they have educated their children to
appreciate this new medium and exactly how it works.

But there is something intrinsically wrong with our methodology,
and something even more wrong with the student who completes a
degree course, who qualifies as an expert, who does not question our
methodology. We turn out students wedded to the idea that the only
meaningful research in psychology is that conducted in the laboratory
where we can exercise a great deal of control over the variables in
which we are interested. 'It is supposed that the reduction of questions of a higher order to questions of a lower order will explain the
former. But an explanation is never obtained in this way. What
happens is merely that, descending ever lower and lower in one's
investigations, from the most important questions to less important
ones, science reaches at last a sphere quite foreign to man, with
which he is barely in touch, and confines its attention to that sphere,
leaving unsolved the questions most important to him' (Tolstoy,
On Science). We have here the explanation of the nonsense syllable
syndrome, and of the syndrome of the artificial laboratory studies of
Berkowitz who has so influenced the American National Commission
on the Causes and Prevention of Violence. Berkowitz has for ten
years shown his own students, who gain credits to their degrees by
participating in his experiments, seven minutes from the film *The
Champion*. They then are asked to reward a student, who may or
may not have insulted them, who has drawn a floor plan for a school
by giving him electric shocks. Of course the student is Berkowitz's
collaborator, the floor plan never varies, the film never varies, and

the electric shocks do not reach the student. Apart from these minor factors the experiments are supposed to answer questions of a high order. Not surprisingly he finds students who have seen *The Champion* administer more dummy electric shocks than those who see films about canal boats. Berkowitz concludes that televised aggression adversely affects our children, having descended in his laboratory to a sphere quite foreign to the effects of everyday television in people's houses. And as Tolstoy would predict he is immensely self-confident.

'It is as if a man, wishing to understand the use of an object lying before him – instead of coming close to it, examining it from all sides and handling it – were to retire farther from it until he was at such a distance that all its peculiarities of colour and inequalities of surface had disappeared and only its outline was still visible against the horizon; and as if from there he were to begin writing a minute description of the object imagining now at last he clearly understood it, and that this understanding, formed at such a distance, would assist a complete comprehension of it.' Tolstoy's criticism is as true today of social science as it was of natural science in 1898.

Of course the social scientist can, and must, leave the laboratory. When he does so he will investigate the effects of televised aggression at first hand, and as we shall see, he will find first-hand results are not comparable to third-hand ones. This is no doubt the reason why Feshbach and Singer (1971), who studied the effects of televised aggression in residential schools, found that televised aggression, far from stimulating further aggression, actually decreased the amount of aggression shown amongst boys with a history of aggression – in other words, it had a cathartic effect. I have for some time argued that one criteria by which to evaluate research is the amount of time spent by the researcher in a real-life situation, evaluating the problem at first hand. Berkowitz, who controls experiments from afar, would come out rather badly using such a criterion while Feshbach and Singer would come out well.

HOW IS THE RESEARCH DONE?

We have already seen in our discussion of Berkowitz's experiments that not only does he conduct his experiments in the wrong place, he conducts them in a most peculiar manner, worthy of Tolstoy's term 'In a sphere quite foreign to man'. We can summarise this section by saying that it is largely a problem of sampling. Berkowitz does not select a representative sample of televiewers. He selects merely his own students, and rewards them, one suspects, if they do what he expects, and because they are his students they know what he expects. Nor does he take a representative sample of televised violence. In the first instance he makes the classic mistake of equating television with the cinema. We have seen that the two media are very different and that one cannot generalise from one to the other. He works with cinema film projected as in a cinema. Moreover he has exclusively used the film, *The Champion*. For ten years now the same seven minutes of *The Champion* have been used; he has made little attempt to vary it. Not only has he virtually worn out this film, it also is a film people have seen, and it stars a well known hero, Kirk Douglas. It is not representative of televised aggression. Moreover Kirk Douglas is known as a 'good guy', so no matter what Berkowitz tells his students, and they are told all manner of things such as Douglas is the victim, the hero, the goody, the baddy; one can hardly expect them to be greatly influenced by Berkowitz's little stories which he tells before the film.

To complete the picture of a sphere quite foreign to man, we must now consider his sampling of aggressive behaviour. Once again in this respect we find Berkowitz conservative. He and his students have exclusively used the dummy electric shock administration. One must rightly be critical of the validity of this measure. How does it relate to real-life aggression? Unfortunately we can nowhere find out the answer to this elementary question. Again the shock is administered as a reward to Berkowitz's accomplice, but the students are not meant to know this. Again the shock is dummy, but the students do not know this, they are to believe that it is real. At best this device is questionable, at worst naïve. His student subjects are led to accept a large number of untruths so that we may accept Berkowitz's findings as the truth as regards the effects of televised violence. Clearly one cannot make meaningful statements on the basis of such limited research conducted in a sphere so foreign to man. Clearly one must attempt to take an adequate sample of televised aggression, must show it via a television monitor, must adequately sample aggressive behaviour preferably using a measure which corresponds to real-life measures, such as playground fights or conflict between children, and one must select a sample which in some way represents that part of the population which is most at risk. Experiments can be conducted of this type, and I leave the reader to judge whether my own limited experiments more adequately satisfy the criteria I have attempted to list here.

HOW ARE RESEARCH RESULTS PRESENTED?

Finally, and we need not labour this point, research in social science is presented in such a way as to confuse the lay reader. I should like to invoke the mystification hypothesis outlined in Chapter 1, that any profession protects itself by mystifying its subject matter and more importantly by mystifying the reader who comes across a research report. Social scientists write for one another, they do not write for the intelligent layman. The reason, I fear, is obvious – they have so little to say. The smoke-screen of jargon which masks this is so intense that patience and effort are required to debug it in order to establish exactly what the experimenter did do. The experiment hopefully controls experience, yet in the presentation of results this basic fact is lost. Moreover a strong case can be argued that the way the social scientist presents results debases the English language. So many 'new' words are coined, so many elaborate ways are sought to say the most simple things, that eventually the reader is confused not only with regard to social science but also with regard to the English language as a vehicle by which ideas can be expressed. In part this results from the self-confidence of the scientist dealing in an area quite foreign to ordinary men. In part it results from an attempt to camouflage the weakness of a poor study and in part it results from the six years of intensive training which are mandatory before one can call oneself an expert.

An example

Let's consider an early experiment which is still cited as evidence that televised aggression has adverse effects on child viewers: a study conducted by experts. Mussen and Rutherford (1961) studied the reactions of 36 children aged between six and seven years to two films. One film supposedly depicted aggression. In their own words, 'the cartoon showed a continuous sequence of aggressive activity in which an animated weed attempts to choke a flower, and a panda bear struggled to destory the weed'. The film lasted for only eight minutes. Children, one at a time and alone, watched one of the films and were then ushered into a room where an experimenter sat holding a balloon on a string. The children were asked how much they would like to break the balloon but they were not actually allowed to break it. Supposedly, children were meant to say I want to break it very much, much, not sure, not want to break it, and not want to break it at all. In fact children only said I want to break it, not sure, and I don't want to break it. To act as a control, other children individually viewed a film which showed a frog and duck play co-operatively, and which supposedly did not depict aggression. These children were also asked whether they wanted to break the balloon. In addition, half the children who saw the aggression film and half the children who saw the control film were 'frustrated' before they saw the films. 'Frustration' can be variously defined, but stripping the psychological theory from their definition, what the children

B

were asked to do was to copy numbers repeatedly while their teacher frequently criticised their work.

You may not be surprised to learn that children who had seen the 'aggressive' film, more often than children who had seen the neutral film, said they wanted to pop the balloon. In this study 'frustration' had little effect on the aggressiveness measure. This study, according to the authors, was prompted by the widespread concern about the possible harmful consequences of viewing dramatic portrayals of violence. One can only wonder what can be deduced from such results? Could the public make an informed decision on the basis of these findings? Is the film used typical of the aggressive films children see? Indeed is it aggressive? Can you say that the desire to pop a balloon indicates that children are more or less aggressive after viewing the film? How long-lived were the effects?

SUMMARY

The criticisms outlined above may appear rather obvious, but results from so-called classic studies are often generally accepted and not sufficiently criticised – thus Berkowitz's experiments are cited by those who believe that televised violence has adverse effects and Schramm *et al.*'s contention that to attend to televised fantasy is escapist has been accepted by at least two generations of mass communication researchers. These studies are often cited by those who are not familiar with the exact detail of their procedures and it is only when the studies are read first hand and criticised in detail that their shortcomings become evident. I have attempted in this chapter to explain in general terms why research in mass communications, simply because it claims to be scientific, is not inevitably objective nor necessarily relevant to the everyday effects of televiewing by children. Throughout the remainder of this book, therefore, a footnote generally denotes a cryptic criticism of a research measure or technique.

But a more serious criticism of mass communication studies, which will be reviewed in succeeding chapters, is that early 'pioneering' studies are not only generally accepted but, more seriously, such studies define the whole problem area. Because of a lack of theory we tend to have isolated pockets of research, some of which have even been well mined, but these pockets in no way interrelate to give a general picture describing the roles of television in our everyday lives. The limited theory outlined in Chapter 1, in spite of its faults, at least allows for a reinterpretation of much of the data so far collected in a 'scientific' manner, and attempts to show the relationship between what have become 'compartmentalised' problem areas.

Moreover in social science we must allow for the fact that we are dealing with human beings, who because we call them 'subjects' in psychological research, are subjected to the demands of the experimenter and thus respond in a different way in research studies than they do in everyday life. Psychological research has been criticised because of 'demand characteristics' which means that unless we understand how the person sees the psychological questionnaire or test we cannot fully understand the way people have responded. Some social scientists have rebutted this criticism by claiming that the problem of generalisation from the experiment to the real world does not consist of a point to point comparison between one and the other but depends entirely on whether one has reached a correct theoretical understanding of the relevant process – much as the basic process of combustion is the same for both a burning match and a forest fire (Milgram, 1974). This point is valid but the analogy is weak since it is a scientific, rather than a socially scientific statement. Combustion essentially involves elements which do not vary over time, elements moreover which are quite unlike human beings because people can and do sense the subtle nuances of any research situation. In social science therefore we cannot rely on the result of a single experiment nor a single experimental design, but should rather seek to replicate findings in situations where the subtle experimental nuances are systematically varied.

3

Identification or recognition?
How do children become involved
with television characters?

The aim of this chapter is to explain how viewers become involved with television programmes and films; to explain how it is that 'normal' reality is suspended in favour of the manufactured reality of the mass media. Theorising in this area would seem to date from concepts derived from the cinema and which appear to take little account of the unique qualities of television. Most viewers are said to identify with television characters in the same way that they identified with film stars in the cinema. That is, according to Schramm, 'the experience of being able to put oneself so deeply into a television character – feel oneself to be so like the character – that one can feel the same emotions and experience the same events as the character is supposed to be feeling and experiencing'. The emotional experience of viewing is thus heightened, and the likelihood of subsequent influence, in the form of imitation, is thereby increased. It is somewhat naïvely argued that televiewers similarly identify with television characters. Televiewing is therefore an identity loss situation.

Horton and Wohl (1956), however, in an important yet neglected article suggest that televiewers engage in para- or pseudo-social interaction with those television celebrities who appear frequently and whose performance is carefully rehearsed to simulate face to face conversation with the viewer at home. They argue that the viewers, far from putting themselves in the shoes of such characters, remain very firmly in their own and respond to the celebrity as they might if they met him in the street. Reality is suspended insofar as they participate in what has been aptly called the 'illusion of intimacy'. Para-social interaction, therefore, involves no identity loss; rather the viewer takes an answering role to the celebrity when he appears on the screen.

I shall argue that a process akin to para-social interaction accounts for a great deal of viewer involvement in television programmes. I suggest that viewers recognise television characters, simply because of repeated exposure, and come to feel that they know them and can, as a consequence, predict their likely next actions. In terms of the village argument outlined in Chapter 1, I suggest that regularly appearing characters comprise something of a screen community, with whom the viewer will interact in much the same way that in the village the individual interacted on a single stage with the extended kin group. As is the case with para-social interaction the viewer does not forget either who he is or where he is. In order to expand this argument it will be briefly necessary to compare the televiewing and cinema-viewing situations.

TELEVIEWING AND CINE-VIEWING

A night out at the cinema, in darkness, in an unfamiliar surrounding is designed to allow the viewer to forget both who he is and where he is. Apart from the early days of cinema – especially in children's serials – and until after the advent of television, the same character rarely appeared in two consecutive movies. The screenplay is closed in the sense that actors address remarks at each other and not directly at the audience. In order to encourage viewer involvement subjective camera techniques are often employed whereby events are filmed from the point of view of one of the characters; one sees, for example, the response of other characters to his remarks and actions. In order to become involved with the film, the viewer must adopt the stance of one of the actors and hence share his screen experiences while viewing. Cine-viewers leave the cinema in somewhat of a daze as they re-adjust to their environmental reality.

Television, on the other hand, is viewed in the home, with the light on and often in familiar company – a situation likely to remind the viewer of his own identity unless the light is switched off, which Himmelweit *et al.* noted enhanced emotional impact. Moreover, the same characters are seen weekly in television's prime products – the serials and series programmes, and the same compères are exposed weekly in the chat and personality shows. Characters are seen in the detail of what television producers call the 'talking head', and in the case of compères, remarks are addressed directly at the viewer at home. The very size of the television screen ensures that the viewer sees the detail of facial movements as in conversation and the viewer cannot but feel that he 'knows' these characters, much as he knows the people who live close to him. Rather than immersing himself in the production the viewer answers these characters back, feels sorry for them when in difficulty, hates them when they are belligerent and to all intents and purposes responds and replies to them as though they were people he knows intimately. Bearing in mind what was said in Chapter 1, it appears that television simulates conversations over the garden wall, and does not provide for identity loss. If what is argued here is true, we may predict some interesting differences between viewers' responses to television characters and film stars.

RESEARCH COMPARING TELEVISION CHARACTERS AND FILM STARS

If what has been said concerning the illusion of intimacy is correct, we may predict that as regards television, the viewer knows the name of the character since he 'meets' him every week, better than he knows the name of the actor. With cinema film it is argued that the star's name is better recalled than the name of character's portrayed in the film. Noble and Barnes (1972) asked 100 students aged between twelve and sixteen years to list both characters' and actors' names in television programmes they had viewed, and cinema films seen recently. For television programmes they were able to list no less than 1,316 characters' names but only 428 actors' names. With film the situation was reversed; only 56 characters' names were recalled as opposed to 123 actors'. Interestingly enough, the star of *The Persuaders* was said to be the Saint, and the star of *Ironside* was said to be Perry Mason, which indicates that television actors, as they have long complained, become typecast in the roles in which they frequently appear on television. (Actors who appear in advertisements maintain that they become the Aspro-Man and other work is difficult to find. Voices, however, are more ubiquitous and recur frequently.) Further evidence supporting the idea of the illusion of intimacy was found in that 60 per cent of children gave only the first names of television characters in the shows they had seen. Moreover, 36 respondents admitted they talked to television characters, while none reported that they talked to film stars in the cinema. Interestingly too, in the light of the argument in Chapter 1, the most popular television programme in Montreal, where this study was conducted, was *All in the Family* – a situation comedy portraying a typical family with a highly prejudiced father who everybody knows as Archie Bunker, a show which was twice as popular as its nearest rival *The Persuaders*.

THE MOTIVES FOR IDENTIFICATION AND PARA-SOCIAL INTERACTION

Bearing in mind the differences found between television and the cinema, it is apparent that the motives for identification are different from the motives for pseudo-social interaction. Identification allows the viewer to experience in fantasy the film character's screen experiences, is thought to lead to subsequent imitation and it is difficult to see how identification can provide feedback relevant to everyday life. As we shall see in the next chapter, it is argued that identification is escapist in the sense that it involves identity loss and an ostrich-like tendency to bury one's head in the sand. It was argued in Chapter 1 that human animals, by dint of evolution, need to interact with a stable extended kin group which is representative of the larger social grouping in order that the individual learns how to behave in future roles. It is suggested that the motive for para-social interaction is to allow the viewer to converse with the screen community, which in turn is representative of the larger social grouping. Para-social interactions afford the viewer opportunities to interact with characters of the opposite sex, characters of higher and lower status than his own and with people of particular occupations and professions. It is likely that para-social interactions can lead to critical analysis of events and occurrences, and since they involve no identity loss such interaction may well provide practice for everyday social roles, as in the village, and allow the viewer to take roles not yet experienced in real life. As will be seen in the following chapter, it is less easy to label such a viewing style escapist, in the sense that no feedback to everyday life is possible.

RESEARCH INTO THE MOTIVES FOR IDENTIFICATION

In spite of the popularity of the concept of identification, research studies throwing light on to the process are old, sparse and inconclusive. Principally research has concentrated on the motives why children identify with film heroes. Three principal motives, derived somewhat simplistically from Freud (1933), have been proposed: first, that children identify for narcissistic reasons – namely with those television characters who are, so to speak, mirror images of themselves; secondly, goal-orientated identifications whereby the child identifies with those characters who are successful in the way the child would like to be – popular, aggressive and so on; and thirdly, children are said to identify with the aggressor, when the child, because he is frightened by a character, seeks to become like that character in order to remove the fear. While Albert (1957) argues that no one can hope to observe identification processes *per se*, in the same way that one cannot observe electricity, researchers have assumed that identification will inevitably take place when film viewing. As we have seen in Chapter 2, social scientists often assume that their hypotheses are correct and seek to prove them by means of very inadequate measuring techniques. Maccoby and Wilson (1957), for example, simply asked boys and girls who had seen an all-male cast, 'Which of the main characters did you like best?', and assumed that children who said 'Bob' had identified with 'Bob' – that is had put themselves into his shoes while viewing, covertly reproduced in themselves both the actions and emotions of that character, watched for cues from other characters in the same way as their hero, and would as a consequence selectively recall those events with which their hero was primarily involved.

Maccoby and Wilson were concerned to discover if working-class children would identify for narcissistic reasons with a working-class hero and middle-class children with a middle-class hero. They showed 139 boys and 130 girls aged twelve years, two 20-minute episodes from *Junior G men* serial film, featuring a working-class and a middle-class hero. Children were asked one week after viewing whether they wanted to be like either Billy or Harry, were most like either Billy or Harry and whether they most liked either Billy or Harry. It is not therefore surprising to find that identification choice could not be predicted on the basis of the social class of the child viewer. Not daunted, the authors argued that children who aspired to middle-class membership would identify with the middle-class hero. Even when the data were reanalysed in this way, the authors were only able to account for three-quarters of the identification choices. They claim that children do not identify with those characters most like themselves, but with those characters that they would most like to be like. Nor, in spite of their prediction, did they find that identification choices bore any meaningful relationship to the types of material recalled after the film, since regardless of identification choice children recalled the same incidents. However, when given a choice in a second study, it was found that girls identified with heroines and boys with heroes, yet even so they did not find that girls selectively remembered incidents enacted by the heroine, nor boys incidents enacted by the hero. Yet, since children were forced by the experimenters' methodology to say they had identified with a film hero, these results are hardly surprising. It would seem that if identification takes place at all when viewing films, it only takes place momentarily and many child viewers are far from immersed in the actions of the film characters.

Zajonc (1954) wished to discover whether nine to thirteen-year-old children would identify with a successful character even if he portrayed values alien to the child. Children heard either an autocratic or democratic leader succeed in one of two versions of a radio space serial. Those children who heard democracy succeed favoured the democratic leader and vice versa; at face value it would appear that children identify with the successful character – for goal-orientated reasons. To see whether children would imitate the character with whom they had identified children were asked to imagine that they were the captains of the space ship and whether it was more important that everybody obeyed orders, or got along well with everybody. Children most valued the régime which the radio serial associated with success, but since only 70 per cent of those who heard the autocratic leader succeed most valued his régime, Zajonc concludes that children will not always identify with a successful character if he shows values alien to the child. Children would not, he maintains, identify with a successful criminal. However, since Zajonc asked children only, 'Would you rather be like the autocratic or democratic leader?', it is to be doubted whether much importance can be attached to these results.

CONSEQUENCES OF IDENTIFICATION

Zajonc asked whether children would imitate the actions of the character with whom they had identified. Clearly much concern regarding the effects of the mass media has concentrated on whether or not child viewers will imitate the actions of successful television characters. So far imitation has been assessed only in terms of hypothetical judgements of the child, and actual behavioural imitation has not been demonstrated. Bandura, whose work we shall more closely review in Chapter 7, has been concerned to demonstrate that children are as able mimics of what they see on television as they are of real life adults, as we would predict from the social learning evident in the village. In a typical experiment Bandura, Ross and Ross (1963b) showed four-year-old nursery children either a five-minute film in which an adult's aggressive actions are successful in gaining possession of attractive toys or a film where an adult's aggression is severely punished. Children then played in a room containing similar toys and their play was observed by judges to see which film induced the greatest amount of imitation. While most of the play behaviour was not sufficiently close to that exhibited in the film to be called imitative, children were more likely to copy the successful, rather than the unsuccessful, adult's actions. Bandura concludes that 'successful villainy may outweigh the viewers' value system'.

While Bandura argues that imitation and identification are synonymous since they 'encompass the same behavioural phenomenon, that is the tendency for a person to match the behaviour, attitudes or emotional reactions as exhibited by actual or symbolised models', it is by no means clear that children who imitate have put themselves into the character's shoes while viewing. It seems more likely that children merely observed outcomes, as they would have done in the village, and demonstrated to Bandura that they are able to benefit from another person's experience.

IDENTIFICATION WITH THE AGGRESSOR

Results obtained by Albert (1957) add little to the confusing findings so far reported. However, it is worth noting that the studies cited are largely those which are the basis for the conceptual thinking concerning the identification process. Indirectly Albert's results throw some light on identification with the aggressor, although his study is so confusing to read that different reviewers reach contradictory conclusions after reading his study. Two hundred and twenty eight- to ten-year-old children were shown one of three versions of a *Hopalong Cassidy* film, in which the viewing order of the reels was reversed so that in one version Hopalong won, in a second he appeared to lose and in a third there was no result. Children were not fooled by this degree of experimental sophistication, since they overwhelmingly identified with Hopalong regardless of whether or not he was successful. While boys identified with male characters and girls with females, children deemed 'aggressive' did not identify with aggressive characters, although 6 per cent of viewers did identify with the villain. Although identification may be invisible like electricity, there is little need to stick your fingers in the plug to prove it exists, as does Albert by merely asking children after viewing, 'Which of the characters would you rather grow up and be like?'. Apart from sex differences in identification choice, there is no clear-cut rule suggesting that identification results from narcissism, from goal-orientation, or because of the frightening power of the aggressor.

A REINTERPRETATION OF IDENTIFICATION STUDIES

There seems little doubt intuitively that identification is a meaningful concept, because cinema viewers are often carried away while viewing. Regrettably most of the studies concerning identification tell us little about the process, because of their poor scientific designs. Most of the questions put to the children demanded an answer, and there seems little reason to infer that children have put themselves into a character's shoes simply because they like him best, or would rather be like him. It seems rather that in many of the studies the child observes the outcome of the film character's behaviour and is able to benefit from that character's experience. There is no need to imply that the child concentrates on the actions of the character, and attempts to match his behaviour to that of the film character. Even in Bandura's imitation experiments, the children did not exactly copy the actions of the film character. Moreover Albert received more clear-cut answers to the question, 'Who don't you want to grow up and be like?', than to his identification questions, which suggests that children recognise the villain rather than identify with him. It was previously suggested that children in the village recognise all the social roles enacted there.

Yet there can be little doubt that children and adults do identify with stars of both cinema and popular music. Such identifications, moreover, lead to imitation, especially of dress and appearance, and in many cases the viewer does attempt to match his behaviour to that of the star, who one assumes is seen as something of a mythical hero.

PARA-SOCIAL INTERACTION AND THE ILLUSION OF INTIMACY

In many of the studies so far reviewed, it is as if children, far from putting themselves into a character's shoes, recognise the good and bad characters and play opposite them. We shall argue in Chapter 5, that children are unable, until about nine-years-old, to perceive the world from a point of view other than their own because of ego-centrism, which no doubt explains why at children's matinées they respond to the film characters by hissing the villain and cheering the hero. There are adequate theoretical reasons to assume that prior to the ability to identify, children must first be able to discern the good character from the bad. Explanations as simple as this have been neglected by social scientists with the notable exception of the psychoanalysts, Horton and Wohl (1956). It is, according to Horton and Wohl, as if televiewers meet and interact with the most illustrious and famous men when they appear on the television screen. Such characters are met as though they were in the circle of immediate friends. The illusion of intimacy is encouraged by those celebrities who frequently address remarks directly at the viewer in the same way as a real-life friend might do. As we have seen, a number of viewers report that they talk back at the television screen; it is clear that the illusion of intimacy is potent. Far from losing his identity the viewer responds to these compères, as he might respond to village celebrities.

The persona

Horton and Wohl refer to the type of television character who speaks directly to the audience as a persona, whose performance is carefully rehearsed so as to give the impression that he is talking to the viewer in an intimate way. The persona is a television personality who regularly hosts chat or entertainment shows which are often named after him. He will attempt to copy the gestures, conversational style, and facial expressions of the informal face-to-face conversation – the 'How are you?' question, the nods and winks into the camera, the pained expression after a bad joke and so on. In order to encourage further the illusion of intimacy an air of general informality will pervade such shows, first and nicknames will be preferred, interesting hobbies and pursuits of both guests and personas are frequently referred to.

To encourage the viewer still further into believing he is 'present' during such broadcasts, considerable stress will be made that the programme is 'live', the whole approach will be casual and frequently both floor-men and camera-men will be seen. Nearly always in persona shows a studio audience is employed. This audience is carefully coached so that chatter between the persona and the audience is encouraged. Audience members appear before the cameras to give the impression of face-to-face contact. The audience also serves to tell the viewers at home when to laugh,* when to applaud and are invited before the camera to emphasise to the viewer at home the compère's greatest attributes.

Finally very considerable use is made by personas of the close-up camera technique, so that during the greater part of the programme the viewer is in fact watching nothing other than the persona's 'talking head'. The viewer thus sees eyebrow, mouth and other facial movements as they would be seen in face-to-face contact. Unlike dramatic presentations the persona's performance is open in that his remarks are addressed directly to the viewers at home, and not as in drama addressed directly at other characters.

Audience response to personas

The persona directs his attention to the viewer at home, and calls upon the viewer to respond to him, cued in by the studio audience. Mere witnessing of the programme is not evidence that the spectator has played the required part. Viewers should respond either overtly by laughing or saying 'ah' when viewing, or even answering the compère back. It is not uncommon in research studies to find that 40 per cent of viewers admit that they talk to their television sets. It may be assumed that even more viewers respond to the personas covertly, in thought rather than action, while viewing. In a very real sense, therefore, television chat shows involve viewers in ways that are unique to television. As argued in Chapter 1, television resembles the extended kin community in the village, with whom the individual would frequently interact on a face-to-face basis. Moreover, as in the village, the interactions with significant others on television are subjected to critical analysis and either rejected or accepted by the individual viewer. In particular, discussion with other people will

* Smyth and Fuller (1972) noted that when laughter was 'dubbed' on to recorded jokes listeners laughed more frequently and for longer.

lead to an unfavourable or favourable consensus of opinion concerning the programme. Pseudo-social interactions become the topic of conversation, just as village interactions were the topic of conversation amongst the extended kin.

Motives leading to para-social interaction

The motives which prompt para-social interaction are, as might be expected, very different from those which prompt identification with film stars. One salient motive for para-social interaction is that such exchanges show the spectator how to behave in a variety of different situations. Para-social interactions afford the viewer an opportunity to interact with characters of the opposite sex, characters with higher or lower status than his own and with people of particular occupations and professions. Soap opera, for example, can be seen as an interminable exploration of the events which could be met in home life. Para-social interactions may provide an exploration and development of 'how to behave' possibilities in situations likely to be met in the future (particularly if one believes one's opportunities will be greater then – which is the case for children), or which have been met in the past, or might be met in the present. Para-social interactions may provide information likely (or imagined) to be relevant concerning suitable behaviour for present and future situations. In other words para-social interactions with television personas have similar functions to real life social interactions in the village – they provide essential social learning – namely, how to respond to members of the larger society.

More obviously para-social interactions may also compensate for a lack of real life interactions by the invalid, the sick, the lonely, the aged, the timid, the rejected or the isolated. In extreme cases some lonely individuals will fall in love with the personas and may even reject real-life partners. Such cases are likely to be rare, but para-social interaction may be motivated by loneliness and the desire to interact with anyone, albeit a television persona. As will be seen in Chapter 4, research does indicate that isolated individuals use television presentations in different ways from the socially integrated individual. It was argued in Chapter 1 that interaction with the extended kin grouping prepares the child for interaction in the larger society; it seems logical to suppose that children deprived of extended kin groupings will make use of television personalities, which we have argued have similar functions to the extended kin grouping.

Moreover, bearing in mind what was said in Chapter 1 about the basic communality of experience within the extended kin grouping, it seems likely that para-social interactions may be motivated by the concern personas express about 'ordinary' people. Personas continually congratulate people for achieving old age, marriage, children and all the other inevitables of everyday life. A skilled persona may therefore convince the viewer that he is extraordinary and that his opinions and life experiences are to be valued. There would seem in our society few enough agencies which reward individuals for their ordinariness that para-social interactions with television personas may be motivated for such reasons.

RESEARCH INTO PARA-SOCIAL INTERACTION

In order to see whether personas created the illusion of intimacy I showed 30 children aged seven to eleven years an American television version of *This is Your Life* presented by a professional persona not known to the children, while an equal number of children viewed a dramatic children's film with child actors, *Sports Day*. Children were asked, 'Did anyone in the film speak just to you?' and were told that some children asked this question had replied 'Yes' and others 'No'. Fourteen children who saw *This is Your Life* thought the persona had spoken to them and six of them said they had answered him back, whereas only nine children who saw *Sports Day* said a character had spoken to them. It would seem that the professional persona created the illusion of intimacy half as often again as the child actors in *Sports Day*.

In order to discover whether or not children had placed themselves in a character's shoes, they were asked, 'Have you at any time so far been watching the film so carefully that you forgot you were in school?' Fourteen children who saw *Sports Day* forgot they were in school compared with only nine children who saw *This is Your Life*. It would appear from this limited study that child viewers more often responded in a self-conscious way when viewing a persona show than when viewing a cinema film. As argued in Chapter 1, television differs from the cinema in several fundamental ways, although it would also appear that identification is not the only involvement process when cinema viewing.

THE RECOGNITION PROCESS

Whereas Horton and Wohl argue that para-social interaction only takes place between a viewer and a persona, I shall attempt to argue that children also interact with well known television characters if they are recognised as similar to people known to them. It was argued that in the village the extended kin unit represented society in microcosm, and that children come to know how to respond to people outside the kin unit by extrapolating their experience with extended kin members to the larger social grouping outside the village, perhaps best expressed in the term 'generalised others'. I shall suggest that children learn how to interact in larger social groupings by dint of their interactions with regularly appearing television characters, who also become 'generalised others'.

It is not an enormous logical step from the notion of a persona in a compère show to the notion of little personas in television serials, apart from the fact that in a serial programme characters do not actively invite audience response. But when viewing serials or series programmes we clearly recognise Barlow, Marcus Welby and the Virginian every week, with the result that we feel we know these characters well enough, for example, to say hello to in the street. We recognise, that is we get to know, these characters in much the same way as the child in the village comes to know his extended kin members. Noble (1969e) argued that viewers can recognise whether a character is good or bad, foolish or clever by comparing that character with people known to them, or with other film or book characters with whom they are familiar. If a television hero is enacting a part which is familiar to the viewer, for example father, mother or child, which is in turn similar to the way the viewer's father, mother or brother behaves, the viewer may become involved in that presentation. Viewers frequently make explicit the physical similarities which they see between a television character and someone they know by saying, for example, 'He's like our Bob – same hair – same smile.' When asked viewers can also frequently point out behavioural as well as physical similarities between characters in television programmes and people they know. Indeed it is suggested that the process can work in reverse. Just as the child in the village becomes familiar with the whole range of relationships likely to be encountered in the outside world because they are represented in the extended kin, so too the child viewer becomes familiar with the range of relationships in the wider society by means of interaction with screen characters he has seen regularly, many of whom in these days of mobility are not likely to be represented in his extended kin grouping.

The motive for recognition

Imagine for one minute that you have been introduced to a new group of people. At first you are unsure how to behave and would begin to look for someone you know. Should you know no-one, you will most probably try to categorise the people present according to whether you have met people like them in the past, since you then will have some idea what to say to them and how to behave towards them. I suggest that we behave in similar ways when we watch television programmes. We watch the characters to find out something about them and to predict how they will behave later. The child who has yet to experience many social relationships will probably use those television characters with whom he is familiar, as a basis for subsequent classification of new people.

Reinforcement for recognition: Prediction of outcome

If we recognise television characters as like people we know then uncertainty about the film and its plot is correspondingly reduced. The viewer feels gratified when he correctly predicts the character's next behaviour, and in so doing reduces the uncertainty associated with an undefined situation. Foote (1951) has argued that recognition is a basis for motivation, in that when one enters a new situation one attempts to relate it to old ones by familiar signs. Similarly the child encountering new people in new places is likely to relate them to something familiar – and it is suggested that television can often provide a starting point for such situations as hospitals, police stations, and even moving to a new housing estate.

Types of television programme which encourage recognition

Identification with characters is usually said to occur during dramatic presentations. Para-social interaction is most likely during compère shows. It is suggested that characters are most frequently recognised in those programmes in which the same hard core of characters appear week after week. The viewer recognises them, knows what to expect from them, and is consequently involved with these characters. We can predict that such characters are at least as 'real' to many viewers as distant aunts and uncles. Moreover, if one examines the top twenty programmes in any week's viewing, one-third are likely to be serials or series programmes designed for recognition; one-third compère shows designed for para-social interaction and the remainder news and dramatic programmes. Television shows which present 'the people to the people' to quote Wilfred Pickles are regularly the most popular programmes viewed, especially the long running *Coronation Street*.

Playing opposite recognised characters

Given that the viewer recognises a character as like someone he knows or as a character in his own right, how does the viewer become involved in that particular programme? If the viewer recognises a character as like his father he may respond to that character as he did, or does, to his father – be pleased if the father-like character is thwarted, be annoyed when the father-like character is autocratic, and be submissive when the father-like character is demanding. The viewer therefore plays opposite the recognised character and responds to his actions with no loss of identity. It is not likely that the viewer will overtly respond by talking back out aloud to the characters in television serials and series; it is more probable that he will respond covertly or in thought alone. Should a viewer talk back at his set, he is unlikely to remember what he has said; although one reviewer wrote; 'On the fourth day with nobody else in the house – I suddenly realised that during the previous fifteen minutes I had been vehemently talking back to the screen.' The response taken by the viewer to a film character may be similar or identical to the response which is taken by another film character. For example the viewer may feel angry as a response to the villain's misdeeds. The hero may similarly act out a response of anger. In this case the viewer may identify with the hero and live through his experiences, since both viewer and film hero respond similarly to the villain.

Maccoby and Wilson argue that the viewer identifies with only one character in the film since the plot centres so fully around him. However, many television programmes are panoramic, rather like Tolstoy's novels, whereby the viewer is kept in touch with a large number of characters who only occasionally come into mutual contact. It is therefore likely that viewers will recognise and respond to several characters in a single television programme. The viewer may respond to these characterisations in the same way as he would respond to a similar real life group – by selectively paying attention to, and responding selectively to, many of these different, but familiar characterisations. Within the framework of a regularly appearing cast employed in series and serials programmes and with whom viewers are familiar, a guest star may enact a role which is unfamiliar to the viewer. The viewer may respond to this character in a way that he has never done in real life. Television may, therefore, provide a unique opportunity for social learning, since it is possible that in playing opposite recognised television characters he can take a role never experienced in life, a role he has ceased to take, or a role he will take later.

Stereotypes and verbal labelling

The process whereby a viewer recognises a character on television as being like someone he knows, or recognises somebody in life as like a television character he knows, is associated with the concept of the stereotype. Language plays a critical part in labelling characters' roles and is almost inevitably an abstraction from what were originally behavioural characteristics of people known to the child. Thus saying that a character is kind, or a bully, leads the viewer to expect that the character will behave in a certain predictable way. Children, for example, have said of certain characters that they 'are like Daddy, because they are kind and helpful, but in other ways they are not like Daddy'. However, we tend to overcategorise and have a stereotyped perception of people we know less well. Stereotypes, whether favourable or unfavourable, are particularly relevant when applied to occupational and national roles. Television clearly can shape stereotyped perceptions of such groups, since for many viewers their first contact with policemen may be via the television screen; consequently when real-life policemen are encountered they are expected to behave like television policemen.

RESEARCH INTO THE RECOGNITION PROCESS

One hundred children aged between seven and twelve years were shown the Czech puppet programme, *Clown Ferdl,* which is described in Chapter 5, and asked for each of the three main puppet characters, 'Who that you know is character X like and why?' Very nearly two-thirds of the children interviewed said that the puppet characters were like someone they knew, even when they knew they could answer 'nobody'. By and large, the three characters in the programme were seen as similar to three groups of people known to the child – like family members (32 per cent), like close friends (44 per cent) and like acquaintances and people less familiar to the children (24 per cent). Children most frequently recognised the bullying ringmaster in the film as like the school bully. While the children seemed to have recognised the role of the bully, was there any evidence that they had responded to this role while viewing?

Children's response to recognised roles

Of particular interest in the children's answers was the frequency with which they spontaneously mentioned themselves when saying why television characters were like people they knew. Fifty per cent of answers were of the type, 'they both hit *you*', or 'they both threaten *you*', which suggests that the recognition of characters' roles is indeed a self-conscious process. Children were also asked if they wanted to help anybody in the programme, since it was thought that children might respond to the dilemmas in which a programme character found himself by wishing to help him, which is a self-conscious response to a character's actions. Fifty-four per cent of those children who recognised two or three of the characters as like

people they knew said they wished to help somebody in the programme. Fifty per cent of those children who had recognised one
character in the programme as like someone they knew said they
wished to help, while only 24 per cent of children who recognised
nobody said they wished to help anybody. In this research, therefore,
it would appear, that children only responded to the actions of
programme characters if they recognised them as like people they
knew – which is as expected.

RECOGNITION LEADING TO INVOLVEMENT

We have argued that viewers who recognise television characters
and play opposite them become involved in that television presentation. If the viewer responds to the recognised character by wanting,
for example, to help him, that viewer – however temporarily – is
deluded into believing that the programme is real rather than a
dramatic presentation. One of the most striking characteristics of
mass communication studies is the frequency with which viewers
confuse the reality and fantasy of their favourite programmes. A
serial character has only to be written out of the script moments
before the wreaths begin to arrive. Children who had seen *Clown
Ferdl* were therefore asked whether they thought the programme was
real or unreal. Real was defined in terms of whether events seen in
the programme could or could not occur in real life. Those children
who recognised all three characters thought the programme most
real; those who recognised two of the characters thought the programme real; those who recognised only one character thought the
programme fairly real while those who recognised no character
thought the programme was unreal. Such data suggest that children
who recognised the characters even in a puppet programme as like
people they knew, responded to those characters and were less inclined immediately after viewing to deny that the programme was a mere
dramatic presentation.

RESEARCH COMPARING IDENTIFICATION AND RECOGNITION

Having, as it were, groped my way to the concept of recognition in
the *Clown Ferdl* study, I addressed a second study in a more systematic way to a comparison between recognition and identification.
Ninety boys and girls, from seven to eleven years old, in a middle-
class school situated on the outskirts of the city of Leicester viewed
one of the three films described below: *Sports Day* – a film with child
actors in which the boy hero is wrongly accused of maltreating a
dog, refuses to specify who maltreated the dog and is wrongly
punished until his sister makes the truth known; *Terror from the
East*, a slick but feeble-minded American television series concerning

Californian policemen who aid a man masquerading as a vicar (Charles Laughton) whose intention is to kill; and *This is Your Life* – American version with a professional persona who presents a lady survivor from the *Lusitania*.

Both males and females played important parts in these programmes which were all equally unfamiliar to the child viewers. The procedure adopted was as follows. First, a skilled interviewer established rapport with the children before the film was seen, and the names of their friends both at home and school were recorded. Children watched one of the films in six groups each composed of 15 children; thus 30 children watched each film which was stopped at a critical moment in the plot. Each child was individually interviewed a second time and asked amongst other things, to role-play the hero and the villain; to predict what would happen next in the film; whether they had identified with a firm hero; and whether they had recognised a film character as like someone known to them. After the rest of the film was seen children were individually interviewed for a third time, and asked questions concerning their involvement with the film seen.

Extent of identification and recognition

When the films were prematurely stopped, each child was asked, 'Is there anyone in the film you would like to be exactly the same as?' and were told some of the children interviewed had said, 'Yes', and others, 'No'. While no child identified with the villain, 39 per cent of children said they wanted to be exactly like a film hero or heroine. Children were also asked, 'Is there anyone in the film you would like to be like in some ways?'. It was thought more children might partially, rather than totally, identify with a film hero. Fifty per cent of children replied 'Yes' to this question. Answers to this latter question are from now on taken as the index to identification with a film hero.

Children were also asked at the film break, 'Is there anyone in the film who is like someone you know?', and again were told that some other children had replied 'Yes' while others had said 'No'. Forty-two per cent of children replied that there was a character in the film like someone they knew. Film characters were said to be like members of their family (35 per cent), like close acquaintances at home and school (46 per cent) and like acquaintances known less well (19 per cent). These figures replicate those previously found in the *Clown Ferdl* study. Most children (69 per cent) recognised a film character as like someone they knew because of behavioural similarities, while the remaining 31 per cent recognised characters because of physical similarities.

Comparing identification with recognition results, it was found that 67 per cent of children in some way related the film to themselves – either by identifying with a hero (26 per cent), recognising a film character (17 per cent), or by both recognising and identifying with a film character (24 per cent). Moreover, 85 per cent of those children who only recognised film characters, recognised more than one character as like people they knew. In contrast to identification, which can only take place with one film actor, children frequently recognised several of the film characters as like people they knew. Finally one-third of the children did not appear to be in any way involved with the film seen since they neither identified with nor recognised film characters.

Sex differences in identification and recognition

Researchers have long been puzzled because girls tend to 'identify' with both male and female performers – at least in the sense that Maccoby and Wilson define and measure identification. Boys, on the other hand, tend to identify only with male film heroes. Himmelweit *et al.* comment 'considering that half the audience consists of girls, it is indeed surprising to see how few children's plays seem to take account of this factor; their themes tend to relate to boys' rather than girls' interests providing adequate heroes for the former, but inadequate heroines for the latter'. Bearing in mind what was said in Chapter 1 – namely that television is a 'female' medium insofar as it simulates conversations over the garden wall, we are entitled to expect that girls will probably tend to recognise more than boys, and that boys will tend to identify more than girls. Each of the three films seen portrayed a female heroine, but whereas 60 per cent of boys said they wished to be like a film hero in some ways, only 40 per cent of girls did so. It appears that girls, even when the opportunity is available, will not identify as often as boys. Girls, on the other hand, recognised film characters as like people they knew (49 per cent) more often than boys (34 per cent). Girls seemed to prefer to play opposite performers when they appear on television. One suspects that girls preferred to play opposite film stars, such as Valentino, even in the cinema. Boys, however, prefer to live through and share a film character's experiences while viewing via the process of identification. It is suggested that the sexes are fundamentally different as regards the need for identity loss experiences, the male almost needs to lose his identity when attending to the mass media, while the female, who is usually also the family biographer, prefers to keep her identity intact and take answering roles. Indeed as will be seen in Chapter 5, girls learn to empathise with film characters at an earlier age than boys.

These results may perhaps explain why Maccoby and Wilson found firstly that girls recalled, better than boys, the words and actions of the girl character *when* they occurred in a context of interaction with the boy, and secondly why boys recalled the aggressive content better than girls *only* if the boy hero was the agent of aggression.

CONSEQUENCES OF IDENTIFICATION

In this section I shall compare the reactions of children who identified with a film character with the reactions of those who did not. It was expected that children who identified with a hero would:

1. More easily than non-identifiers be able to imagine themselves in the role of the hero/heroine.
2. Take the hero/heroine's role less self-consciously than non-identifiers.
3. Be more involved in the films than non-identifiers.

Imagining themselves in the role of the hero/heroine

At the point where the films were prematurely stopped, each child was asked, 'Who is the hero/heroine?' and, 'If you were the hero/heroine what would you be feeling now?'. Children were asked whether they found it very hard, hard, not so hard or easy to imagine themselves as the hero. Had the children identified with the hero, they should while viewing already have taken his role and thus it was argued should not find it difficult to imagine themselves as the hero. It was somewhat surprising to find that 45 per cent of the children said they found it hard or very hard to imagine themselves as the hero, 33 per cent found it not so hard, while only 22 per cent found it easy. These results suggest that the majority of viewers had not put themselves into the hero's shoes while watching. But did children who identified with the hero find it easier to role-play the hero than non-identifiers? Results indicated that identifiers found it marginally more easy (60 per cent) than non-identifiers (50 per cent) to imagine themselves as the hero.

Imagining themselves in the villain's role

The notion of identification with the aggressor in the televiewing situation would appear to suggest that some viewers might put themselves in the shoes of the villain while viewing either *Terror from the East* or *Sports Day*. Children were asked, 'If you were the villain, how would *you* be feeling now?' and asked how easy it was to imagine themselves as the villain. While no child said he wished to be like the villain in any way, it was surprising to find that 50 per cent of children thought it not so hard, or easy, to imagine themselves as the villain – the same proportion as found it not so hard, or easy, to imagine themselves as the hero. It would seem that this question refers to the ease or difficulty experienced by the child when asked to imagine himself in any role – whether hero or villain. Examination of the answers to the questions, 'How silly do you feel imagining yourself as the hero and as the villain?' lend support to this latter interpretation.

SELF-CONSCIOUSNESS OF THE VIEWER

It is difficult to assess how self-conscious a child viewer is when watching television, but clearly a child who plays opposite a recognised character, rather than immersing himself in a character's experiences, will be more aware of his own identity. It was argued that people generally feel silly when they are self-conscious, aware that they have done something stupid, or alternatively are asked to do something stupid. Children were, therefore, asked at the film break whether they had felt very silly, silly, not so silly or not at all silly when imagining themselves as the hero. Twenty-six per cent said they felt either silly or very silly, 34 per cent felt not so silly and 40 per cent felt not at all silly when they were asked to take the hero's role. Approximately three-quarters of the children were able to take the hero's/heroine's role without feeling too self-conscious. These results support Maccoby and Wilson's contention that many viewers can spontaneously put themselves into the shoes of television characters while viewing.

The obvious next stage was to discover whether those children who had identified with the hero/heroine felt less silly imagining themselves as the hero/heroine than non-identifiers. Results suggested that this was the case, since twice as many non-identifiers (35 per cent) as identifiers (18 per cent) felt either very silly or silly when imagining themselves as the hero. Moreover whereas only 26 per cent of children felt either silly or very silly imagining themselves as the hero/heroine, 54 per cent (twice as many) felt either very silly or silly imagining themselves as the villain. It would seem that asking children how silly they felt when taking a film character's role does indeed reflect on how self-conscious children feel when putting themselves into a character's shoes. As we have argued it appears that children cannot self-consciously identify with a film character – in other words identification is an identity loss process.

Viewer involvement in film presentations

These children who have put themselves into the hero's shoes and shared his experiences while viewing can clearly be expected to be more involved in the film presentation than children who have not identified with a film character. I have previously argued that one result of identification is that viewers will be inclined to deny that the film is a mere fiction. Children who have identified with a film character should be more inclined to say, firstly, that the film is real rather than acted; and, secondly, they will maintain that they can meet people similar to those seen in the film in real life, rather than say they could not meet such people in real life. Children were therefore asked whether the people in the film acted (as in a school play) and asked to say either – obviously acted, I think it's acted, I am not sure, I think they behave like that all the time, or they behave like that all the time. Just under half the children interviewed (a surprising 45 per cent) said that the film characters behave like that all the time. It is perhaps easy to see how serial characters become real to the majority of the viewing audience if something akin to the illusion of intimacy operates when televiewing serials.

While objective reality was temporarily suspended by half the children the suspense was not total since only 17 per cent of children said they could often, or very often, meet 'anyone who behaved like the people in the film', rather than replying 'not very often' or 'never'. Children who are involved in film presentations are likely to feel that the situations are real rather than acted, but that these situations are not those in which they are likely to find themselves. However, it should be remembered that the films shown in this study were chosen because they were all equally alien to the children, so this latter result is not surprising. I hope, now that I have acquired video-tape equipment, to repeat this experiment with programmes such as *Coronation Street* for which I would predict much greater reality-fantasy confusion.

As expected, some 60 per cent of identifiers maintained that the film characters 'behave like that all the time' as compared with only 32 per cent (half as many) of non-identifiers. Identification with the film hero did, therefore, involve children in the film to the extent that they saw the film as real life, and not as a dramatic presentation. Similarly children who identified with the hero/heroine more often than those who did not, maintained that they might meet someone in real life 'who behaved like the film character', 22 per cent and 13 per cent respectively.

Summary of identification results

Initially comparison was made between children who said they wished to be like the hero/heroine in some ways and children who did not wish to be like the hero. It may be remembered that only half the children said they wished to be like the hero in some ways. Compared to non-identifiers, identifiers, firstly, felt less self-conscious (silly) when imagining themselves as the hero/heroine; secondly they found it slightly less difficult to take the role of the hero/heroine; thirdly, more often stated that film characters did not enact parts but behaved like that all the time and, fourthly, more often thought that they could meet people in real life similar to those seen in the film.

Overall, identification seems to involve the viewer putting himself unself-consciously into a character's shoes and consequently he believes that the events seen in the film are real.

CONSEQUENCES OF THE RECOGNITION PROCESS

The process whereby film characters are recognised as like people known to the child is very different from the process of identification with film heroes, although both processes involve the child viewer in the film seen. While both identifiers and recognisers will maintain that the characters do not enact parts but are real, identification is likely to lead to greater involvement in the film than recognition. It is suggested that children who recognise film characters as like people known to them, in contrast to children who do not recognise characters and children who identify, may be expected to:

1. Feel self-conscious (or silly) when asked to imagine themselves as the hero – since recognition requires no identity loss.
2. Experience considerable difficulty when taking the villain's role – since recognisers are likely to play opposite the villain.
3. Respond to the film characters' actions by, for example, worrying when characters get into trouble in the film – because recognisers self-consciously interact with film characters.
4. Play opposite recognised characters by maintaining that the film characters spoke just to them – again because recognition involves no loss of identity.
5. Correctly predict, while film viewing, what is likely to happen in the film – thereby reducing uncertainty concerning the film's outcome.

Viewer involvement with recognised characters

Children who recognised a film character as like someone they knew were expected to respond to that character, perhaps not overtly, but as though the character was present in a face-to-face situation. Recognisers were expected to deny that the people in the film merely acted parts. Results presented in Table 1 show that recognisers (line 4) slightly more than non-recognisers (line 5) said that they could more often meet such characters in real life and maintained that

TABLE 1

INVOLVEMENT IN THE FILM FOR CHILDREN WHO IDENTIFIED WITH
CHARACTERS, AND CHILDREN WHO RECOGNISED CHARACTERS

Identification or Recognition	Involvement: Did the children perceive (1) the characters as real or merely acting their parts (2) whether they could/could not meet film characters?			
	Not acted real	Acted	Could meet often/very often	Could not meet
	Per cent			
1. Overall	45	55	17	83
2. Identification with a character (like him/her in some ways)	60	40	22	78
3. No identification with a character (not like him/her even in some ways)	32	68	13	87
4. Recognition of a film character (a character is like someone known to the child)	50	50	21	79
5. No recognition of a film character (no character like anyone known to child)	40	60	14	86

these characters were not acting but were real. If we assume that confusion between the reality and fantasy of a film presentation can be taken as a measure of involvement, children who recognise characters become more involved in television presentations than children who do not recognise characters.

Since identification, unlike recognition, involves identity loss, we might expect identification to lead to greater involvement than self-conscious recognition and interaction with television performers. As can be seen in Table 1, children who identified (line 2) were most inclined to say that the characters behaved like that all the time, and most often say they could meet such characters, followed in turn by recognisers (line 4), while children who neither recognise nor identify are least involved of all (lines 3 and 5). Identification and recognition lead to involvement in television presentations but the recogniser stands further back from the action than the identifier.

Recognition as an identity intact process

If recognisers stand further back from the action, watching and responding to characters, they should feel more self-conscious and silly than non-recognisers when asked to imagine themselves as the hero/heroine. As can be seen in Table 2, recognisers (line 4) felt

TABLE 2

HOW DIFFICULT AND SELF-CONSCIOUS CHILDREN FELT WHEN ROLE-
PLAYING THE HERO/HEROINE, ACCORDING TO WHETHER THEY HAD
IDENTIFIED WITH OR RECOGNISED FILM CHARACTERS

Role-playing the hero/ heroine (imagine that you are the hero/heroine)	Feeling		Difficulty	
	very silly, silly	not so silly, not at all silly	very hard, hard	not so hard, easy
	Per cent			
1. Overall	26	74	45	55
2. Identified with hero/heroine (like him/her in some ways)	18	82	40	60
3. No identification with hero/ heroine (not like him/her even in some ways)	35	65	50	50
4. Recognition of a film character (a film character is like someone known to the child)	30	70	40	60
5. No recognition of a film character (no film character like anyone known to the child)	24	76	45	55

slightly sillier than non-recognisers (line 5), while it is apparent that
identifiers (line 2) felt least embarassed. Results suggest that identifiers easily put themselves in the hero's shoes while recognisers
self-consciously interact with the hero.

When children were asked how difficult it was for them to imagine
themselves as the hero, no differences were found between recognisers and identifiers. As previously suggested this question does not
appear to directly relate to the self-consciousness of the child viewer.

How do children react to the villain

As we have seen, children rarely identify with the villains seen in
films. How then do children cope with villains? As we might expect
(Table 3), children feel equally self-conscious when taking the part of
the villain whether seen through the eyes of the hero via identification, or through their own eyes via recognition. But it would appear
that the recognition process places the villain's role in high perspective, since more than any other child, recognisers said it was hard
for them to imagine themselves as the villain. It would seem that
children in general, and recognisers in particular, recognise villains
on their television screens just as they once realised who were the
'whores and thieves' in their extended kin group in the village.

TABLE 3

HOW DIFFICULT AND SELF-CONSCIOUS THE CHILDREN FELT WHEN ROLE-PLAYING THE VILLAIN, ACCORDING TO WHETHER THEY HAD IDENTIFIED WITH OR RECOGNISED FILM CHARACTERS

Role-playing the villain (imagine that you are the villain)	Feeling		Difficulty	
	very silly, silly	not so silly, not at all silly	very hard, hard	not so hard, easy
	Per cent			
1. Overall	54	46	50	50
2. Identified with hero (like him/her in some ways)	55	45	51	49
3. No identification with hero (not like him in some ways)	55	45	51	49
4. Recognition of a film character (a film character is like someone known to the child)	56	44	65	35
5. No recognition of a film character (no character is like anyone known to the child)	54	46	35	65

Viewers' response to recognised characters

Children were expected to respond to recognised characters on the television screen much as they would respond to members of their extended kin in the village – for example, by worrying when they get into trouble and by talking with them. Children were therefore asked, 'When the hero was in trouble in the film, did you feel very worried, worried, or not at all worried?' As can be seen in Table 4, twice as many recognisers as non-recognisers or identifiers said they were worried when the hero was in trouble. If we remember that the heroes did not appear worried when in trouble on the screen, it would seem that only children who recognise characters respond by feeling worried when that character is in trouble.

Similarly, it was thought that children who identify with film characters and share their screen experiences can hardly hold conversations with them at the same time. Children who recognised characters were expected to converse with them via the illusion of intimacy. Children were therefore asked, 'Did any of the film characters speak just to you?', asked to say whether this had occurred very often, often, not so often, or never. As can be seen in Table 4, one-third of the children replied that a character had spoken just to them and predictably it was recognisers rather than identifiers or non-recognisers who experienced the illusion of intimacy. Children who recognise characters can, and it would seem do, feel that they have

TABLE 4

RESPONDING TO A CHARACTER'S ACTIONS WHETHER THE CHILD HAD
IDENTIFIED WITH A CHARACTER OR RECOGNISED A CHARACTER

Identification or Recognition	Responding to a character's actions (1) worried when hero in trouble in film (2) whether character talked to them or not			
	worried or very worried	not at all worried	spoken to them	never spoken to them
	Per cent			
1. Overall	38	62	35	65
2. Identified with a character (like him/her in some ways)	33	67	29	71
3. No identification with a character (not like him/her even in some ways)	42	58	41	59
4. Recognition of a film character (a film character is like someone known to the child)	52	48	40	60
5. No recognition of a film character (no character like anyone known to child)	26	74	29	71

been spoken to. If, as has been argued, the social self is shaped by conversation with significant other people, it would seem that the recognised television characters in serials, whom one feels one knows, might help to shape the social self of the viewer at home.

Motive for recognition: Prediction of the film's outcome

Just as in the village the extended kin represents society in microcosm, and shows the child how to behave in all possible situations, so it was thought that children who recognise television characters as like people they know would be likely to predict how these characters will behave in the future. Thus it was thought that recognition would reduce uncertainty relating to the outcome of the film plot. Each film was stopped at a crucial moment in the plot, and children were asked what they thought would happen next. *Sports Day* was stopped after the hero had been wrongly accused of hurting a dog and was sitting in detention while the school sports were in progress. *Terror from the East* was stopped when the bogus clergyman had secretly left his house to kill a girl, and *This is Your Life* was stopped when children were watching the sinking of the *Lusitania*. Each child was asked, 'What will the hero do now?', and in the case of the first two films, 'What will the villain do now?'.

Results summarised in Table 5 show that slightly less than half

TABLE 5

ABILITY TO PREDICT WHAT CHARACTERS IN THE FILMS WILL DO, ACCORDING
TO CHILDREN WHO IDENTIFIED WITH THE HERO OR WHETHER THEY HAD
RECOGNISED A FILM CHARACTER

Identification or Recognition	Prediction: what will hero and villain do next in the film?				
	Correct prediction for hero	Don't know for hero	Incorrect prediction for hero	Correct prediction for villain	Incorrect prediction for villain
	Per cent				
1. Overall	46	30	24	32	68
2. Identification with a character (like him/ her in some ways)	43	30	27	30	70
3. No identification with a character (not like him/her even in some ways)	45	34	21	28	72
4. Recognition of a film character (a film character is like someone known to the child)	59	18	23	46	54
5. No recognition of a film character (no character like anyone known to the child)	35	41	24	20	80

the children were able to predict correctly what would happen to the
hero in the film and a third were able to predict correctly what would
happen to the villain. Which children, however, were best able to
predict outcome? Children who have identified with a film hero,
who share the here-and-now of his ongoing film experiences, do not
need to look forward in the plot, and as expected were no better
than non-identifiers at predicting outcome for either villain or hero.
On the other hand, children who recognise characters as like people
they know were expected to generalise from this information to
know how the character is likely to behave. Recognisers were
nearly twice as good at predicting outcome for both hero and
villain than non-recognisers, and likewise were half as good again as
identifiers at predicting outcome. Moreover compared with both
identifiers and non-recognisers alike, fewest of all recognisers
failed to make a prediction. It would appear that children recognise characters in order to predict their likely future behaviour,
unlike children who identify, who do so to share the film character's

ongoing experiences. It seems reasonable to suppose that children can acquire a repertoire of how-to-behave models from the predictable behaviour patterns which they see enacted weekly by television characters whom they feel they know. Such hypotheses will be tested in future studies.

CONCLUSION

I suggest that viewers can do one of four things when watching film or television programmes. In the cinema, or alternatively watching television alone at home with the light off, a viewer is likely to identify with a film character, submerge his identity in order to share his film experiences, imagine that the characters are real, but not look forward in the film plot – rather enjoy the character's ongoing film experiences. Viewers who have identified with a film character, because they do not compare their life experiences with the film experiences, are presumably likely to imitate indiscriminately the behaviour of the film character with whom they have identified. As we have noted such viewers are more likely to be male than female, although we probably all enjoy losing our identities via identification at some points in time. The cinema seems designed for identity-loss experiences since the films are viewed in darkness, in unfamiliar surroundings and we generally watch the close interplay between characters who address remarks at each other rather than to the viewer at home. If what is said here is correct we could possibly use the frequency of cinema attendance as a measure suggestive of an individual's need to lose his identity.

Secondly, a viewer can self-consciously recognise a television character as like someone he knows, or alternatively come to know a regularly appearing character as well as he knows many people in real life, interact with this character by responding to his actions, imagine temporarily that the character is real and correctly predict what this character is likely to do in the programme. Since television so frequently shows us little other than the talking head, and since so many remarks are addressed directly to the viewer at home rather than to other characters, it is not surprising to find that so many viewers are temporarily deluded into believing that the character speaks just to them and that many answer him back. Viewers who watch television in their homes in company are not likely to lose their identities. Moreover, because they recognise the behaviour of the character as like someone they know, and hence compare their life experiences with television experiences, they are not likely to imitate indiscriminately the behaviour of characters recognised weekly in series and serial programmes. Rather, these characters serve as something akin to a screen community with whom the viewer regularly talks and interacts. Viewers who feel they know these characters well may indeed compare new people they meet in real life with such characters in order to be able to predict how these new people are likely later to behave. I suggest that this regularly appearing screen community serves for many as an extended kin grouping, whereby the viewer comes into contact with the wider society beyond his immediate family. These regularly appearing characters show the individual at home how to behave in a surprising variety of situations with which the viewer has had little real life contact. This function I suggest was once achieved by the extended kin within the village grouping.

As I have noted, women appear to recognise television characters more often than men. For many women the antics of the characters in soap operas become points of gossip, just as women presumably gossiped about the antics of people within their extended kin groupings in the village. It is therefore highly probable that what they have seen in television serials and series programmes is later critically discussed with friends. Just as both men and women can put the light out to watch a film on television, so both sexes can choose a recognition experience by watching serials and series programmes at home in company. For men, no less than women, what they have seen the night before becomes a talking point at work the next day.

Thirdly, a viewer can both identify with a character and recognise other characters as like people he knows. In this case the characters will be seen as real, he will share the experiences of one character and interact by responding to the actions of the other film characters. At the same time such viewers are likely to understand what is to happen in the film. In highlighting the differences between recognition and identification I would not wish to give the impression that they cannot both take place simultaneously. More viewers may both recognise and identify than either recognise or identify exclusively.

Fourthly and finally, a viewer may not recognise a character as like someone he knows: such a viewer will think that the film is acted and will be probably not interested enough in the programme to predict the outcome.

4

The mass media as an escape

In Chapter 1 it was argued that children need to withdraw from the
bewildering management of social stages in industrial society, and
that television while providing respite also allows children to take
part in that society at the same time. I shall argue in this chapter
that mass communication researchers have by and large accepted the
idea that children 'escape' by attending to television, but have overlooked the very important function that television has in providing
for social learning – that is, the way children take part in society by
attending to television. As we have seen in Chapter 2, once a value
position becomes entrenched in social scientific research, that value
position remains unquestioned and accepted as dogma. Unfortunately the prevailing value position regarding television has been that
it can provide no learning relevant to everyday life, or if it does teach,
it compares unfavourably with books and school. I shall argue that
because viewers interact with recognised television characters, and
do not lose their identity via identification, that television uniquely
affords children opportunities for exploring social roles; that via
interaction with recognised television characters children again
become part of the wider society, just as in the village they became
'social' because of interaction with extended kin members.

Moreover, I shall suggest that the mass communication research
tradition, because it has failed to understand the function of 'art',
has labelled fantasy programmes as escapist, and reality programmes
as useful. In Chapter 1 we argued that art ideally should be available
to everyman, and that art is not the prerogative of the specialised
few as the high culture tradition would have us believe. The notion
that everyman is an artist was perhaps most clearly expounded by
Tolstoy (1898a), when he defines 'art' as 'an activity by means of
which one man, having experienced a feeling, intentionally transmits
it to others'. 'This', Bernard Shaw says, 'is the simple truth: the
moment it is uttered, whoever is conversant with art recognises in it
the voice of the master.' 'Art' is therefore a peephole into the mind,
and any television programme which manages to transmit feelings
to others is art, and must of necessity provide the viewer with feedback relevant to everyday life. Like all other media, television at its
best must constitute an art form, and if we accept Tolstoy's definition, it seems likely that fictional programmes will allow children

C

to experience feelings which they may not yet have experienced in real life.

Nor, even if we search for one, shall we find a society exclusively concerned with reality. Each society has its myths which are usually expressed in story or fantasy form, and these myths have the very real function of being charters for social action, or put another way, metaphoric expressions of value. In the village we recognise myths in parable and story form; in industrial societies we must look elsewhere and it seems self-evident that television's fantasy programmes may well express myths, and consequently the charter for social action which the child may not learn in school.

The scene is set: televiewing undermines family communications

As with identification studies, research concerning the notion of escape is American in origin and dates back to Maccoby (1951) who studied 622 children in the Boston area, half of whom had access to television. These latter children did less recreational reading, less radio listening and less picture-going than children, matched for age, sex and class, without television. Similarly televiewers spent less time playing, less time helping with household tasks and, Maccoby claims, less time talking together than non-televiewers. While the television set increased the amount of time which family members spent together, she claims that 58 per cent of parents said there was very little or no talking while televiewing. Unfortunately we are not told how often family members converse when washing up, reading, or even eating. It seems somewhat dangerous to conclude that television is asocial, when four out of ten viewers talk to each other when viewing. In this first study it appears that the investigator set out to prove that televiewing has negative effects.

TELEVIEWING IS ESCAPIST

Not daunted Maccoby (1954) set out to prove that five- and six-year-old children subject to harsh parental discipline would retreat 'as an escape' to their television sets, although she seemed unconcerned with what such children might gain from televiewing. Middle-class children who were not treated warmly or permissively watched about one and a half hours a day, while warmly treated children not subject to harsh parental discipline watched about one hour a day – hardly a surprising difference. Moreover in working-class families children watched for between one and a half and two hours a day regardless of parental discipline. She concludes that middle-class children watch television both to escape from parents and to annoy them.

What exactly is there in the 'restricted' five-and six-year olds' televiewing which is defined as escapist? Maccoby outlines three escape modes – the ostrich tendency whereby the child forgets his problems while viewing, the identification mode where the child by putting himself in a character's shoes can be aggressive, sexual and disobedient without fear of punishment, and the wish fulfilment mode where, by identification again, the child can kill with the aggressive hero, love with the sexual hero and so on. Maccoby argues that these vicarious satisfactions are presumably of a lower order than real-life satisfactions, and are thus chosen as second best solutions when real-life satisfactions are lacking.

As such, watching fantasy television programmes constitutes for Maccoby an escape, presumably because each mode involves identity loss. If, however, parents are unreasoning and unreasonable, it seems possible that children may have better conversations by para-social interaction with recognised television characters than with the parents. Whether television conversations, in such a case, are of a lower order than the real life alternative seems a moot point.

TELEVISION OVERWHELMINGLY MEETS 'FANTASY' NEEDS

Bailyn (1959), studying children of school age, was concerned to find out which ten- and eleven-year-old children were heavy 'pictorial users'. She found that girls who did better in school than would be expected from their intelligence scores were less exposed to pictorial materials than children who performed less well in schools than their intelligence scores would predict. The heavy televiewer was also the heavy comic-book reader and heavy cinema-goer. Such children were boys, rather than girls, Catholics, rather than Protestants, working rather than middle class and less, rather than more intelligent. Bailyn concludes that the chief goal sought in televiewing fantasy programmes was escape, since unintelligent boys who were assessed as rebelliously independent* were found to prefer pictorial media in which there was an aggressive hero with whom they could identify. It is clear that in this author's opinion watching televised fantasy programmes detracts from school performance.

Bailyn notes, however, that those children who most liked pictorial media confused the reality and fantasy of the television portrayals they saw. As we have seen such confusions result not only from identification but also from para-social interaction with

* Children were asked, 'If you were going to the circus would you want to go with your father, best friend, brother or sister, mother or by yourself?' If children said 'by myself,' they were said to be rebelliously independent.

recognised characters. If, as seems likely, these children came from families which Sanford (1959) would describe as authoritarian, namely working-class Catholic, where children are disciplined by convention and not by principle, it also seems possible that such children may grow to recognise television serial characters as friends, who at least allow the child to feel rebellious.

It should be remembered that not only are the bulk of our television programmes American in origin, but the bulk of mass communications research is also American. It is not surprising, therefore, to find a large number of studies which confirmed the *zeitgeist* of the late 'fifties: that televiewing fantasy is escapist. Pearlin (1959) asked 736 viewers what they watched on television and how much stress they experienced. He finds a strong relationship between fantasy viewing, which he defines as drama, films and series rather than news, current affairs and politics, and the amount of stress experienced in everyday life – yet more confirmation for the ostrich mode of escape whereby fantasy merely helps us forget our personal problems.

'INSTANT' RESEARCH: STUDIES CONCERNING THE INTRODUCTION OF TELEVISION

It is in this tradition that the results of Schramm, Lyle and Parker (1961) and Himmelweit, Oppenheim and Vince (1958), whose authors were concerned to catalogue the effects of the nationwide introduction of television, should be discussed. Predictably, in mammoth studies comparing communities with and without television in North America and the United Kingdom respectively, they discover that television reduces film going, radio listening, comic and magazine reading. Children very rapidly rate television as the medium they would most miss, because for Himmelweit *et al.* it is easily available, it helps to fill in leisure time, it makes the child feel secure by screening programmes with familiar themes, it provides a talking point, it allows for escape from the problems of life and because of identification it allows the child to experience emotions without danger. Schramm *et al.* conclude that children use television both for information and escape, as a social tool and in order to withdraw from real life.

While these authors concede that five- and six-year-old televiewers have vocabularies a year in advance of non-televiewers, more intelligent teenage viewers do less well on knowledge tests and in school than non-viewers. Perhaps it was this tacit comparison with school performance which prompted McLuhan (1964) to write of Schramm *et al.*: 'their approach was a literary one, albeit unconsciously so, and they made no study of the peculiar nature of the television image'. Himmelweit (1962), however, noted that in the longer term televiewers read as many books as non-viewers, and that dull children even read more books than before televiewing, while Lyle and Hoffman (1972) find that bright students manage to cram televiewing, reading, athletics and school activities into their 'life space'. Thus, while these are valuable, introductory studies because of the novelty of the new situation, they do not perhaps give a clear indication as to long-term effects.

Schramm *et al.*, by comparing children's leisure activities before and after the introduction of television, conclude that it is over-whelmingly the fantasy needs of children that television is meeting. Fantasy, for Schramm *et al.*, as for Pearlin and Maccoby, invites the viewer to take leave of his problems in the real world, invites surrender, relaxation and passivity, offers pleasure and wish fulfil-ment, affords relief from threats and anxiety, annuls the rules of the real world and invites emotion. For unconscious literates, these authors have remarkably little feeling for 'art'. On the other hand, 'reality' content refers viewers to the problems of the real world, invites alertness, effort and activity, encourages thinking, offers information and shows situations which make the viewer even more aware of threats and more anxious – hardly one would imagine education for leisure. Thus it follows that westerns, crime, drama, serials and popular music shows are mainly fantasy, and news, documentary, interviews and educational television portray reality. Their analysis is positively value laden in favour of reality or print materials which for these authors are synonymous. They speak of the schizoid side of televiewing which leads to withdrawal into the private world of television fantasy.

TYPES OF CHILDREN WHO WITHDRAW INTO THE FANTASY WORLD OF TELEVISION

At eleven years, Schramm *et al.* noted, children were predominantly orientated towards fantasy – that is, high television and low print usage, but at fifteen years more children were reality orientated – that is, low television and high print usage.* These latter children had internalised the social norms of the middle class namely – self-betterment, self-restraint, saving, deferred gratification and were orientated to the future. Working-class children tended to continue to 'use' television rather than print. Predictably, children of higher intelligence tend towards reality materials and less bright children towards fantasy materials. Similarly, where there was a difference between what the parent wanted the child to do and the child's

* Schramm *et al.* seem unconcerned that print offers an endless variety of imagined images, while television offers only one.

ambitions, the higher was the consumption of television, radio and comics. Himmelweit *et al.* similarly found that 'television addicts' (a surprisingly value-laden term used to describe those 30 per cent of children of all ages who most watched television, when only 39 addicts were interviewed), were likely to be less intelligent and working class. Moreover, addicts differed from light viewers in that they were ill at ease with other children, lacked security and were shy and retiring. Himmelweit *et al.* maintain that, with 'escape' through television readily available, outside contacts which have met with little success in the past will decrease, as such children escape into the certain and undemanding companionship of television.

Yet when we examine precisely what programmes constitute an escape, we find that addicts prefer either mystery/adventure plays, which allow the child to experience an active dangerous life via identification, or, more importantly, family serials, which are sought for companionship and reassurance. Moreover, we find addicts are more worried than light viewers about getting married, leaving school, finding jobs, correct manners, feeling different from other children, feeling left out of things and are not popular. Such children seem ready targets for body odour and dental hygiene advertisements. It seems likely that their self-concept is not stable in relation to a fixed community group, and that such children watch family programmes in order to play opposite recognised characters and experience 'what it would be like' to be married, popular and so on. After all, are 30 per cent of the adult population unmarried, unpopular and unemployed? Later in life these children may put into practice the social learning depicted in such television programmes.

RESEARCH IN THE SCHRAMM ET AL. TRADITION

Schramm *et al.*, far from labelling fantasy as working-class viewing materials, maintain that fantasy drains off discontent resulting from the hard blows of socialisation and lead the child to withdraw from the real world. This value position is unquestionably accepted by Hazard (1967). Each of 430 adult viewers was asked to plan a perfect evening's viewing, complete an anxiety test; his social status was measured as high or low, and each viewer was asked whether or not he went to art galleries, museums and theatres. This latter measure is described by McQuail (1969) as one of 'cultural participation' and by Hazard as one of 'cultural activity'. Hazard then elaborately classifies each person's perfect evening's viewing as realistic, namely news and documentary, or as realistic fiction – where reality is changed to suit the needs of the programme and so on to extreme fantasy which has no basis in expected reality in which he places science-fiction and horror stories. Regardless of cultural participation, that is visits to art galleries etc., only 18 per cent of viewers prefer an evening of total reality, only 12 per cent an evening of medium fantasy content while 70 per cent prefer an evening of fantasy. Neither anxiety nor cultural activity affected viewing choices, which causes one to ask whether 70 per cent of the population have to escape from the realities of everyday life?

Televiewing style and social relationships

In what is regarded as a classic study Riley and Riley (1951) sought to discover whether there was a relationship between acceptance or rejection by the child's peer group and televiewing style. While it is by no means clear how acceptance by the peer group was established, the Rileys found that 80 per cent of children who referred only to the family – that is, evaluated themselves only in terms of family standards – liked 'little animal comics' which were liked by only 55 per cent of children who referred both to peers and family. For ten- to twelve-year-old children expected to do well in school by their parents 'Bugs Bunny' is a rascal who gets away with it, and who can evade parental standards. Similarly 51 per cent of children who referred to their family, but not to their peers, preferred fantasy programmes such as westerns, mysteries, horror and adventure stories, compared with 40 per cent of children who referred both to family and peer groups. Moreover, the best predictor of which child would not outgrow an interest in action and violence programmes was that a child tried to use his peers as a reference group but was rejected by them. Such children, they argue, experience more stress, which is reflected in a 37 per cent preference for violence, than children referring only to family (17 per cent), or children accepted by the peer group (21 per cent). The Rileys conclude that children use television in different ways. Sixty-nine per cent of children accepted by their peer groups liked the *Lone Ranger* because he could be used as a basis for social play, knows what to do in a tough spot and sometimes brings in the history of the USA. On the other hand 85 per cent of children who referred to, but were not accepted by their peer group, liked the *Lone Ranger* but for different reasons. They said he was 'scary, hard to get out of your mind when going to sleep, and creepy' and as such, the Rileys argue, provides an escape from the real world in which demands are unrealistically high. Escape in this instance is provided by identification, but far from reassuring the child seems, if anything, to make him more anxious.

There would seem little doubt that different children 'use' the same television programme for different purposes and that televiewing styles are related to the social context in which the viewer finds himself. Friedson (1953) noted that children who were attached to their parents used television to draw themselves closer to the family by viewing with their parents. Similarly Johnstone (1961) found that children accepted by peer groups listened to popular music or watched television together while 'isolated' children listened and watched alone in order to pass time and avoid loneliness. But the fundamental question remains unanswered; that is, what do lonely children find when they attend to the mass media?

Escape: Clarification of the concept

As Katz and Foulkes (1962) point out, even if it is true that aliena- tion or deprivation tends to drive people to seek refuge by tele- viewing fantasy, it is not clear what they find when they get there. If people watch fantasy materials to obtain relief from, or compensa- tion for, their own personal inadequacies, it does not mean that these media do not have positive uses for these individuals – in other words the satisfaction of the escape desire may not itself be escapist.

The question, essentially, revolves around the uses that people find for the mass media in their everyday social lives. As argued in Chapter 1 the latest news from Ruandi-Urundi, about church unity or globe-trotting American officials is essentially beyond the pale of the individual's effective sphere of influence, which makes him essentially a spectator, rather than a participant, in life's dramas. Moreover such news, since it is beyond his control, may essentially contribute to a feeling of alienation from the outside world. On the other hand, fantasy materials, so often labelled escapist, may be put to uses not implied by that label, since they may provide social learning which can be applied in everyday life and thus provide some feedback to the viewer's real life social roles. If, instead of behave we say act, we immediately confront the Greek word 'drama'. If we consider escape in its most literal sense, it means to put on another cap, in other words to experience these feelings the artist wishes us to feel, to know in advance which hat to wear in as yet unmet and possibly as yet undefined social stages. Viewed in this way, it is a suspect procedure to claim that television's fantasy programmes are escapist merely because they have little to do with the school curriculum.

The social functions of media fantasy

Bogart (1955) noted that working-class adults used comics so that they could compare people known to them with comic characters, and as a basis for conversation. Wolfe and Fiske (1949) found that 'normal' children used comics as a means of successfully coping with reality by first projecting those desires which their parents found unacceptable on to characters, and later, in what they call an adventure stage, by gaining self-confidence by identifying with an invincible hero. Finally, they observed that older children used more mature comics to find out about life itself. Even less well adjusted children substituted omnipotent *Superman* for the less tolerant and successful father which enabled them to perform their daily tasks without too much anxiety. In both cases the fulfilment of a desire to 'escape' did provide feedback of use in everyday life.

Even more striking are the uses which female radio listeners found for daily radio serials. Herzog (1944), in what remains a unique study which needs to be replicated with television serials, found that the serials were used as a means of emotional release – a good cry; as wish fulfilment – whereby listeners with unfaithful husbands and rebellious children listened to the serials featuring successful wives and mothers; and for advice which explained things or taught the listener 'how to behave' in certain situations – 'If you listen to these programmes and something turns up in your own life, you would know what to do about it.' No less than 41 per cent of 2,500 listeners, including 38 per cent of university graduates, said that the radio programmes had helped them to deal better with the problems in their everyday life. Listeners said, for example, that they had learnt how to get on with people, how to handle their husbands and boy friends and how to bring up their children – 'most mothers slap their children. She deprives them of something. That is better. I use what she does with my children.' Other listeners learnt how to express themselves in certain situations, how to accept old age and how to comfort themselves when worried.

If, as we have argued, the extended kin within the village teaches such skills to its members, it is not difficult to see that the people one feels one knows on television similarly teach even the 'educated' viewer at home to cope with real life social situations. While, as Herzog points out, what is learnt may not essentially be practical for all real life situations, her data do suggest that the mass media could indeed provide such learning experiences. As Trenaman (1967) found, Jack Archer's mental illness resulted in sympathetic attitudes to mental disease after, rather than before, listening. At the very least these data point to a non-escapist use of fantasy materials. It may well be that such advice is more often used in everyday life than the formal knowledge imparted by the school system. The media habits of the alienated and deprived may even be motivated by a desire to re-establish effective interpersonal contacts.

Escape in relation to identification and recognition

Undue emphasis on the processes involved in identification with media stars, since identification involves loss of identity, tends to obscure the variety of consequences which follow exposure to 'escapist' programmes. If, as in the recognition process the viewer is reminded of his identity, it is more likely that he will relate his pseudo-social interactions with characters he feels he knows to his everyday life, especially if he correctly predicts how a character will act. It is argued that interactions with television characters may help, in Schramm *et al.*'s terms, to provide insights which aid the alert viewer see himself better, and may 'drain off discontent resulting from the hard blows of socialisation' whereas identification may lead the child to withdraw from the real world and confuse fantasy and reality.

FRIENDSHIP PATTERNS AND VIEWER INVOLVEMENT

In three independent studies* a strong relationship has been found between the degree of viewer involvement in a film seen and the number of friends listed by the child viewer. In each study those children who thought the film seen was most real were those with less than four friends. Children with an average number of friends denied that the film they had seen was real, while children with a large number of friends thought the films were quite real. In the *Clown Ferdl* study, involving 100 children aged from seven to eleven years, 50 per cent of children with one to four friends said the characters were very real or real, 14 per cent of children with five to eight friends thought the characters very real or real and 37 per cent of children with more than nine friends said the characters were very real or real; a relationship which would not occur by chance more than twice in a hundred times. Initially guided by the mass communication research tradition outlined above, I was at first tempted to argue that 'isolated' children escaped by identifying with film characters. However, it later became apparent that there were clearly discernable developmental trends in the way children, as they grew older, became involved with the television programme seen – which is the theme of the next chapter.

DEVELOPMENTAL TRENDS IN VIEWER INVOLVEMENT

We have argued that children become involved with programmes they have seen by either identification or recognition. In each case

* Eyre-Brook (1972) *Scarecrow*; Noble (1969c) *Patrick and Putrick* and Noble (1969d) *Clown Ferdl*; all Prix Jeunesse prize-winning films described in Chapter 5.

involvement results in a confusion of the reality-fantasy of the materials just viewed. The obvious next stage was to discover the extent of recognition and identification among children of different ages. Seven- and eight-year-old children (55 per cent) who had seen either *Sports Day, This is Your Life* or *Terror from the East* said they wanted to be like the film heroes seen in some ways slightly more often than did nine- and ten-year-old children (48 per cent). Younger children (56 per cent) more often than older children (12 per cent) forgot or completely forgot they were in school while viewing. Similarly, younger children were more often worried or very worried (43 per cent) when the hero was in trouble than older children (29 per cent). It would seem, therefore, that younger children more easily lose themselves via identification and more often escape in Schramm *et al.*'s terms when televiewing fantasy programmes.

However, while younger children more often identified with television heroes, older children more frequently recognised the television characters as like people they knew. Seven-year-olds recognised fewest characters of all (26 per cent), followed in turn by eight- and nine-year-olds (43 and 41 per cent respectively). Ten-year-olds, twice as often as seven-year-olds, recognised a character as like someone they knew (49 per cent). Thus while younger children submerged their comparatively unmoulded identities into the films, older children – their new sense of identity intact, played opposite the film characters seen in these typical programmes. There would seem little reason to label the younger child's identification with film heroes as escapist, since it appears that as the child grows older he will increasingly play opposite the characters seen in television programmes. Moreover, as previously noted, girls tend to recognise while boys tend to identify. Once again it seems somewhat dangerous to maintain that either televiewing style is escapist, more especially since fantasy television serials and series tend to induce recognition whereas cinema films tend to call for identification as a means of involvement.

Individual differences in viewer involvement

The 40 five- to eight-year-olds who saw *Patrick and Putrick* were assessed by their teachers as either introverted, extroverted or neither. Introverts were defined as children whose interests were in their own thoughts and feelings, while extroverts were defined as children whose interests were directed outwards at the people in the world around them. Introverts, it was felt, would be more inclined to incorporate film experiences into their lives than would the out-wardly orientated extroverts. As predicted introverts thought the film was more real (25 per cent), than either extroverts (10 per cent), or normals, none of whom said the film was real. It would appear likely that more introverted children identify and more extroverted children recognise. This is not to say that either child 'escapes' by watching televised fantasy, but rather that children bring different orientations or predispositions to the media which do not seem to result from conflict with either peers or parents.

SOCIAL ANCHORAGE AND TELEVIEWING STYLE

If, as we have argued, the child in a stable balanced community comes to see himself realistically by means of interaction with significant others, the development of a self-concept suitable for all occasions will be impeded if the number of mirror images available to him is restricted. We have already seen that in part the Rileys have established a relationship between programme preference and the social context in which the child finds himself. It seems likely that children with restricted and contradictory mirrors will acquire an identity which is inconsistent. Such children may be prompted to 'lose' inconsistent and painful identities by identifying with the television heroes in those mystery and adventure programmes which Himmelweit *et al.* noted were popular with insecure children. These same children may also interact with the characters recognised in the family serials, which Himmelweit *et al.* also found popular for insecure children not in order to lose their identities but to gain practice in predictable interactions which possibly help to establish a more stable identity. Himmelweit *et al.* tell us that these programmes are sought for companionship and reassurance.

We must therefore ask whether such insecure children can only identify with television heroes, or whether they can also interact with recognised television characters with their sense of identity intact. An attempt was made to answer this question in the study where children viewed either a dramatic film, a professional compère show or a typical television series show. Each child was asked to name all his friends, which in previous studies has been found a reliable indicator of the child's acceptance by his peer group (Newcomb, 1956). The number of friends listed was then compared with the child's capacity for identification and recognition – the results of which are summarised in Table 6.

It is apparent that as the number of friends listed by the child increases, so identification decreases yet recognition increases and vice versa. Thus children with few friends, with restricted peer mirrors, identified with television heroes almost half as often again as did children with plentiful peer mirrors. These latter children, indeed, recognise more than they identify, which suggests that they do not need to lose their identities as often as children with restricted

TABLE 6

NUMBER OF FRIENDS LISTED BY THE CHILD TABULATED BY RECOGNITION,
IDENTIFICATION, AND WHETHER CHILDREN THOUGHT THE CHARACTER
HAD SPOKEN JUST TO THEM

Number of friends listed by the child	Children identifying with a character	Children recognising a character	Children who thought a character had spoken just to them
	Per cent		
1–3 friends (N=26)	58	36	32
4–5 friends (N=40)	50	40	30
6 or more friends (N=22)	42	55	47

peer mirrors. Moreover, these children more often than children with few friends maintained that television characters spoke just to them. It appears that gregarious children believe in the illusion of intimacy; their identities are stable and they can confidently interact with anyone, whether in life or on the screen.

Equally important, however, is the frequency with which children with access to restricted peer mirrors recognise television characters and think these characters have spoken just to them. One-third of these children recognised, and thought they had been spoken to, by television characters. Children who are prone to identity loss, therefore, do not lose the capacity to play opposite recognised characters with their sense of identity intact – and it should be remembered that these children did not see a television series programme that they knew well, that some of these children saw the dramatic film with child actors, and these films were projected as in the cinema. All these factors reduced the likelihood of recognition.

Nor should it be forgotten that even children with access to a large number of peer mirrors also identified with film heroes. The difference between gregarious and more isolated children is one of degree, rather than an absolute difference. When need arises and programme types which demand identification are screened, gregarious children are also able to lose their identities if they so desire. In comparison with children with an average number of friends, both the more isolated, and consequently more introverted child, and the more gregarious and consequently more extroverted child, tends to confuse the reality and fantasy of programmes just viewed. Such confusions, according to Schramm *et al.*, cause the child to withdraw from the real world and, moreover, cause the child more trouble than he should have in learning the rules of the real world. But need this necessarily be the case?

The intentions of fantasy writers

Many artists create fantasy. They do not do so to cause the child problems in the real world but rather to allow the child to experience emotions and feelings which enable him to gain a peephole into his own mind, so that he may come to terms with some of those enigmatic feelings which the artist perceives as a result of being human. Television no less than any other media is an art form, but one which is still in the developmental stage. We have argued that it is uniquely suited to enable the viewer better to understand the complexities of ordinary everyday social relationships.

Yet according to Hazard, science-fiction programmes provide the most extreme example of media fantasy materials, which implies that they cannot provide any feedback to everyday social roles. Science-fiction viewers are therefore escaping, by evading the problems of their everyday life. It is worth noting that science fiction writers, unlike researchers, do not perceive fantasy in this way. Aldiss (1962) argues that science-fiction writers often describe everyday problems, but that the setting is removed in both time and space. The unrealistic setting allows the writer to explore basic problems and defects in modern society, which if set near to home might prove disturbing. Fiction is therefore 'an arrangement of symbols and images' which 'if in negotiable currency, we can adapt to our own situation'. Like Aldiss, I am puzzled why fantasy should be held in disrepute. 'The feeling is, perhaps, that indulgence in "idle dreams" is unhealthy and tends to divorce the spectator from reality.'

Thus while the edited 'drama' of the news story, which Halloran *et al.* (1970) found created its own momentum, is regarded as nonescapist, those experiences and feelings which in Solzhenitsyn's words unite the 'lump of humanity' by dint of the artists' vision, are regarded as escapist. Some of these feelings are no strangers to any of us, and if we cannot acknowldege them openly, we can at least acknowledge them through fiction. Identification, therefore, may be regarded as a mechanism by which we come to share experiences and feelings which the artist thinks warrant our attention. Having peeped into the intricacies of our own minds we should therefore be better able to see both the world and ourselves, which is perhaps why the Rileys found that children involved with the *Lone Ranger* were not reassured and lulled into a false sense of security, but found him scary, creepy and difficult to get out of their minds.

Indeed Elkin (1950) and Emery (1959) suggest that it is precisely the ostensible unreality of the western, precisely the apparently 'escapist' content that enables the child to identify with the hero and live through his experiences. Had television actually presented father-son conflicts in the raw, rather than through the disguise of the western, the content may have been too near to home for the child to become involved in the situation. Redl (cited in Schramm *et al.*) reports that disturbed and delinquent children could not sleep in their institutional beds after they had seen loving parents and warm families on television. These children were not disturbed by the violent and frightening programmes which Redl reports were avoided by 'ordinary' children. Such results even suggest that violent programmes may help to drain off the aggression experienced by disturbed children, and indeed prevent such violent feelings finding expression in everyday life. As we shall see in Chapter 7, televised violence, provided it is portrayed in stylistic form, does prompt aggressive children to play more imaginatively than before viewing. But we need to explain why it is that stylistic, rather than realistic, aggression has a cathartic effect.

TELEVISION FANTASY AS EXPRESSIONS OF MYTHICAL THEMES

The enduring popularity of the western has prompted some writers to argue that westerns reflect those conflicts which are universally experienced by man. Emery and Elkin maintain that the old-fashioned black and white western may indirectly reflect Oedipal conflicts. The western typically shows youth being aggressive towards older men in order to gain possession of the attractive heroine. They argue that this situation parodies Oedipus's dilemma, and every boy's desire for his mother and antagonism towards his father, as part of his Freudian development. While an extreme argument, very little is known about the ways viewers 'use' westerns.

The notion that television fantasy reflects mythical themes is, however, an interesting one. As Malinowski points out, no society can exist without its myths which have the very real function of acting as 'charters for social action'. In other words, myths reflect primal values in metaphoric form. No civilised people can avoid expressing their value system to their children in story or parable form. Viewed in this way, the western may be a vehicle for the transmission of cultural values in which, after all, good usually prevails over bad, even if the going is violent. Nor should it be forgotten that westerns are virtually the only pictorial representations of white man's history. They present man's struggle with nature, with himself and above all man's struggle with his innate aggressiveness. They depict societies without law and order; if you wish, they show Darwin's notion of the survival of the fittest, in raw pictorial form. And the survival of the fittest is the charter which governs our social action, it is the charter the child must encounter when he leaves school, and is the charter he must accept to succeed at school.

SOME RESEARCH INTO THE MYTHICAL VALUES PORTRAYED IN CARTOONS

I was fortunate to have a French student Dejean (1972) prepared to compare French cartoons available in Quebec with American cartoons similarly available. She found that French cartoons stressed the propriety of social relationships: the employee was submissive to the employer; the men had a good time while the women waited at home and the good characters helped the weak ones. In American cartoons such as *Bugs Bunny*, social relationships were virtually non-existent, the characters were mere parodies whose key sentences were, 'I am going to be rich'. The French cartoons were neat, simply drawn and the sound level was appropriately low key. Of the American cartoons all Dejean could say was that they were 'gross comic' portraying lots of 'gestures, kicks and the noise was overwhelming'. In the French cartoons a moral was clearly evident, the good fairies prevailed over the weak humans whereas in the American cartoons there was no moral and no feeling – 'only fun'. While she conceded that the American cartoons were professionally executed, with plenty of gimmicks such as close-up, panoramic shots, and well synchronised music, she also found them noisy, brash, loud and slap-happy. Moreover, she found French Canadian cartoons much nearer their American cousins than to French cartoons. While I would not accept this analysis of the structure of national cartoons as evidently correct, what is important is the way in which these cartoons reflect the national values and the culture of which they are an integral part. It is not difficult to see that a French child exposed to French cartoons is going to acquire a different perspective on the world than the American child exposed to American cartoons. Indeed, I would even suggest that the respective cartoons metaphorically portrayed the differing values and social charters of the two countries. Viewed in this way the child could even acquire something of his national character from early exposure to television's fantasy materials. In other words television fantasy has very real functions of which mass communication researchers are only dimly aware.

CONCLUSION

We have argued in Chapter 1 that the stresses of life in modern industrial societies were such as to drive the child to his television set for respite. What he finds when he gets there, though, is another matter. We have argued that children use television both to retreat from society and to take part in it at the same time. It has been suggested that even children with inadequate social anchorage learn to recognise and interact with television characters, which, in part, restores contact with the wider society when the immediate social surround is unsatisfactory. Such children do indeed identify with television characters and lose their identities, but identification is part of a developmental process which normal children eventually outgrow. Even so, identification does allow the child to experience those feelings the artist wishes us to explore and as such does not provide a complete withdrawal from everyday life. Indeed, when art, television allows us to explore the basic enigmas of the human condition. Moreover, even those most stereotyped programmes which children view may socialise them to accept the charter for social action which they will discover before they leave school. As such it is dangerous to label fantasy programmes as escapist, as though they had no relevance to everyday social life. Finally there is no need to dwell on the methodological inadequacies of many of the studies reviewed here. Escape as a concept seems to leave much to be desired – it has essentially been a middle-class, school-orien-tated label which more often denotes a value position rather than a worked-out theoretical concept applicable to your child as he sits in front of the small screen.

5

Child development and televiewing

Anybody who watches television with children cannot help but realise that their response to television changes dramatically as they grow older. The aim of this chapter is to try to map out these changes using the developmental psychology of Piaget as a starting point. Piaget has demonstrated how chronological age, above all other factors, determines the way the child thinks and reacts to the world, so it is not perhaps surprising that his theories, which are based on intimate observation of young children, are equally applicable to televiewing. But there is another reason why the developmental study of televiewing is rewarding. Piaget (1950a) argues that children's thought develops as human thought developed through history. In Chapter 1 we argued that adults who listen attentively to their young children will gain a fresh perspective on the world, one which they have forgotten. If what was said about the evolution of communities is true we may expect to find that children when describing television will employ concepts which were applicable to the learning of social roles in the village.

Contrary to the notion that children are little adults, Piaget (1950b) demonstrates that the child's world is not only different from the adult world, but that some twelve years of steady development are required before the child thinks as an adult. In the twelfth year the child enters the fourth major stage in intellectual development – the stage of formal operations. The adolescent, like the child can live in the here-and-now of the present, but unlike the child he can also use thought so that in his imagination he can live in the future and cope with the hypothetical and spacially remote. But we shall find it difficult to understand the television responses of the child in the preceding stage, that of concrete operations which lasts from about six/seven years until the onset of formal operations. These children live totally in the present and are only capable of dealing with the 'concrete' problems immediately before them. The knowledge acquired manipulating materials has yet to be abstracted from the problem in hand. An appreciation of the difference between the here-and-now thought of the younger child and the hypothetical thought of the adolescent helps in our understanding of the varying reactions of differently aged children to the same television programme.

Even the adult who understands the adolescent, and who can vaguely recall the ways of thought he used in concrete operations, will find it difficult to understand or recall the 'world' of children prior to the cognitive revolution which takes place at about six/seven years. The basic fact of the young child's thought, whether in the sensory motor stage (the first eighteen months of life), or the pre-operational thought stage, is egocentrism, whereby the child conceives himself as both the centre and cause of all events. Such children cannot see the world from any point of view other than their own; they believe their dreams are in the room where everybody can see them. They live exclusively in the present. Television is simply incorporated within the child's experience and becomes part of the child's inner world.

Each of Piaget's three developmental stages – pre-operational, concrete, and formal operations – exert influence on televiewing. Starting with younger children, the aim of this chapter is to present a developmental view of children in front of the small screen divided into three main sections to correspond to Piaget's developmental stages. For each stage hypotheses derived from Piaget's theory are presented and subject to empirical test.

PRE-OPERATIONAL THOUGHT STAGE (EIGHTEEN MONTHS TO SIX/SEVEN YEARS)

Clearly the televiewing experiences of younger children are likely to prove most intriguing. Often when talking about a programme we have seen together I wonder whether the young child and I have seen the same programme. Piaget's conception of the pre-operational thought stage helps to explain such discrepancies. Egocentrism in thought is likely to colour the young child's televiewing in five distinct ways. Firstly, the young child is likely to think in a binary way, that is, to respond in an all-or-nothing manner to television. If children are asked to place a number of rods of different lengths in order, from smallest to longest, the egocentric child compares every rod with every other rod which indicates that he has no concept of largest or smallest. Children aged from two to five years, therefore, can be expected to perceive no shades of grey in television characters: they will be perceived as either all good or all bad.

Secondly, because of egocentrism in thought, the child is unable to perceive events from any point of view other than his own. Children aged up to five years cannot differentiate between internal experiences, such as dreams, which they think everybody can see, and external experiences such as television. Young children may be expected, therefore, to consider television as reality because they are not capable of imagining that people can act dramatic parts.

Similarly, both puppet and cartoon characters are likely to be thought of as real and alive, having an existence independent of the screen so that in extreme cases television characters are 'their friends' who come and talk to them at night. It should, however, be noted that children gradually grow less egocentric in thought as they grow older during the stage of concrete operations and thus the child's belief that television is reality will gradually decline.

Thirdly, egocentrism in thought should lead the child to imagine that either he or his friends are involved in television programmes. As far as the young child is concerned he makes the clouds move. All external events occur because of his intervention. Such children are likely to think that they influence the events that take place on the television screen. Children unable to admit to viewpoints other than their own, however, are likely to put themselves into the programmes alongside the characters, rather than identifying with the heroes.

Fourthly, we may expect the young child to classify objects and events, both on and off television, in unique ways. During this stage an object is defined by its location and thus when a scene changes in a television film and a character appears in a new situation, or as larger or smaller than before, this character may be seen as a different person or puppet than the one previously seen.

Fifthly, because young children cannot use operations in thought, they are unable to reverse the constituents in a chain of reasoning, perhaps best illustrated by Piaget's famous jug and water experiments. If two identical jugs are filled to the same level with liquid the child will admit that the amount of liquid in the two jugs is the same. If, however, the liquid is poured into a long thin jug and a squat fat jug respectively, the child will deny that the amount of liquid in the two jugs is the same because he cannot mentally reverse the operation – that is he cannot imagine what would happen if the liquid was poured back into the original jugs. It would seem reasonable, therefore, to expect that young televiewers, who cannot reverse operations, are unlikely to recall the beginning of a television programme, nor be able to predict what will happen next. They will not perceive that the story of a television film has a beginning, a middle and an end.

The young child in the village

If evolutionary development is reflected in individual development, we may expect the ways of thought of the young child to have functions necessary for the socialisation of the child into a mature member of his community. It is apparent that the young child is dominated by his visual field in an existence which concentrates on the here-and-now. Children learn to read pictures before they understand language. In the village all the child sees is 'reality', and events do not have the serial order of the story. We have suggested that it is by observation of social relationships and by mirror reflections of self that the child is socialised. Dumped almost prematurely into the twentieth century, it is hardly surprising that the child still relies on what he sees as the description of reality. Nor, if we accept Mc-Luhan's notion that linearity in thought commenced with the onset of print, is it difficult to imagine that the child fails to grasp story lines until he commences reading, since the young child is exclusively concerned with the 'here-and-now' of the present which is sufficiently demanding of his intelligence, without concern for the morrow. As Tolstoy points out, we adults are perhaps so concerned with explanations of causality that we tend to overlook the very real way chance and non-rational factors exert influence on events. Nor is it difficult to imagine why the child should employ binary thought. In the village he knows how to relate to members of his extended kin group, he interacts with them regularly, these are people he knows. Aliens from outside his social grouping are likely to be viewed with fear since the child does not know how to respond to them.

Young children's binary responses to television characters

In a remarkable but unobtainable study, Gomberg (1961) recorded the reactions to television of 56 four-year-olds in three play-school centres in New York. When talking to the children, a number of widely held binary conceptions of the television world became apparent. The people on television were either all good or all bad; all the cowboys were good people whereas all the Indians, except *Tonto*, were bad. Similarly, all the men in the army were good. These conceptions in turn led to some interesting but less widely held views, for example, bad people bleed but not good people; a sheriff may not be caught; a bad man never does anything that is good; the job of the cowboy is to kill the Indians; and the good guy wears a white hat and rides a white horse, while the bad man wears black and rides a black horse. The conceptions, moreover, spilled over into real life. Gomberg reports that one four-year-old found hysterically crying in the playground when he had grazed his knee, was shouting, 'I am not bad, not bad'. The association between bleeding and badness was irrevocable.

Perhaps the most sinister conceptions were those relating to aggression. Gomberg found that the children widely held the view that, 'all the good people have to kill the bad people; you can't really talk to a bad guy – you must shoot him; all the heroes kill only the bad guys; a gun means you are strong; only the good guys should have a gun; the bad guy always started the fights; all quarrels between good and bad end in killing; and settling quarrels with a gun was neither good nor bad – it was just how everybody did it'. Once again these conceptions derived from the television screen were equally applicable in everyday life. Some children reported – 'if bad people try to kill you, call your mother and she will get a gun and kill him; every good person loves little children. To protect children they must kill the bad people; dynamite is used to blow up a country and kill the bad people: policemen ride in aeroplanes and cars and kill the bad robbers and Indians.'

The child in the village sees only reality and learns future social behaviour by observation. Our children, it would seem, see mainly aggression and thus begin to perceive the world in fundamentally stereotyped ways. It appears that television has imparted to children a view of the world where aggression and usually death are seen as the normal way to resolve conflict. Granted that childish modes of thought are largely superseded by more adult discriminatory ones, there is still a danger that these modes of thought will persist in later life, since few of us can remember how or what we thought in childhood. Memories stored prior to the cognitive revolution become almost inaccessible when the child enters the concrete operations stage; therein lies the source of our childhood amnesia, our inability to recall our earliest experiences. Proving that such conceptions do persist is difficult. I asked a Canadian student to probe teenage children's concept of Indians, in a country where Indians are not fictional but also form part of the Canadian community. O'Shaughnessy (1972) found that teachers felt impotent in communicating about Indians compared with the media, and that at nine years children said 'real-life Indians looked black-haired, head-banded, and mean', eleven-year-olds said they looked 'dark skinned, dark eyed and messy' while thirteen-year-old children, while describing the injustices suffered by the Indian, still maintained that they were second-class citizens, destined to remain in the poverty cycle and just not bright enough to avail of higher education. These children said they had learnt most about Indians in school, but media-induced attitudes transferred from fictional to real life groups, comparable with Gomberg's four-year-olds, are still frighteningly evident even among maturing adolescents. We should perhaps question the television fodder that we dish out to our youngest and most vulnerable television viewers who as we shall see are not highly regarded amongst programme-makers as an audience.

Moreover the obsession with aggression as the natural way to solve problems is not a particularly healthy attitude to inculcate in the young, especially if that aggression is always portrayed as clean fun. Indeed the codes governing the depiction of aggression in the UK have been changed so that the young are now exposed to the consequences of aggression. As will be seen in Chapter 7, while the consequences of aggression disturb young viewers, it also seems to inhibit the overt imitation of such aggressive acts. In summary, it would appear necessary to resolve to depict more reality for the youngest televiewers.

Social learning from television programmes

We have argued that children in the village are exposed to the roles they are likely to enact in the future, and are able to practise such roles in play before they enact them at a later date in real life. Gomberg reports that children used television commercials as a source of authority. These four-year-olds talked of products, foods, vitamins and toys as though it was necessary for everybody to own them. Such conceptions, every bit as much as the conceptions of good and bad people, are binary in nature since to be deprived of what is seen on television as normal implies badness and inferiority. It is perhaps significant that students in Canada who talked to their children about advertisements found that while children often mentioned different programmes as their favourites, they all mentioned the same advertisements. Six-year-olds said of the scenes depicted in commercials, 'Sometimes Mummy does that, but Granny always does that', and of the coke advert, 'They are my friends'. Older children were somewhat more explicit: 'Commercials always show a problem anyone could have in their home or playground or anywhere, then they show the product; ads show you how people live with a natural problem and then tell you how to solve the problem. People really do such things'; 'The cream took off the lady's hairs. They do it because it grows and is prickly and it looks awk'; 'In the ads you never see unhappy people, but in the programmes you never see unhappy people because they don't look at the camera', and one Israeli boy stated, 'Ads show how Americans live, many people I know do the things shown on commercials'. The authority of television advertisements seems to persist from young binary conceptions into later life. Moreover they come to help to define real life, in the same way that the scenes witnessed in the village also defined the future acts of the child spectator.

Gomberg significantly found television inspired play evident amongst 80 per cent of the boys, and overall amongst 50 per cent of her four-year-old sample. The children enacted television roles just as we have argued the village child enacts the roles of his extended kin group. Gomberg found children practising roles as varied as spectator at a television show and television weather man as well as *Lone Ranger*, sheriff, *Superman*, *Tonto*, and *Mickey Mouse*. She reports the following play session inspired by *Pop-Eye*.

Glenn: 'I bought a book, a *Pop-Eye* book. Teacher is gonna read it.'

Jamie: 'I'm *Pop-Eye*. I'm *Pop-Eye* the Sailor Man.' [Note the word for word repetition of *Pop-Eye* dialogue]. He flexed his arms, spread his legs, tilted his head forward and stalked ahead in a rolling gait. Glenn followed immediately behind, imitating every gesture that Jamie made.

Jamie and Glenn (singing aloud): 'I'm *Pop-Eye* the Sailor Man, toot-toot, I'm *Pop-Eye* the Sailor Man, toot-toot.' (They came up to Cary who was pulling Jimmy and Billy in a wagon.)

Jamie: 'I'm *Pop-Eye* the Sailor Man.'

Billy: 'Who?'

Jamie: '*Pop-Eye*, *Pop-Eye*. And I'm gonna sock you.' (He made a fist and hit Cary. Cary ducked the first time but Jamie swung again and this time Cary was hit. Jimmy leapt out of the wagon and began to hit Jamie. Jamie hit Jimmy. Jamie got a blow under his eye. He began to scream.) . . .

Teacher: 'Jamie, why did you hit Cary?'

Jamie: (Sobbed quietly, then stopped.) 'Cause, cause, I'm *Pop-Eye* and *Pop-Eye* hits people.'

Teacher: 'Oh, does he?'

Jamie: 'Well, *Pop-Eye* always hits and knocks Pluto up to the sky. He always hits.'

It is to be noted that the play session above reflects binary thinking – in that whenever a television symbol was used, the play took on a stereotyped character. They used their equipment in a set and stereotyped way, they walked and ran in a set manner and their phrases were exact replicas of *Pop-Eye*'s. Gomberg comments, 'whatever their background, there was, because of television, a communality to their play', just we might add as there would be a communality to the play of children in the village who witness the same real-life village occurrences. As Piaget has noted, prior to the age of six and seven years, understanding between children occurs only where there is contact between two identical modes of thought existing in each child. The egocentric child cannot seek or find some basis in the other child's mind on which to build conversation or play unless they have experience in common. Television, like the village, appears to provide common experience which enhances the possibility of co-operative, if stereotyped, play.

Television seen as reality by young children

We have suggested that young children believe what they see, since throughout time the evidence before their eyes has been the most reliable source of information, especially with regard to the learning of future social roles. Thus we may expect young egocentric children to believe more implicitly what they see on their television screens than older less egocentric children. Similarly Gomberg's four-year-olds said, 'if it is on television, it is true'. One lonely four-year old girl was quite sure *Superman* was more than just a screen character: '*Superman* comes to visit me all the time. He brings me presents . . . and takes me flying wherever he goes. He always kisses me good night and then I go to bed.' We have already noted that intent televiewers, whether because of identification or recognition, temporarily delude themselves that they are viewing reality; it would seem that young children in the televiewing cradle also believe they view reality. Moreover, children without adequate social anchorage persist in the belief that what they view is real. Himmelweit *et al.* describe Henry, aged nine, who was nervous and diffident at school but of average intelligence. He relished the fact that the *Dragnet* stories were true, insisted that there really was a *Dixon of Dock Green* and half-believed in the fantasy of *Superman*. Such confusions are less common amongst normal children aged seven years and above, but they are an integral part of the four-year-old's televiewing style, since at this age the child cannot fully differentiate between internal experiences such as dreams and external experiences such as television. An alert parent can, however, train young children to discriminate between reality and fantasy, merely by questioning them.

In order to put these case study results on a more systematic footing, I have asked children of differing ages whether they think a recently viewed television programme is real or unreal, and true or false. Noble (1969c) showed 40 children aged five, six, seven and eight years the puppet film *Patrick and Putrick* and asked them, 'Could puppets make pastry like they did in the film?'. Five-year-olds were significantly more likely to say the film was real and true than six-, seven- and eight-year-olds who are likely to have entered the concrete operations stage. These children, for example, said, 'It's only a film – things don't happen like that in life – it's not really true is it?' Similarly in Canada the cartoon *Hercules* was shown on video-tape to 27 children aged between two and twelve years. They were individually asked after viewing, 'Is *Hercules* . . . "for real"?', 'Can people fly like *Hercules*?', and 'Is *Newton* [a centaur-like character] real?'. The majority of children aged four or less said the film was real, people could fly like *Hercules* and *Newton* was real. The majority of children aged five and more said the film was pretend, people could not fly like *Hercules* and *Newton* was unreal. These data suggest that younger pre-operational children on both sides of the Atlantic see even puppet and cartoon characters as real. Younger children do not seem able to distance themselves from television sufficiently to ask whether what they see is real. In spite of the crude methodology employed in these studies, the data suggest that the child's belief that the films are real progressively decreases as the child grows older and gradually learns to distinguish between the fantasy and reality of television programmes.

Do egocentric children enter television programmes?

Egocentric children, unable to admit to viewpoints other than their own, should be unable to identify with television heroes, since they are cognitively unable to lose their identities. Such children should, therefore, put themselves into the action of a film, or even while viewing insert events from their own imagination into the film. When asking children about the story of *Scarecrow*, a Czech cartoon in which a cat attempts to steal a bird's egg, one five-year-old said, 'I smacked the cat'. Another five-year-old said, 'But you cannot get on the film', a clear example of the child confusing events in his own imagination with events which occurred in the film. Similarly a five-year-old girl, when asked 'Who was in *Blue Peter*?' which she had seen the night before replied, 'Val, John and little Norman'. Val and John are the regular programme presenters, and little Norman, it transpired, was 'the boy next door'.

Immediately after children had seen *Patrick and Putrick* they were asked what objects the puppets had used in the film. While six- to eight-year-olds recalled twice (5) as many objects as five-year-olds (2·5), five-year-olds recalled an average of at least one object not seen in the film. Only one in four of the six- to eight-year-olds recalled an object not seen in the film. While these differences were small they were consistent and reached statistical significance.

Character consistency in television programmes

It is argued that prior to the concrete operations stage, children do not know that television characters are the same in different settings. Thus it might appear to a young child that a puppet in a bucket is a different puppet when placed under a table. Gerhartz-Franck (1955) reports that some six-year-old children thought the mouse hero in *Town and Country Mouse* was a different animal in close-up than in long shot. When in close-up children thought they were watching a different older mouse. Similarly insect-pest films had the effect of reassuring Africans who were pleased that they did not have insects as large as those depicted in close-up shots. It would appear that the pictorial literacy required to comprehend television has to be learnt, while in the village all events are seen in their true scale.

In a study of children's reactions to *Blue Peter* (Noble, 1969a) each child was individually interviewed the day after he had seen the programme and asked who had presented it. Five-year-olds, in spite of the fact that 40 per cent were regular viewers, were not able to recall all the three compères seen in the programme. Five-year-olds added such characters as Norman and the 'little girl'. Children aged six years and over were correctly and significantly more able to list the three regular compères of *Blue Peter*. This result suggests that children aged less than six years will not always recognise the same characters in different surroundings, and that this may be true even when the same programmes are viewed week after week.

However, children aged five years were correctly able to recall that only two puppets were seen in the film *Patrick and Putrick,* even though they were covered in both flour and pastry during the course of the plot. Thirty-seven of the 40 children correctly recalled but two puppets, although one five-year-old replied 'seven' and one seven-year-old thought there were three. Yet when presented with photographs from various puppet films, neither five- nor six-year-olds were able to recognise more than three photographs from the film, whereas seven- and eight-year-olds correctly recognised all five. It would seem that the ability to recognise a photograph from a film, necessarily involves both recalling the film and relating the photographs to the recalled film – a skill involving the operation of reversibility which we have argued is not evident until the stage of concrete operations.

Comprehension of the story

The French film director Godard was once asked whether his films had a beginning, a middle and an end. He replied that they did but not necessarily in that order. Pre-operational children, we have argued, do not even have the concept of beginning, middle and end because they are unable to reverse operations. A number of continental writers* have commented on this inability. For example, Zazzo (1951) comments that before the age of seven, French children are only interested in the separate incidents that they see and understand little of the story. I was initially drawn to this type of research when I viewed *Thunderbirds*, an elaborate puppet series, with two boys aged five and six years. At each commercial break the five-year-old would ask, 'Is that the end?' and was quite prepared to go to bed, while his six-year-old brother would reply, 'Of course not, stupid, they have not rescued the trapped people yet'. The difference that resulted from one year of age was striking.

I, therefore, attempted to examine systematically how well

* Mialeret and Melies (1954); Franck (1955).

children aged from five to eight years could recall the story of the Prix Jeunesse prize-winning film *Patrick and Putrick*. French colleagues worked out that 127 incidents were scripted for the fifteen-minute puppet film. Immediately after viewing each child was individually interviewed and asked to tell the story, which was tape-recorded. Whereas six-year-olds recalled a similar number of incidents to seven- and eight-year-olds (11·5 and 12·5 respectively) five-year-olds recalled only six incidents. It is perhaps surprising that five-year-olds recall a bare 5 per cent of the incidents depicted, significantly fewer than the 1 in 10 incidents recalled by six- to eight-year-olds.

Moreover, detailed analysis of the film stories, when retold by children who had seen *Patrick and Putrick*, revealed that of the 7 major sequences enacted, five-year-olds recalled an average of 1·5 in the correct order. Six- to eight-year-olds recalled an average of 3·5 sequences in the correct order. While Franck and Zazzo have suggested that six-year-olds are unable to understand the story of a film, my results suggest that it is the five-year-old who is incapable of tracing the plot back to the beginning and does not therefore perceive the story line, whereas six- to eight-year-olds do understand the film's plot. The 'suddenness' with which plot comprehension develops suggests that the term 'cognitive revolution' when used to describe the differences between pre-operational and concrete operational children may be appropriate.

However, we may be asking too much of the five-year-old's limited vocabulary when asking him to retell the film's story. We, therefore, presented each child with five photographs representing various stages of the plot development in the film. Children were asked to place these photographs in the order in which they had occurred in the film and a score was derived for each child of the number of photographs correctly sequenced, making due allowance for guesswork. Five-year-olds placed only 1·2 photographs in the correct order, six-year-olds 2·1, while seven- and eight-year-olds placed 4·7 photographs in the correct order. These results initially suggest that the six-year-old has but a tentative grasp of the film story since his scores are significantly lower than those of seven- and eight-year-olds. But further analysis showed that neither fives nor sixes could correctly select five *Patrick and Putrick* photographs from five others. The recognition of photographs from a film seems to involve cognitive skills other than the ability to comprehend a film story.

Remaining discontent at the somewhat pedantic proof so far presented, I resolved on a more dramatic method. Forty five-year-olds and 40 eight-year-olds were shown *Scarecrow* (Prix Jeunesse Unesco prize 1968), an eight-minute cartoon film in which a scarecrow protects a baby bird from a cat. The film was stopped at a critical moment in the plot as naturally as possible. Children were then asked, 'Is that the end?'. Thirty of the five-year-olds and 16 of the eight-year-olds replied that it was the end. When asked why they thought it was not the end, five-year-olds replied, 'It has broken down', and could not suggest what might happen next. Eight-year-olds were, however, able to predict what would happen. When the remainder of the film was shown and children again asked, 'Is that the end?' many five-year-olds were confident that it was because 'I sawed the writing' (credits) whereas eight-year-olds replied that the baby bird had escaped unharmed.

Armed with tentative methodology and videotape equipment I attempted to further verify this hypothesis with Canadian children. Two fairly typical *Hercules* cartoons were shown to 27 children aged between two and twelve years. The first cartoon was stopped at the height of the drama when a large rock threatened to kill *Hercules*. Each child was individually interviewed and asked, 'Is that the end?' Three-quarters of the children aged five years and less thought it was the end while only one of the older children emphatically said that it was the end. After the children had viewed the two complete episodes of *Hercules* they were asked, 'Was that all the same story?' Once again all but two children aged five and less replied that it was one story while all but two of children aged six years and more replied that there had been two stories. When asked, 'Why did the rock fall on *Hercules*?' none of the children aged five and less could reply, while all bar two of the older children gave answers indicating understanding of causality. To the query, 'What will happen next?', younger children did not know, whereas older children gave answers of the type, 'He will be saved', which indicated knowledge that they had some idea of story development.

Both in North America and in the UK there appears to be something of a critical difference between five years and six years as regards comprehension of filmed stories. We have argued that in the village the child merely observes events which he knows are real and which do not necessarily conform to the serial order of the 'story'. It would appear that children unable to use the operation of reversibility in thought similarly respond to television programmes by maintaining that they are real and are unaware that they tell stories. As we have seen, Piaget's child development theories best explain the young child's televiewing style. Children, for Piaget, are simply unable to use operations in thought prior to the cognitive revolution, which entails a physical maturation of the brain. Even when five-year-olds have been taught to admit that the amount of water poured into differently shaped jugs is the same (Smedslund 1961) these five-year-olds quickly revert to pre-operational thinking after a short time. It would appear that Piaget's assertion that pre-operational thought structures exert real influence in the young child's intellectual life is correct, and are also applicable to televiewing.

— Summary of pre-operational children's televiewing style

Taken overall, results suggest that:

1. Young children see a series of separate and fragmentary incidents rather than the story of a television film.

2. The content of these incidents suggest that children will see either all good or all bad characters, and usually the good will proceed to kill the bad.

3. It is likely that the three and four-year-old child will not invariably recognise the identities of the principal characters throughout the film. The perception of the film characters is dominated by the setting in which they are filmed.

4. Moreover, young children tend to believe implicitly what they see on television to be real.

5. Young children while viewing may read incidents into the plot from their own imaginations, or add incidents and events that they think should have occurred.

6. It seems likely that young children will use television programmes as the basis for social play – although such play is likely to be of a highly stereotyped nature.

7. Children may acquire their future how-to-behave models from watching television. As will be further seen in Chapter 7, young children are excellent mimics of what they see on the television screen.

In spite of what we adults may label a lack of comprehension of what they are viewing, young children are ardent televiewers. Schramm *et al.* report that at three years they typically watch for 45 minutes a day, by five years they view two hours daily and by six years some two and a half hours a day is spent televiewing. It would appear that children will watch whatever is on the television screen simply because of the fascination of moving images in unusual situations. But is this the whole story?

Young children in the village, and young children in front of the small screen

Central to the theme presented in this book is the idea that television satisfies those needs of children which were met by the extended kin group in the more primitive village. Here, it may be recalled, we argued the total life of the community was visible, and the child saw the whole pattern of social relationships which he was likely to encounter later enacted before him. We know that monkeys reared in laboratories and deprived of extended kin groupings are later unable to survive in the wild since they do not seem to know how to relate and fit in with the larger monkey troop they find there. It would seem that the earliest, and most crucial learning, is acquired by observation in interaction with a larger community grouping. It seems possible that the village child was provided with such learning by dint of his position within the larger social context. The urban industrial child, if deprived of an extended kin group in life, will use television in order to view and learn about the wider society he must fit in with later. We know that he readily imitates those social roles he has seen enacted on television, albeit weatherman or spectator at a television show. We know that the play of 80 per cent of the boys observed by Gomberg showed the influence of television, and more importantly television provided a basis for communal play which was not available from any other source. It may not be surprising therefore that children believe what they see on television to be true, nor that they fail to comprehend television's stories since in the village they would have only perceived reality, and the events they viewed would not have had a linear sequence. It is suggested, therefore, that television may well provide that socialisation necessary to allow the child to fit in with the larger social grouping, as the extended kin socialised the child in the village. If this analysis is correct, is it true that children get the television they deserve?

Television producers' conceptions of their child audiences

If children attend to television to learn about life, do they view a sufficient variety of programmes which fulfil this function? The answer would seem to be no. Elliot (1969) in a survey of European television production agencies discovered that children's television was the 'Cinderella' of the programme companies. Most of the institutions say they provide more non-entertainment programmes for older children, but younger children under seven years of age are regarded as an audience for light entertainment and variety. Nor as we shall see in Chapter 9, do children's television producers (regarded by agency chiefs as in the best position to decide what is good and suitable for children) take due regard of those unique qualities which the young child brings to televiewing. Producers seem to conceive of the young child as a miniature adult, who, because he is young, should be fed only the adult pap rather than the meat.

Nor should we rest content with *Sesame Street*. The producers of this programme are to be admired for their will-power in commissioning 247 pounds weight of research at a cost of 15,300 dollars a pound. Most of this research concentrated on finding out what

/amme characteristics drew children's attention to the screen.
sequently the programme presents a whole series of gimmicks of
ven utility in dragging the four-year-old's attention to the screen,
gimmicks such as loud noises, monkeys, bouncy music, other
children, and repetitive commercial breaks – in other words an
expensive catalogue of attention-getting devices, which are most
unashamedly used as a vehicle for adult jokes and purely the rote
learning of numbers and letters without teaching children how to
count any real objects. A devotee of *Sesame Street* sat down with
her three-year-old daughter to watch the programme and come to an
understanding of her daughter's comprehension of the programme.
Toohey (1972) discovered that after fifty minutes, 'I am tired of
sitting down'; 'I learnt an (draws) R. I forget what it is called':
'What is the number for Mummy?' When viewing a sequence on
garbage collection, 'What's happening, Mom?', and when it is put
into a barge at the close of the sequence, 'Why was it in the boat,
Mom?' More importantly Toohey found that of 36 sequences her
three-year-old understood but 9, while a six-year-old understood
28–30 sequences, which came as something of a revelation to the
committed parent. As one consultant to the programme told me,
'Yes they did ask my advice, but they did not take it when I suggested that much of the proposed content was above the pre-
schoolers' heads'.

It is tolerably clear that the television programming for the under-
sixes should involve more, rather than less, resources than the
programmes for older children. If young children don't understand
stories and believe what they see to be true perhaps, as we have
argued, television should be primarily a window into the real world.
Indeed if physical maturation determines whether or not a child
thinks egocentrically, television producers should perhaps cater for
such egocentricism and present to the child realistic flashes of the
world in all its aspects. Collage programmes with regular personas
to create the illusion of intimacy, showing different societies at work
and play could enrich the televiewing experience of the young child.
We can safely leave the primary socialisation of the child into the
culture's prevailing values to the cartoons as described in the previous chapter.

TELEVIEWING IN THE CONCRETE OPERATIONS STAGE (FROM SIX TO ELEVEN YEARS)

According to Piaget, somewhere between the age of five and seven a
cognitive revolution takes place, which means the universe of the
six-year-old child is not merely the same old universe of the four-
year-old with the simple addition of certain new facts. The world of

the child in the stage of concrete operations is organised, imagined and thought about a new and more efficient way, which actually changes the way things look. The child is no longer exclusively concerned with what he sees immediately before him since he can use operations in thought, and mentally reverse the pouring of water in the jugs experiment. However, while children can use operations in thought, they are still limited to solving 'concrete' problems which are immediately before them.

The revolution explains why six-year-old children understand the story of a television film; they can mentally retrace the events seen, and of course predict forward, in a way that is just inaccessible to the younger child. We may expect therefore, as our first hypothesis for the concrete operations stage that the child will gradually improve plot comprehension and recall as he progressively grows older during this stage and gradually exercises his new-found cognitive abilities.

Secondly, because Piaget argues that egocentrism increases whenever the child begins to cope with a new and untried field of cognitive action, we may expect the child at the beginning of the concrete operations stage to be so absorbed in his new logical powers that he will concentrate on the incidents rather than the major plot development in a film. Such children will not, therefore, be able to see the wood for the trees.

Thirdly, it is likely during this stage that mental age and social class, in addition to chronological age, will be important determinants of the child's ability to comprehend a film's story fully. Mental age, after all, refers to the child's ability to use operations in thought – and is thus likely to be of greater importance as regards film comprehension than during the pre-operational thought stage. Similarly because middle-class children, more frequently than working-class children, are encouraged to talk and reason with their mothers (Newson and Newson, 1963) middle-class children may be expected both to talk about and to comprehend television films at an earlier age than working-class children.

Fourthly, because egocentrism in thought diminishes but slowly even during the concrete operations stage, we may expect children of different ages to comprehend differentially the emotions, motives and feelings of film characters. Egocentrism at this age is essentially the inability to perceive events from any point of view other than one's own. It is not until the end of the concrete operations stage that the child becomes able to take roles – that is to imagine himself in the shoes of other people. Piaget's research, in which children are shown a scale model of a mountain and then asked how does the mountain look from both here and over there, suggests that it is not until ten years that the child is cognitively able to see the mountain

D

from a viewpoint other than from where he is standing. Children aged up to and including nine years may be expected, therefore, to understand only the concrete physical behaviours of film performers, and it is the ten-year-old who will first understand the feelings and motivations of filmed characters. Similarly the ten-year-old child may be expected to comprehend first that symbols in film represent some other and less direct meaning.

The seven-to eleven-year-old in the village

In Ireland the age of criminal responsibility commences at the concrete operations stage – seven years. Clearly in a very real sense such children are adult, sufficiently so to contribute via their labour to the welfare of the community. Their work roles will essentially be tailored for miniature adults, and matched to the skills which the child makes evident. These children are expected to relate cause and effect, and their status in the village changes accordingly. It is, however, interesting that it is not until ten years that the child is able to empathise, that is, to put himself in another person's shoes and imagine how he is feeling. Prior to this age the child concentrates on correctly perceiving the behavioural display of emotions, which would seem in evolutionary terms to precede the ability actually to feel what another person is experiencing. This virtually unique human trait most probably requires that the child is forced to evaluate his viewpoint in the light of the viewpoints of significant other people in his community grouping.

Progress in plot comprehension during concrete operations

We have already seen that it is the six-year-old child who first shows that he understands that films do, indeed, have a beginning, a middle and an end. This perhaps explains why Himmelweit *et al.* found that seven- to nine-year-olds most enjoyed westerns because they had 'learnt' the format so well they could predict the ending. It was the six-year-old who exclaimed to me, when watching a cartoon dog in a rubber raft, 'I know what is going to happen, I know what is going to happen – the raft will be punctured and, whoose, it will shoot across the lake'. He was correct, of course.

It was noted that whereas five-year-olds recalled an average of but 6 incidents from *Patrick and Putrick,* six-year-olds recalled 11·5 incidents and seven- and eight-year-olds recalled an average of 12·5 incidents. Clearly as chronological age increased so did the number of incidents recalled. Similarly, results obtained from eight-, nine-, ten-, eleven- and twelve-year-old children who saw the puppet film *Clown Ferdl* also suggest that children in the concrete operations stage make gradual progress in plot understanding. Ten boys and ten girls of each of the ages listed above were shown *Clown Ferdl* (Prix Jeunesse prize for seven- to eleven-year-olds, 1968) after which each child was individually interviewed and asked to tell the story of the film as it had occurred. Each interviewer was provided with a checklist of the 92 incidents scripted by the Czech producers, and as children told the story, both ticked off and numbered the incidents in the order they were recalled. The film's story is complex but essentially depicts a puppet clown who is taught by a human puppet-maker to play musical instruments before he attempts in vain to join the circus. After many adventures and failures he finally is accepted into the circus. As anticipated, progress in the recall of film incidents increased gradually, rather than abruptly. Eight-year-olds recalled 15 per cent, nine-year-olds 22 per cent, ten-year-olds 23 per cent, eleven-year-olds 27 per cent and twelve-year-olds 30 per cent of the incidents listed in the script. It is still noteworthy that immediately after viewing children recall on average only a quarter of the incidents seen in a film made for their age group.

While statistical analysis revealed that eight-year-olds recalled significantly fewer incidents than either eleven- or twelve-year-olds who have reached the stage of formal operations, the number of incidents recalled increased only gradually with age. Age was the best predictor of the number of incidents recalled by the child. Sex differences – boys 24 per cent, girls 22 per cent, were negligible. In order to assess plot comprehension more strictly, rather than mere recall of incidents, the number of incidents recalled in order was computed for each child. Eight-year-olds recalled an average of 13 per cent of incidents in order, nine-year-olds 18 per cent, ten-year-olds 22 per cent, eleven-year-olds 25 per cent and twelve-year-olds 29 per cent. Once again, there was a very strong relationship between chronological age and the number of incidents recalled in order. While there were no sex differences, statistical analysis showed that eight-year-olds recalled fewer incidents in order than ten-, eleven- and twelve-year-olds and that nine-year-olds recalled fewer incidents in order than twelve-year-olds. We shall further explore the reasons why there should be a difference between nine- and ten-year-olds in the fourth hypothesis of this section.

The wood from the trees hypothesis

Because egocentrism is likely to increase when the child enters the concrete operations stage, it may be expected that younger children will recall incidents, perhaps at the cost of the story line – whereas older children will be able to relate the incidents recalled within the basic fabric of the story line as they perceive it. Younger children were less able to separate the wood from the trees; that is, recall incidents within the framework of the plot than older children. Eight-year-olds (8 per cent out of order) and nine-year-olds (14 per cent out of order) did not correlate incidents with story line. Ten- eleven- and twelve-year-olds (with, respectively, 5, 8, and 3 per cent of incidents out of order) seemed able to recall incidents within the rubric of the plot. These results suggest that some sort of balance has to be maintained between plot comprehension and recall of incidents. It seems likely that the nine-year-old child in particular becomes egocentric once more to signal that he is about to learn how it feels to be in another person's shoes, which ability will clearly aid the recall of a film's story.

Further support for the idea that a critical gap exists between nine and ten years appeared when results from a photograph-sequencing task were examined. Each child who had seen *Clown Ferdl* was presented with 12 photographs from the film and asked to place them in the order in which they occurred in the film. As the wood from the trees hypothesis suggests eight- and nine-year-olds (35 per cent and 27 per cent respectively) placed more photographs out of order than ten- to twelve-year-olds (18 per cent, 21 per cent, 24 per cent respectively). While the oldest children made more mistakes than the ten-year-olds this may reflect the hostility they felt to the film; the fact remains that statistical analysis indicated a significant gap between the ability of the nine- and ten-year-olds to recall incidents seen within the basic rubric of the story line.

Mental age and social class differences in concrete operations

It was expected that intelligence would exert more influence on the child's ability to recount the story of a film in the concrete operations stage than in the pre-operational thought stage. Older children, be-cause they link logically rather than intuitively, should be better able than younger children to perceive relationships (the most frequent test of intelligence) when recalling the story of a film. Results obtain-ed in the *Patrick and Putrick* study lend support to this hypothesis. At five years, pre-operational thinkers of above average intelligence re-called only marginally more sequences in order (1·6) than did average and below average pre-operational thinkers (1·4). The gap between more intelligent and less intelligent children had consid-erably widened by seven and eight years – the ages which mark the onset of the concrete operations stage. At these ages, children of above average intelligence recalled nearly twice as many sequences in order (4·5) than children of below average and average intelligence (2·5). Similarly Eyre-Brook (1972) found that eight-year-olds of above average intelligence recalled twice as many incidents in order (41 per cent) than did eight-year-olds of average or below average intelligence (22 per cent). There would seem little doubt that more intelligent children in the concrete operations stage appreciate plots at an earlier chronological age than less intelligent children. While more intelligent children who had seen *Patrick and Putrick* recalled four out of seven sequences in the correct order, significantly more than the average 2·5 sequences recalled in the correct order by children of average and below average intelligence, there were no significant differences between the groups as regards the number of incidents recalled – 14 and 11 respectively. Thus, while both groups recall a similar number of incidents from films, intelligence in this instance would seem to be the ability to separate the wood (plot) from the trees (incidents).

Results presented above suggest that one of the factors, other than the chronological age of the child, which determines film understanding, is the child's mental age – at least in the concrete operations stage. Unlike mental age, however, social class differences in reactions to televised material have been noted even for five-year-old pre-operational thinkers. Eyre-Brook examined the ability of children in a middle-class school and in a working-class school to retell the story of the film *Scarecrow*. Both five- and eight-year-old middle-class children recalled more incidents in order (33 per cent) than did children from a working-class school (23 per cent). According to Newson and Newson (1963) middle-class children, more often than working-class children, are read stories and encouraged to speculate about the likely ramifications of their behaviour. It may be that middle-class socialisation practices encourage children to comprehend the stories seen in television films at an earlier age. Social class differences in television usage can be observed among children in the pre-operational thought stage and serve to emphasise the importance of parental example in the way young children approach television. We shall have more to say about social class differences in televiewing styles in Chapter 8. As an additional example of parental influence, I found that five- to eight-year-old coloured immigrant children did not watch children's television at all – whereas white working-class children of the same age watched Independent Television programmes for children and white middle-class children of the same age watched BBC television programmes for children.

Understanding film characters' motives

We have argued that some ten years of steady development are required before the child is spontaneously able to admit that points of view other than his own are possible, which marks the final decline of egocentrism in the child's thought. Moreover, we have suggested that the ability to empathise, to imagine how the other person is feeling, is acquired when a stable community provides the child with a consistent image of self in mirror interaction. This could explain, *inter alia*, why children with limited social contacts recognise less than children with stable social contacts.

Children in the pre-operational thought stage will, therefore, be unable to comprehend the emotional interplay between characters; they will understand only physical actions. Nor may we expect that the child in the concrete operations stage will suddenly understand the motives and emotions of film characters. Thus when Flapan (1965) asked six- and nine-year-olds to describe segments of a film they had just seen, six-year-olds reported only gross overt actions and, even though they understood the story, did not report the characters' intentions nor emotional feelings. When compared with nine-year-old reactions, six-year-olds rarely mentioned the feelings or thoughts of the adult in the picture or communication between adults. Six-year-olds recognised anger, hurt or happiness but only from the physical actions of the character.

Results obtained from *Patrick and Putrick* suggest that the understanding of emotional interplay between film characters develops more slowly than the grasp of the main sequences in the film. When each child was shown the photographs of the puppets and asked, 'What are the puppets doing in this photograph?', very few of the five- to eight-year-olds interviewed gave answers which implied knowledge of the characters' feelings. While answers implying knowledge of the characters' feelings marginally increased with age, very few children, even at eight years, did more than describe the photographs. Children said, 'They are mixing flour,' and did not, even when asked, 'Why?', answer, 'They are mixing flour because they are hungry'.

In *Clown Ferdl* the clown is shown to fall in love with a dancer in the circus by means of symbolic representation. When children were asked, 'What happened in the film between the dancer and the clown?', eight- and nine-year-olds replied either that they did not know, or merely described the clown's physical actions with the dancer, such as holding her poster or looking at each other. Only 6 per cent of eight- and nine-year-olds were able to give an adequate reason why the two had fallen in love. Ten- to twelve-year-olds were more inclined to mention symbolic cues such as the dancer juggled a heart shape when describing the clown and dancer relationship and 25 per cent gave an adequate reason why the two had fallen in love.

When assessing concepts of left and right with five- to eleven-year-olds sitting opposite him, Elkind (1961) found that it was the nine-year-old who spontaneously said, 'I thought you meant from where you were sitting'. The tendency to judge spontaneously from another's point of view never appeared before the age of nine and became increasingly frequent thereafter. Similarly Feffer (1959) found the most striking rise in role-taking abilities was noted between the ages eight and nine when compared with ten- to eleven-year olds. In the experiment six- to thirteen-year-old children had to make up a story using three characters in a cardboard theatre and subsequently tell the story from the point of view of each character. Empathic abilities were also related to mental as well as chronological age. Clearly the child with the mental age of nine or ten years, who can spontaneously take the point of view of another person, is likely to take the points of view of filmed characters and interpret their actions and motives.

Thus, when two- to twelve-year-old Canadian children were shown *Hercules* and asked how Newton felt as he watched a character climb an erupting volcano, only 2 out of 19 children aged eight and less mentioned worry or fear, while 7 of the 8 children aged nine and more replied that he was worried or frightened. Piaget's standpoint regarding the understanding of other people's points of view and feelings are clearly salient to the child's comprehension of the motivation of film characters' behaviour.

Understanding film symbols

Television is ideally suited to visual metaphor. If, as we have argued in this chapter, children come to comprehend film but slowly during their development, we may similarly expect only a gradual understanding of visual metaphor as children grow older. The Prix Jeunesse organisation which sponsors and awards prizes for children's television programmes, probably awards too many prizes to films employing symbolism not understood by the child audiences on whose behalf the prizes are awarded. In *Scarecrow*, for example, the changing of the seasons is depicted symbolically; similarly *Clown Ferdl* enacts his amorous advances by means of elaborate heart shapes wrought from lions' tails, and the juggling of heart shapes by interested spectators. Predictably, we discover that children don't even seem to notice this fine detail which so impresses the Prix Jeunesse judges. Ninety-three per cent of five-year-old children, asked when they had seen *Scarecrow*, 'How could you tell spring had come?', simply did not know. Indeed only 38 per cent of eight-year-olds could interpret the concrete visual signs they had seen, 'Because the sun came out, because the flowers came out, or because the snow melted.' Similarly only 8 of 100 children who saw *Clown Ferdl* noticed the symbolic way in which the clown-dancer relationship was filmed, and these children were all aged from ten to twelve years. It would appear that accurate plot comprehension is linked to the ability to understand how a character is feeling, which in turn relates to the recognition and comprehension of symbolic cues. Such abilities would seem to develop between nine and ten years.

Summary of televiewing style in concrete operations

The notion that films have a story seems to develop rather abruptly at about six years of age. In contrast, the ability to perceive beyond events and comprehend the motives and feelings of filmed characters develops rather slowly. Not surprisingly, the ability to understand material requiring a higher degree of interpretation develops later than the ability to sequence items into the outline of the essential action of the plot. Children aged between eight and nine years, because of a resurgence of egocentrism prior to the development of empathic abilities, are still influenced by what they see. They still experience difficulty reconciling the theory that films have a story with observation of the numerous incidents in a film. The ten-year-old and older child does not seem to experience the same degree of difficulty; at this age they fit incidents seen into the story line and in consequence recall more incidents from the film.

Some children are capable of understanding the story of a film at an earlier age than others. Results suggest that middle-class and more intelligent children accurately perceive and recall films at an earlier chronological age than working-class and less intelligent children. These latter children will also be slower to perceive and understand the motives and feelings of film characters, particularly if they are somewhat isolated from their friends. Most children aged ten, unlike their younger counterparts, seem able to take roles spontaneously; they also seem able to appreciate the motives underlying the actions of film characters.

Concrete operations in the village

According to Piaget the main reason why egocentrism declines is because children in the concrete operations stage learn in interaction that many points of view are possible and the child's own notions are not invariably correct. It would seem worth emphasising that once treated in an adult fashion in the village the child in concrete operations regularly interacts with a large extended kin group which make known their viewpoints to the child, and correct his viewpoint where necessary. Perhaps this is why children more frequently recognise television characters not only as they grow older but also if they have firm feet in a stable social anchorage of other people. We do not at this point in time know whether recognised television characters can force the child to re-evaluate his viewpoint in the way

his real life significant others may do. But at least it is a hypothesis
worth testing.

TELEVIEWING IN THE FORMAL OPERATIONS STAGE (ELEVEN/ TWELVE YEARS ONWARDS)

Piaget and Inhelder (1958) maintain that the adolescent, like the
child, lives in the present, but also unlike the child he can live in the
future and the domain of the hypothetical. It is only during adolescence that operations become abstracted from concrete instances,
and formal logical arguments to which facts are less revelant can be
conducted. His conceptual world is full of informal theories about
self and life, with plans for both his and society's future, and with
the personally relevant problems of work and marriage – all made
possible by the adolescent's ability to think reflectively.

The onset of formal operations marks the final beginning of the
end of egocentrism in thought. Adolescents may be expected to
share the adult's conception of the world and therefore, hypothesis
one, will comprehend films as efficiently as adults.

Secondly, having rejected the 'here-and-now' world of the child,
the twelve-year-old, especially if he is middle class, is concerned with
his future and self-betterment. Such adolescents can be expected to
reject those fantasy programmes so popular with younger children
and orientate towards those realistic materials which may be
perceived as useful with regard to future careers.

Thirdly, in complete contrast to the pre-operational thinker, we
can expect that adolescents, because they codify knowledge and
extend it in ways that only abstract and formal thought can support,
will no longer respond in binary ways to filmed material. These
teenagers will be able to appreciate merit in the ideas and skill
employed in a film while at the same time dislike certain aspects of
that same film.

Fourthly, adolescents who can postulate 'it's as if' such a state of
affairs exists are likely to imagine hypothetically the sorts of relationships which may exist between film characters even if they are not
portrayed in front of the camera. Thus, teenagers should be able to
explain hypothetically apparent inconsistencies in the behaviour of
film characters. Moreover, during adolescence the young adult is
likely to have an emotional relationship with a member of the
opposite sex. No doubt adolescents will also comprehend emotional
relationships portrayed on film.

Formal operations in the village

I am not convinced that the ability to think hypothetically was much
valued in the village, since hypothetical thought is often not prag-

matic or useful to the task in hand. Indeed, as we shall see, such thought is not over-encouraged in working-class households, where village values, rather than mobile 'industrial' values, tend to be dominant. Essentially, therefore, hypothetical thought may result from education, and may be the precursor of a desire for mobility and a change in status, and as such a threat to the stability of village life. Moreover the ability to think hypothetically requires a considerable training available only to those whose life-style yields considerable leisure time free, in part, from the worries of everyday life. Children in the village who showed a capacity for such thought were no doubt, and probably still are in primitive societies, encouraged to join an esoteric profession, possibly the priesthood.

Adolescents' ability to recall television programmes

Children in the formal operations stage can be expected to recall films as well as adults. Mialeret and Malandain (1962) found that, even when films had been seen twice, seven-year-olds recalled but 4 per cent while twelve-year-olds recalled 50 per cent. Holaday and Stoddard (1933) report that eleven-year-olds recalled 62 per cent of feature films whether immediately after viewing or three months later, while sixteen-year-olds recalled 80 per cent and adults 86 per cent. Paulsen (1957) comments that twenty months after viewing, eleven-year-old German children recalled the film plot more fully than adults. Like the twelve-year-olds who saw *Clown Ferdl* I recalled some 30 to 40 per cent of the film and I similarly placed 2 of the 12 photographs out of order after I had first seen the film.

Rejection of fantasy programmes

Schramm *et al.* report, 'We are now in a better position to explain what happens at the "turning point", the time near the beginning of the teens when adult patterns begin to replace childish ones and spectacular changes in media behaviour occur. In the case of lower socio-economic levels, less change is necessary to go from childhood to adult patterns. But in the case of middle-class children, the norm of self-betterment, activity and future time orientation becomes demanding. If their mental ability is equal to the ambitions encouraged by the norm, they tend to high print, low TV behaviour; if not, towards high use of the media generally.' The turning point would also seem to be related to the child's ability in formal operations to use logical and abstract thought.

Children who saw *Clown Ferdl* were asked to say whether they thought the film was real or unreal, true or false, and whether the events seen in the puppet film were lifelike. Twelve-year-olds, significantly more than children aged eight to eleven years, denied that the film was life-like, real or true. As might be imagined twelve-year-olds looked askance at the questioner and exclaimed, 'Of course the film is not real – it is merely fiction'. Likewise Gemelli (1951) concludes that film experiences belong to the Italian child's 'realm of fantasy' until he is ten or eleven years of age, and that films which do not belong to the play world as opposed to the real world are of little interest to the child before formal operations. Such evidence as is available strongly suggests that it is the twelve-year-old, entering the formal operations stage, who first rejects those fantasy television programmes so popular with younger children.

Appreciation of ideas in disliked films

However, the rejection of childhood fantasy does not imply that children in formal operations will reject out of hand those ideas expressed in fantasy programmes. Unlike the younger child, twelve-year-olds can respond in non-binary ways to film material. In *Clown Ferdl* as well as puppets and people, characters are portrayed as two-dimensional posters. When children were asked if the posters were actors, twelve-year-olds were adamant that they were not actors, significantly more so than eight-to eleven-year-olds who thought they were actors. Yet at the same time, twelve-year-olds considered the use of posters as a novel and good idea. Younger children reacted in a more 'all-or-none' way – in that they either liked the idea and the posters, or they did not like the idea and the posters. Twelve-year-olds could react in such a way as to dislike the posters as actors yet see the merit of the idea.

Understanding interpersonal relationships in film during formal operations

Because of the adolescent's ability to think reflectively, and his growing interest in the opposite sex, we can expect adolescents to make gradual progress in the comprehension of motives for emotional relationships and attempt to explain inconsistent behaviour. Gollin (1958) showed 700 ten-, thirteen- and sixteen-year-olds a five-scene silent film in which the hero, a boy of eleven, is introduced and alternatively seen doing good (helping a boy who has fallen off his bicycle) and then bad (taking the ball away from children playing catch). Each viewer was asked to give a full description of what he had seen, including his own evaluation of the boy and his behaviour. The narratives were scored for inference – that is, parts of the story which went beyond simple behavioural descriptions and explained the motives of the boy in the film. Similarly, children's stories were scored for consistency in accounting for the divergent behaviour of the boy hero.

Only 2 per cent of children in concrete operations, at ten years, were able to resolve the boy hero's inconsistent behaviour and only 10–20 per cent of these children inferred motives to the boy. By thirteen years, in the formal operations stage, 15 per cent of children could resolve inconsistencies and 60 per cent of children inferred motives to the boy. At sixteen years, however, half the children 'explained' the boy's inconsistent acts and 9 out of 10 provided a motive to explain the boy's behaviour. Gollin's results demonstrate fairly clearly that adolescents gradually resolve inconsistency and attribute motives as they grow older during formal operations and become familiar with answering hypothetical 'as if' questions. Moreover, these abilities were not merely dependent on chronological age; more intelligent children and middle-class children were better then their less intelligent and working-class counterparts. Interestingly, girls were better able to attribute motives and explain away inconsistencies than boys. This latter finding could reflect the fact that girls more frequently recognise than boys and are thus better able to predict outcome.

Summary of televiewing style in formal operations

We need not labour these results, since they are so similar to adult viewing styles that they are readily comprehensible. We see in the middle-class adolescent almost the antithesis of the pre-operational child. The one rejects fantasy, the other believes fantasy to be true. The one reacts in an 'all-or nothing' way, the other weighs arguments and ideas and while not liking something can appreciate merits in the idea. The one has no comprehension of either story line nor can attribute motives to characters, the other has such a highly sophisticated concept of story that he reconciles inconsistencies into the one basic plot which he does by concentrating on the motives of the character. The one televiewing style reflects innocence, the other the embryonic sophistication which will take final shape at the university film club.

Formal operations in the village

That it is the middle-class child concerned with self-betterment who rejects television's fantasy in favour of the learning afforded by reality materials need not surprise us. These are children in preparation for a mobile life, chasing the best opportunities. They must make their own communities, they must manage the presentation of self on a variety of stages, which ability demands reflective thought capable of resolving inconsistencies. The unambitious, and hence socially inferior, working-class teenager is less concerned – like his counterpart in the village before him – with the presentation of self, since he will probably remain in the community into which he was born and finds his identity. His televiewing style, as will be seen in Chapter 8, reflects both a need for excitement after work and a desire to encounter the wider society as it is unfolded to him via his television screen.

By way of qualification: Film structure in relation to comprehension

The analysis applied in this chapter was very heavily tuned to child development theories suggested by Piaget. I may, however, have overstated the case in an attempt to explain why children of different ages respond so divergently to the same television programmes, but that seemed preferable to a list of purely empirical (that is, observed) findings with little explanatory power. However, it must be stressed that much of the work reviewed in this chapter is concerned with children's reactions to television films such as are currently available, and children have watched mainly in schools rather than in the home. These factors constrain the generality of results presented here, which may not be applicable to all televiewing situations.

Continental researchers have been concerned, for example, to understand how the structure of a film affects children's comprehension. Keilhacker and Vogg (1965) showed eleven prize-winning documentaries, dramas, comedies and magazine programmes to 225 'children' aged between five and fifteen and to 246 adolescents aged fifteen to twenty years. In the German tradition data was collected by a variety of methods, which means results are largely interpretative. 'Children' aged fifteen years, according to Keilhacker, will accept coincidental solutions to problems depicted in films, whereas adolescents aged sixteen years and above reject such chance solutions and prefer programmes which spell out the logical continuity of the plot. While adolescents showed more highly differentiated programme preferences than younger children, they reject the over-theatrical, the overplayed and in general the stylised portrayal which, as we have seen, enable younger children to cope with the story line. Similarly adolescents prefer plots relating to human relationships, to self-concept and to identity. While they prefer realistic to stylistic portrayals this does not mean that they prefer 'informal' programmes, but rather they prefer drama which is shown as realistically as possible.

For children aged up to fifteen years, films should be predominantly presented in terms of visual action rather than clever dialogue, and emotions should be expressed physically in terms of laughter and tears rather than through words. Dialogue should be simple and quick. Production techniques, such as abrupt transition between scenes, the introduction of sequences not immediately related to the story and special distortion effects, should be avoided. Moreover, Keilhacker argues that children's television should be stereotyped in terms of an infallible hero who always defeats the clearly recognisable villain.

A more experimental approach was adopted by Mialeret and Melies (1954) who showed children aged four, eight or twelve years one of three versions of a film about a mother and child with the same beginning and happy end. One version was filmed without gimmicks; a second employed transition and change of scene; a whole range of camera tricks such as flashbacks and silhouettes were used in a third. Only twelve-year-old children understood the relationship between the child and the mother; neither four- nor eight-year-olds could describe the film accurately especially in those versions where scenes changed.

One of the distinct advantages of a theory over haphazard results such as these, is that we could easily have predicted Mialeret's results from the hypotheses outlined in this chapter. Similarly had Keilhacker defined children as those in concrete operations, his results are also predicable from the hypotheses presented in this chapter; likewise his adolescents would seem to have the characteristics we have ascribed to the stage of formal operations. A theory, after all, attempts to explain maximum empirical variation from the minimum number of assumptions. We have attempted to explain the developmental televiewing experiences of the child on two continents by means of Piaget's assumptions. The reader is invited to test the hypotheses outlined here for himself. In the next chapter we shall again employ Piaget's theory to attempt to explain how television defines everyday real life social roles.

6

Media definitions of real-life social, occupational and national roles

Many viewers will first encounter a variety of national, occupational and social groups on their television screens. Children who recognise and interact with, rather than identify with and imitate, television mothers, policemen, clowns and Indians (red) are likely to form lasting impressions of such groups and expect the real-life occupants of such roles to behave in the predictable manner defined by tele-vised presentations. Such initial social learning of 'how to behave' towards such people and how such people will behave towards the viewer is likely to be crucial. In this chapter I shall argue that the media help to define the child's expectations of real-life social, occupational and national roles. Again employing Piaget's theory I pinpoint the age of maximum vulnerability at ten to eleven years, when children are first aware of the motivations and feelings of televised personnel with whom they have had no first-hand contact.

THE GROWTH OF STEREOTYPES IN THE VILLAGE AND IN INDUSTRIAL SOCIETIES

We have argued in Chapter 1 that the child is socialised within the village because he is intimately acquainted with the full range of social and occupational roles necessary for the maintenance of the village unit. These roles are occupied by his extended kin members with whom he regularly interacts. In very full degree, therefore, he has first-hand experience of such social and occupational roles. In the mass society, though, due to increasing specialisation, any one individual's contact with the full range of occupational roles is limited. Often the child will have no direct experience of these roles; and if television is used to gain knowledge of the workings of the wider society, the child's first contact with many such roles is afforded by television. Industrial societies are bewilderingly complex, television and other mass media bring its members into contact with an extraordinary range of issues and problems, many of which are beyond the effective sphere of influence of the individual and more importantly beyond the range of his personal experience. It seems likely, therefore, that the individual, far from claiming ignorance about such issues, requires and needs to have an attitude or mental stance towards them. Such stances often identify him as a member of the wider society – but if, as seems likely, his first contact with many such issues is via the mass media, the media stereotypes will become his stereotypes, especially if he is told about such issues by a person he recognises, that is a person he feels he knows, on television. Thus it is that many people, who have never seen soft drugs, for example, intrinsically know that they are dangerous.

MEDIA DEFINITION OF OCCUPATIONAL ROLES

Siegel (1958) was concerned that many children first become acquainted with violence and aggression, not in real life, but via the mass media. She therefore attempted to discover how media presentations of the role of taxi-drivers rubbed off on seven-year-old children, who, it was thought, would have had little contact with taxi-drivers in real life. One group listened to a radio drama in which a taxi-driver was in conflict with a client and in order to solve the problem was violently aggressive. A second group of children likewise heard the taxi-driver in conflict with a client but in this drama the taxi-driver discovered a constructive way to resolve the problem. In order to discover whether the radio programme had helped to define children's real-life expectations of taxi-drivers' behaviour, each child was given a newspaper text. Only those children who demonstrated they knew a newspaper reported only reality were asked by a second investigator, who was not associated with the radio programme, to complete a variety of stories for their local newspaper. Included amongst stories about the local weather and local school holidays was a story about a local taxi-driver getting into difficulties with a client. Two-thirds of the children who heard the non-violent radio drama completed the stories with no mention of aggression while one-third of these children reported intermediate aggression in the solution of the problem. On the other hand, half the children who heard the violent radio drama completed the news account so that the local taxi-driver was very aggressive towards his client and only one-third of the children completed the story without mention of aggression. It would appear from this limited study, which is virtually the only one in its area, that the radio definition of 'how a taxi-driver behaves' helped to define children's real-life expectation of taxi-drivers in their local community.

The televised labour force

Given the fact that media portrayals of occupational roles help to define the real-life expectation of how such role holders will behave we need to know the characteristics of the televised labour force. DeFleur (1964) has described the televised labour force as it was then presented in ordinary American television programmes, and he and his wife (1967) studied children's perceptions of televised occupational roles. In America in 1964, very nearly a third of all jobs seen for at least three minutes in programmes other than commercials, news and westerns were related to the law and about 10 per cent each related to entertainment, to medicine, to personal service and to secretarial and office work. Scientists, it would seem, were only seen in commercials. Comparisons with census information showed that the televised labour force overrepresented managerial and professional roles and seriously underrepresented those jobs of lesser prestige which many child viewers would later occupy. These programmes associated glamorous surroundings with personal servants and with law work, showed foremen, teachers and salesmen in 'ordinary' surroundings and service, semi-skilled and unskilled workers in 'humble' settings. Not only did television define the likely venue of many occupations, it also clearly portrayed a distinct pecking order between different occupations. Foremen, judges, policemen, clergy and doctors all gave orders and received respect from secretaries, drivers, skilled, semi-skilled, and unskilled workers. These definitions of how various occupations behave to one another could have influenced child viewers since when children were asked which job characteristics most attracted them, they chose jobs which let them boss other people to jobs which let them travel, helped people or made a lot of money.

Moreover, those in higher prestige occupations were invariably portrayed as well dressed, socially skilled, intelligent and handsome, while it fell to the menial worker to be boorish, slovenly, badly dressed and ugly. The bulk of tomorrow's workers are hardly encouraged to take up the latter types of job. The various occupations seen on television were usually stereotyped. As Siegel discovered, taxi-, as well as bus- and truck-drivers, were burly and aggressive. In the televised labour force nurses were cold and impersonal; salesmen were glib; artistic professions were temperamental and eccentric; policemen were hardened and often brutal while private detectives were resourceful and cleverer than policemen; lawyers were clever and unorthodox and journalists were callous. These stereotypes both correspond with and reiterate the conceptions held of such work roles in society, yet children meet and interact with many of these roles first on television rather than in

real life. We need to know whether children who first encounter
these occupations on television think, for example, that real-life
nurses are cold and impersonal. Were we to compare conceptions of
nurses amongst children who had been to hospital with children who
have only met nurses on the small screen we could discover just how
much television has helped to define children's expectations of
real-life nurses.

DeFleur and his wife tackled this question by comparing children's *knowledge* of three types of occupational role – first, those
seen in real-life by 85 per cent of children such as teacher and post-
man; secondly, those which were most frequently seen on the television screen but which only 2 per cent of children had seen in real-
life such as lawyers and reporters, and, thirdly, those which children
did not see on television and which only 1 per cent had seen in
real-life – such as electrical engineer and skilled printer. Regrettably
each of the 237 children aged between six and thirteen years were not
individually asked about the personal characteristics associated with
these occupations but rather were tested about the type, place and
training involved in each occupation. We would predict that pseudo-
social interaction with the televised labour force should lead to
almost as much knowledge about televised occupations as personal
contact. Indeed only a quarter of children's answers (28 per cent)
were accurate for invisible occupations whereas 44 per cent of
answers were accurate for televised occupations, and slightly more
than half (56 per cent) of answers were accurate for personal contact
occupations. In spite of the stereotyped portrayals, television was an
effective teacher of information concerning occupational roles.
Heavier viewers knew significantly more about televised occupations,
but not about personal contact nor invisible occupations, than
lighter viewers. Similarly, while girls were more ignorant of invisible
occupations than boys, girls knew just as much as boys about both
personal contact and televised occupations – again reiterating the
argument that television uniquely makes society visible.

Media definition of national roles

Once again, regrettably, data in this area are sparse. Twenty years
after the Second World War, Begitske (cited in DeFleur, 1964)
discovered that American children still nominated Germans and
Japanese as the enemies of the United States and cited television as
their main learning source for this information. These children had
developed conceptions of international relations appropriate to the
1940s but dangerously inadequate for the 1960s. One year after the
introduction of commercial television in England, Himmelweit
et al., when examining how television had shaped attitudes to

foreigners, found that ten- and eleven-year-olds were considerably more influenced by television than thirteen- and fourteen-year-olds. Televiewing seemed to have played little part in the way adolescents perceived Germans, since 14 per cent of both televiewers and non-televiewers said that Germans were 'vicious and arrogant'. However television had influenced the ten- and eleven-year-olds since twice as many televiewers (14 per cent) as non-viewers (7 per cent) said Germans were 'vicious and arrogant'.

However, Himmelweit *et al.* claim, rather surprisingly, that younger televiewers made more objective and fewer evaluative statements about foreigners than non-viewers. Ten- and eleven-year-old viewers, twice as often as non-viewers, mentioned that Jews were 'religious', French were 'gay and witty', Germans 'vicious and arrogant' and Negroes 'black-skinned' rather than 'cunning and unhappy'. The researchers claim that such 'objective' results are in accord with the way television presents such nationalities. It is clear, objective or not, that television does help to define the younger child's expectation of the way real-life foreigners will behave, but has less impact on the older child. We need, perhaps, to explain why this should be so.

A DEVELOPMENTAL EXPLANATION OF THE WAY THE MEDIA DEFINE SOCIAL, OCCUPATIONAL AND NATIONAL ROLES

Keeping in mind the development of televiewing styles in relation to Piaget's theory, a fairly complex relationship between media induced attitude change and stages in thought may be anticipated. As we have seen, until nine years, egocentrism so dominates the child's thought that he is unaware that points of view other than his own exist. When televiewing, egocentric children are likely to be subjectively involved in what they see, which may considerably change their attitudes. Such attitudes are, however, likely to be ephemeral and will change yet again when another programme is seen. At about ten years, the child begins to think objectively, in that he admits points of view other than his own are possible, and is able to imagine how television characters feel in certain situations. Newly able to employ such reciprocity in thought, we may hypothesise that the ten- and eleven-year-old child will be most influenced in the longer term by televised 'propaganda' messages, since they are unsure of their own points of view and are amenable to other view-points concerning occupational or national roles. At the onset of formal operations facilitated by hypothetical thought, the child becomes aware that all standards are relative to others. Older children, therefore, aware of points of view other than their own, may be less susceptible to propaganda than younger children, since older children are able to evaluate televised film messages by comparing them with other points of view known to them.

RESEARCH INTO PERIODS OF VULNERABILITY IN THE WAY MEDIA PRESENTATIONS SHAPE ATTITUDES

Bearing in mind the stereotyped 'vicious' view of Germans presented by the mass media, it was no surprise to learn that one German-born lady in an evening class was unable to persuade her British daughter to visit Germany. What contact, apart from her mother, had this girl with Germans? It seems likely that her principal contact with Germans was via the mass media. Viewers may be led to expect that different occupational and national groups will behave in real-life in those totally stereotyped ways in which workers and foreigners are defined by the mass media. Vulnerable ten- and eleven-year-old children who only see Germans in comics and on the small screen, who are unable to judge media presentations relative to other standpoints, may make the media definition their own, perhaps even for the rest of their lives.

To find out whether children's opinions of occupational roles were defined by the media, and whether younger children were more vulnerable than older children, each of the eight- to twelve-year-olds was asked what they thought about clowns in general in real-life, both before and after seeing the film, *Clown Ferdl*. Children were asked if they thought each of 27 sentences about clowns was very true, true, neither true nor untrue, untrue or very untrue, so that a statistical analysis could be conducted. *Clown Ferdl* does not rely on the conventional stereotype of the clown, but rather shows his full development – learning to play musical instruments, learning to juggle from scratch, and learning the trapeze from square one. Ferdl only achieves eventual success after many rebuffs, failures and moments of sadness.

The film *Clown Ferdl* helped children to define their real-life expectations of clowns in general. Children who saw Ferdl as a person, who was rejected after working hard, were better able to appreciate the human aspect of real-life clowns. The stereotyped assessment based simply on the social face of clowns in circuses was weakened. Before viewing, the children's consensus view was that clowns were stupid, cheeky, lazy, big-headed, flippant and always happy. The same children revised their opinions of real-life clowns after viewing. Clowns in general were significantly less stupid, less cheeky, less lazy, less boasting, more serious and not always happy. The fact that Ferdl was portrayed as both musical and humble also defined what children thought of real-life clowns in general, since after viewing, clowns were seen as more musical, less quarrelsome and less rude than before viewing.

Bearing in mind that all children saw the same film and all were interviewed in exactly the same way, it was expected that children of different ages would respond very differently to the film portraying the clown as a person. Eight- and nine-year-olds, because they think subjectively only know how they would feel in similar circumstances. When the hard-working clown is rejected by the circus, they know how they would feel faced with such disappointment. They feel sad when Ferdl is rejected and, consequently, their attitude to clowns in real-life changes to accord with how they would feel in such situations. At this age children are sympathetic to film presentations and may be expected to change their attitudes frequently and markedly since they are unable to judge events from a perspective other than how they would feel. They do not yet know that other people see the world in ways which differ from their own personal view.

Ten- and eleven-year-olds, in common with the younger children, know how they would feel in similar circumstances but they also play opposite the clown and observe him to see how he feels. They are beginning to take roles spontaneously, and can thus put themselves in the clown's shoes. Where before only one view of the world was possible, now there are two – how they would feel in those situations encountered by the clown, and how they observe the clown to respond in such situations. These children are beginning to think objectively and will thus change their opinion of real-life clowns not to accord with how they would feel in those film situations but to accord with how they observe and imagine the clown to feel. One might, therefore, expect that children of this age will be most influenced in the long term by propaganda messages, since for the first time they are unsure of their own point of view and are amenable to other points of view concerning occupational and national roles.

Children aged twelve years and more become aware, with hypothetical thought, that all standards are relative to others. Consequently, twelve-year-old and older children, aware even before viewing of several points of view about clowns, will change their attitudes less than ten- to eleven-year-olds but in the same direction. Such children may be expected to be relatively immune to televised propaganda.

Younger children were most influenced by *Clown Ferdl*. All children thought that clowns boasted, before viewing. After viewing, eight-year-olds were much less sure (-27 per cent) that clowns boasted; followed in turn by nine-year-olds (-18 per cent), ten- and eleven-year-olds (-6 per cent), and twelve-year-olds hardly changing their view (-2 per cent). How though can the age differences be explained? Is it as Himmelweit *et al.* maintain that attitudes to foreigners become less amenable to change as the child grows older, and if so why? Is it as Garry (1969) suggests that television propaganda is most influential when children are naïve? Garry similarly found that younger American children who saw *Clown Ferdl* changed their opinions considerably more than older children. If naïveté corresponds with Piaget's notion of subjective thought, then one explanation is available.

Eight- and nine-year-olds who are too young to take the role of the clown, who can only think subjectively, only know how they would feel when faced by a bullying ringmaster, who tears up the clown's proficiency certificate and chases him around the circus – less boastful (−23 per cent), sadder (+3 per cent) and more frightened (+4 per cent). These children knew they would be sad, humble and frightened if the ringmaster did these things to them. They evaluated clowns in real-life subjectively from their own point of view, rather than objectively.

Ten- and eleven-year-olds, for the first time aware that not all people see the world in the same way as they do; who are able to think reciprocally and can imagine how the other feels independently of their own reaction, may be expected to differ in their response to *Clown Ferdl*. They were expected to observe how the clown felt during the film regardless of how they would have felt in those situations; namely determined to succeed, confident of eventual success and confident on the trapeze. These children, indeed, thought clowns in real-life were less boastful (−6 per cent), less sad (−20 per cent), and less frightened (−9 per cent) after viewing. It is to be noted that younger children thought clowns both more sad and more frightened.

Twelve-year-olds were expected to judge the 'image' of the clown seen in the film relative to other clown images known to them and least change their attitudes. A powerful presentation is required to shift the attitudes of children who can use relative standards in thought, which the twelve-year-olds told us *Clown Ferdl* was not. Twelve-year-olds thought clowns in real-life were marginally less boasting (−2 per cent), slightly sadder (−11 per cent) and did not change their opinion as to whether a clown is frightened (0 per cent). Since children admit the validity of points of view other than their own from ten years onwards, twelve-year-olds were expected to change their opinions of clowns in real-life in the same direction as ten and eleven-year-olds but less markedly. As can be seen results lent support to this expectation.

DEVELOPMENTAL TRENDS IN CHILDREN'S PERCEPTIONS OF
THE TELEVISED LABOUR FORCE

Results from the specific *Clown Ferdl* experiment need to be placed
within the wider context of televised definitions of occupational
roles. Results obtained by DeFleur accord with the developmental
sequence outlined above. Children's knowledge of occupational
roles, regardless of visibility and personal contact, increased steadily
with age. Children aged six and seven years grappling with televised
story and reality concepts knew twice as much about personal
contact occupations (43 per cent) as about televised occupations
(22 per cent) and least about invisible occupations (14 per cent).
Between eight and nine years when children merely observe characters from an egocentric viewpoint, their knowledge of occupational
roles as portrayed on television has doubled (47 per cent) and is not
far behind their knowledge of visible occupations (57 per cent).
While their knowledge of invisible occupations has considerably
improved (30 per cent), it is apparent that at this age children are
most rapidly learning from television.

Between ten and eleven years, when children are first able to take
the roles of the characters, their knowledge of televised occupations
(61 per cent) is most comparable with their knowledge of visible
occupations (67 per cent) and shows significant gains over invisible
occupations (39 per cent). Results indicate that it is between ten and
eleven years that televised presentations most clearly define occupational stereotypes, since at twelve and thirteen years, as we would
expect, children's knowledge of televised occupations shows a less
rapid increase (69 per cent), than their knowledge of both visible
(76 per cent) and invisible (49 per cent) occupations. As expected
children in the formal operations stage are more immune to televised
propaganda than younger children because they can compare
televised presentations with other sources of information available
to them.

The DeFleurs asked children to rank order the six occupations of
each type in terms of prestige. Six- and seven-year-olds had only
hazy ideas of occupational prestige for each of three types of occupation. Children able to cope with the story line at eight and nine years
were the first to show very considerable agreement about the prestige order of televised occupations but showed much less agreement
about both contact and invisible occupations. At the vulnerable
age – ten and eleven years – children were virtually unanimous
about the prestige order of televised occupations but showed only
moderate agreement for contact and invisible occupations. After
eleven years children's agreement regarding the prestige order of
televised occupations declined, as we might expect from children

able to use relative standards in thought, whereas they began to agree about the prestige order of contact occupations and to a lesser extent invisible occupations. Television, therefore, proved to be a more potent source of occupational status knowledge than either personal contact or general community culture, and at much earlier ages. Ten- and eleven-year-olds, as expected, most readily accepted the televised stereotypes. In this context at least, what they learnt seemed to be reasonably accurate since children's rankings of televised occupations closely corresponded with both parents and experts.

Age differences in susceptibility to televised propaganda

As children grow older they become more objective in thought. Starting from a point where they can think only subjectively at the age of ten they become aware that the film characters do not respond to situations as they do. At ten years the child watches from a distance to see how the character responds. Finally at about twelve years children use relative standards in thought and from a considerable distance compare what they have seen with other propaganda. As we have seen, twelve years has been described as the turning point in the child's life; twelve years is the age when children reject fantasy programmes as 'kid's stuff' and twelve years is the youngest age when a clear distinction is made between the reality and fantasy of television portrayals.

It is suggested that the reason for all these occurrences is the appearance of relative standards in thought at twelve years. Thus, although real people appear in *Clown Ferdl,* twelve-year-olds most emphatically denied that the events in the film were true to life. Eight- and nine-year-olds thought the film true to life, while ten- and eleven-year-olds were ambivalent. These results accord with the notion that eight- and nine-year-olds think subjectively, ten- and eleven-year-olds think reciprocally and twelve-year-olds think in relative terms. To disregard these important age differences in attitude change could lead one to conclude that television presentations of occupational roles have no effect, since attitudes change in different directions at different ages.

Perhaps we can also explain why seven-, eight- and nine-year-olds most enjoy westerns (Himmelweit *et al.*) and why at about ten years children begin to criticise westerns because of their stereotyped presentation. Younger children enjoy the sameness because they can predict both outcome and the peaks and troughs of emotional experience they know they will share with the hero. By ten years they reject the western for more lifelike programmes such as crime and police serials. This change in programme preference seems to occur when the child is first aware that the hero's viewpoint differs from his own. He seems at this age to demand programmes which present a more realistic picture of the environment and one which he will observe and note, rather than share. Care should perhaps be exercised in the production of television programmes for children who are bored with the sameness of the western, so that they do not acquire the attitude towards occupational and national groups which has lead them to believe that Germans are 'vicious and arrogant'.

Definitions of Red Indians – television or school?

Because of the lack of research concerning the way the media help to define national roles and stereotypes, I asked a Canadian student, O'Shaughnessy (1972), to conduct a pilot investigation into Canadian children's notions of the Red Indians who live in Canada. As she points out, the plight of the Indians is a *cause célèbre* requiring a well-informed citizenry, and the subject is one which Canadian children are taught in elementary schools. She began by talking with middle-class children in their own homes to find out what they knew about real-life Canadian Indians. Once again developmental trends were apparent in children's answers. At nine years, when asked, 'What does a real Indian look like?', children said, 'They have no clothes, they wear feathered headbands, black hair and look mean'; at eleven years – 'dark skinned, dark hair and messy'; while at twelve and thirteen years – 'high cheek-bones, reddish skin, flat nose, build depends on how well nourished'. Similarly when asked, 'What would a real-life Indian's house be like?', replies were at nine years – 'tent, tepee or long house'; at eleven years – 'maybe tent, maybe house like ours but smaller'; and at thirteen years – 'perhaps government houses not tents but rundown shacks'. When asked, 'How do Indians get the things they need to live?', nine-year-olds replied, 'Kill people, steal and make stuff'; eleven-year-olds – 'Hunt fur for clothes, catch animals, make things and might buy at stores'; and twelve/thirteen-year-olds – 'Buy from a store, not a supermarket but a general store'. When asked whether Canadian Indians had to go to school or obey laws, nine-year-olds replied, 'No'; eleven-year-olds – 'Sometimes, perhaps their fathers teach them and the council makes the rules'; and twelve- to thirteen-year-olds – 'Yes, but some have to quit school because they are poor and they have to obey tribal regulations and government rules'. All these children claimed that they had learnt most about Indians at school, but it is readily apparent that prior to formal operations, television's influence is far greater than the teacher's.

The nine-year-old's picture of an Indian, derived from lengthy

interviews, was of a far removed, primitive savage. They all associated Indians with Cowboys, and for these children killing was
reflected as a way of life, neither good nor bad, but simply how
Indians survived. None of the children displayed any awareness of
the present-day Indian although several named reservations as where
Indians live. As we would predict, these children showed no ability
to understand an Indian child today with whom they have little
direct contact. Their lack of experience, coupled with their stereotyped notions, might well prevent them extending sympathy in the
future to Indians.

The eleven-year-olds, while adhering to the concepts expressed by
nine-year-olds, seemed also to be struggling with realistic ideas.
Although the Indian still hunted for meat, they thought he would
have normal food like us. 'They have to go to school, but their
schools are not as nice as ours and they obey laws which are self-
imposed'. We would predict such answers, where there is some ex-
perimenting with hypothetical reasoning, accompanied by frequent
falling back on to more comfortable concrete experience.

Thirteen-year-olds presented the most intriguing picture. As we
would expect they were all struggling with big ideas. They described
at length the injustices suffered by the Indians, and were aware of
today's Indian generation. The most disturbing finding was while
these children discussed the need for social change, they exhibited
the attitude that Indians are second-class citizens, destined to remain
in the poverty trap and unable, because 'they are not bright enough',
to avail themselves of higher education. One cannot help but feel
that the stereotype presented by the media, in spite of the sophisticated qualifications made by these formal thinkers, still persists in
residual form.

Indeed when teachers were asked where children learnt most about
Indians, they replied *inter alia*, 'I like to flatter myself that they learn
a lot about Indians from my classes, we spend quite a lot of time on
Indians. But if I'm honest I guess a lot comes from TV – like the idea
that all Indians wear feathers – boy it's really hard to convince them
otherwise' (teaches twelve-year-olds), and 'You can see a real
struggle when they are trying to weigh preconceived notions with
what they are taught. But that's not so bad, if they can get to the
point where they recognise their biases and compare them with so-
called facts' (teaches thirteen-year-olds). Perhaps most interesting of
all, though, was the revelation that none of the dozen teachers interviewed watched children's television, which must reduce the communality between teachers and taught.

SUMMARY

While only a pilot study, these answers reveal the very real way that television creates the stereotype of a national role which children think is applicable in real life. At the very least varied and non-stereotyped programmes concerned with realistic aspects of national and social roles might help the ten- and eleven-year-old child towards a better understanding of the real world, even perhaps an understanding which will stand up favourably when the child enters formal operations and compares propaganda messages relative to what he has seen during these formative years.

7

The thorny problem of television and violence

Regrettably no book on television can omit a chapter on violence, which I fear tends to distract us from the real problem at hand, which is to comprehend those needs which television meets in modern industrial societies. Volume after volume has been written regarding the effects of televised aggression on child viewers, mostly confirming the prevailing *zeitgeist* that televised aggression can only adversely affect them (Bandura and Walters, 1963; Berkowitz, 1962; Goranson, 1969; US Surgeon-General's Report, 1971; Comstock *et al.*, 1972: 4 vols; and Bandura, 1972). We shall argue that most research studies have committed the cardinal error of reducing questions of a higher order to questions of a lower order in an attempt to explain the former. Scientific studies of the effects of televised aggression have indeed reached a sphere 'so foreign to man' that they have left unsolved the questions most important to him.

We have argued that the child in the village learns by observing how significant others behave and subsequently re-enacts what he has seen in play. We have therefore assumed that children are natural mimics, and argue that children will also mimic what they see on television. Research studies at face value indicate that children who have seen actors portraying aggression can subsequently imitate these behaviours. Research also suggests that students who have seen filmed aggression are more likely in the short term to behave aggressively. However, the studies so far conducted are so artificial in terms of their construction and design as to limit the extent to which one can be sure that these effects actually occur in everyday life, rather than within the confines of the psychological laboratory. The limited evidence from naturalistic studies, including my own, suggest that the effects of televised aggression are less marked and can even be beneficial. Few studies have compared the relative effects of different types of filmed aggression such as newsreels and westerns. If, as we have argued, televised portrayals help the child to define real-life situations we may expect, and indeed find, that newsreel violence filmed in locations similar to those in which the child lives does help to define the everyday world of the child as likely to be aggressive, since television is the child's main source of information about the wider society.

If we choose to ask what the child does with televised aggression, rather than what televised aggression does to him, we are forced to a somewhat different conclusion from the prevailing academic *zeitgeist*. Westerns and other types of stylistic violence can be seen as virtually mythical portrayals in which man comes to terms with his innate aggressiveness. Moreover, it is during periods of war and conflict that heroism, sacrifice and comradeship come to the fore and we shall suggest that, far from stimulating children to be aggressive, watching these forms of aggression not only teaches co-operation but helps the more aggressive child to control his aggressive impulses. In other words, the child who watches the western acts out in fantasy his aggressive impulses and is purged of his aggressive tendencies while viewing.

My own view of the effects of televised violence is that nine times out of ten it has no effects on the viewer. In the remaining 10 per cent of cases the effects depend first on the type of televised violence and secondly on how aggressive the viewer feels. When the child viewer feels aggressive and he watches stylistically televised aggression he acts out his aggressive impulses by participating in the 'drama' of the western. Such portrayals help such viewers to sublimate their aggressive feelings – watch the audience's faces at sports to see this process in action. Less frequently, but more worryingly, when the viewer is not overtly aggressive and sees televised aggression occurring in locations similar to those in which he lives, or aggression without conclusion or aggression which overwhelms his capacity to cope with it – a particularly horrific death – these aggressive acts tend to hover in his mind until later he finds a chance to express these pent-up feelings in real-life.

THE NATURE OF THE EVIDENCE

Both clinical and experimental psychologists agree – (in itself a rare occurrence) that television is a school for violence. Wertham (1968) bases this assertion on the clinical study in depth of 200 boys while Larsen (1969) reports 'an extensive program of laboratory research mounts a strong indictment of media performance not only with respect to the amount of violence portrayed but, more particularly, with the manner in which violence is portrayed'. However 'proof', says Raymond Chandler's private detective, Marlow, 'is always a relative thing. It's an overwhelming balance of probabilities.' While the majority of social scientists agree that children who watch televised aggression are subsequently more aggressive, I personally do not consider that the balance of probabilities points in this direction, since research findings conducted in a sphere quite foreign to man must inevitably prove misleading.

THE IMITATION HYPOTHESIS

In the village we have argued that the child learns by watching and doing. If television has some of the functions previously ascribed to the extended kin we may expect young children to be able to imitate what they see on television, because it is by imitation in play that they gain experience of the roles they are likely to enact in the future – roles, we have argued, made visible by the extended kin in the past and by television today. We need, therefore, to establish that children can imitate what they see on television, but more importantly to ascertain under which conditions children will display what they have learnt in imitative play. We have already noted in Chapter 5 that children imitate such diverse television characters in play as weatherman, spectator at a television show, and newsreader, none of which are particularly aggressive roles. We shall argue that Bandura has established that children can imitate what they have seen once on television but by dint of his experimental designs he has overestimated the likelihood that children will only imitate the aggressive behaviour of television heroes.

In a typical experiment Bandura, Ross and Ross (1963a) studied the amount of imitation shown by 96 nursery school children. These three- to six-year-olds from the university crèche were randomly assigned to one of four experimental conditions. Children in a control group saw no aggressive adults, while children in a second group viewed a real-life adult attacking a bozo doll with a mallet. Children in a third group watched a three and a half minute colour film of the adult attacking the bozo doll, and children in a fourth group also watched a colour film in which the adult, this time dressed as a cat against a background of brightly coloured trees and butterflies, also carried out a relentless attack on the bozo doll.

Children watched these attacks one at a time and alone, and in each case the adult hit the bozo, which is a five-foot-high inflatable self-righting doll, on the head with a mallet. Bandura wished to establish that children can learn 'novel' behaviour if it is observed either on film or in real life on one occasion. He argues that children would not spontaneously attack the bozo doll by hitting it on the head with a mallet. Some parents might not be so easily convinced. Immediately after the children had seen an aggressive adult, each child was shown a variety of highly attractive toys in a second room, and then purposely frustrated by being taken away once the child had begun to play with these toys. The experimenter took the child to a third room containing, needless to say, a bozo doll and a mallet as well as dart guns and balls. Children, therefore, were supposedly at liberty to either imitate what they had seen or to play normally with the other toys in the room. After a brief settling down period the adult left the room and the child was left alone with the toys for twenty minutes while his play was observed and scored by judges through a one-way mirror. However, since many of the children tended to leave the room after being left alone for a short period, the experimenter returned midway through the session and told the child she would soon return with some more toys.

In these conditions, Bandura finds that children readily imitated the bozo-doll attacks of the adult whether or not this behaviour was filmed. In the real-life and unadorned film conditions 88 per cent of the children directly copied the posture, the words and the actions of the bozo attacker, while 79 per cent of the children who saw the cartoon also copied the attack. While Bandura does not report the amount or even the percentage of time spent in imitative play, his results show that children who observed the adult imitated (either wholly or partially) that behaviour, and were significantly more aggressive than children who did not see the adult. Children in all conditions, including the control, played equally with the toy guns; this is an example of aggressive behaviour which was not learnt from the adult in Bandura's experiment. He concludes that film models are as effective in teaching aggressive behaviour as such real-life models as parents or teachers. Were this the whole story, we should live in a society where our children constantly imitate the aggressive behaviour of television characters in their play. But if you look out of your window you will find that only a small proportion of children's play is spent imitating aggressive film characters. Children, it would seem, are not indiscriminate mimics, more especially since Bandura finds boys are more likely to imitate televised aggression than girls.

Factors likely to curtail the amount of imitative aggression displayed by children

In a second experiment Bandura *et al.* (1963c) asked whether children would more readily imitate the aggressive behaviour of a successful or an unsuccessful character. Children viewed a five-minute film projected on a television console in which two adults fight in a highly distinctive and unusual way in order to play with some attractive toys. One at a time and alone, nursery school children watched either (1) Rocky being allowed to play with the toys because he beat Johny, or (2) Rocky being thrashed by Johny so that the film closes with Rocky sitting unhappily in the corner, or (3) no film at all. When each child is observed in a second room immediately after viewing, children who saw Rocky beat Johny behaved more aggressively (75·2 aggressive acts) than children who saw Rocky punished (53·5) or children who saw no film at all (61·8). It should, however, be noted that most of the aggression observed was not sufficiently like that of Rocky or Johny to be called imitative. Nevertheless Bandura concludes that children will imitate the aggressive behaviours which they see rewarded on television.

Bandura maintains that in most television programmes the villain often amasses considerable wealth by dint of his aggression and often only obtains his just deserts either after the children have gone to bed or so late in the programme that children do not associate punishment with aggressive behaviour. In a third experiment, therefore, children watched either (1) an adult attack the bozo doll after which a second adult gives him sweets and praises him, or (2) an adult attack the bozo doll who is then punished by being hit with rolled newspaper, or (3) an adult just attacking the bozo doll. When observed in another room containing a bozo doll and a mallet immediately after seeing one of the five-minute films, children were found to imitate the adult's behaviour towards the bozo doll more often if that adult had been given sweets on the film than if he was either not rewarded or punished or if he was hit with the rolled newspaper. Once again boys imitated the 'aggressive' acts more often than girls. Bandura therefore claims that children will imitate the aggressive acts which they see 'pay off' on the television screen.

However, more interesting in this latter experiment was the fact that when children were offered sweets if they could 'show me what Rocky did in the TV programme', both boys and girls demonstrated that regardless of the film seen they would imitate Rocky's aggressive behaviour. In other words, Bandura has established that children can learn 'how to behave' even if they have only seen an adult once on the television screen. Children, it appears, are ready mimics, as we would predict from the theory outlined in Chapter 1. There seems little doubt that children can learn 'how to behave' from simply seeing their elders in action and later imitating them.

Retention of imitative aggression learnt from the media

Given that it is sometimes so difficult to teach children in school and yet they seem to learn so easily from television, do children remember the behaviours they have seen once on television over longer periods than just immediately after viewing. Hicks (1965) and (1968) repeated the Bandura-type experiments and also asked children to return to his laboratory after two and then eight months had elapsed. He found children re-enacted 60 per cent of aggressive responses after two months and 40 per cent after eight months. While these results again suggest the potency of visual learning, Hicks asked children to practise what they had seen immediately after seeing the film for the first time, so we do not know whether they recall the film or their practice.

The influence of the parent while viewing televised aggression

The reader can no doubt sense the line of counterattack to Bandura's generalisations from these experiments. In a word, the experimental setting is artificial. Children rarely view alone; what happens if an adult views Rocky's aggression with the child? Hicks (1968) briefed an adult to watch the Rocky film with the four-year-old children. Children who heard the adult speak approvingly of Rocky's aggression more often imitated his behaviour after viewing than children who heard the adult disapprove of Rocky's behaviour. However, the comments of the adult were only found to be effective if that adult was also present when the child played in the room with the bozo doll.

Summary of Bandura's research on the imitation of filmed aggression

If, for the moment, we accept Bandura's results at face value, which he does in an article in *Look* where he argues that a knife fight in San Francisco was a direct imitation of a television programme seen the night before, and has later argued that skyjackings increase after coverage on television, we may tentatively conclude that:

1. Exposure to an aggressive film model tends to reduce the child's inhibition against acting in a violent aggressive manner after he has seen the film.

2. Exposure to an aggressive film model shapes the form of the child's aggressive behaviour – namely, children who see the model hit the doll with the hammer also hit the doll with the hammer, even when the model is no longer present.

3. Children are more likely to imitate the behaviour of models who are rewarded rather than punished in the film. Bandura rightly points out that most television heroes do, in fact, achieve their goals by being aggressive.

4. Children can imitate the behaviour of any of the film models seen if asked to do so. Television, therefore, provides the child with a variety of ways of behaving which they may or may not copy according to their own wishes, or more cynically the wishes of the experimenter.

Should Bandura's results be relevant for real-life there is, perhaps, cause for concern.

E

Postscript

Intriguingly Bandura has more recently been interested in a positive role for television. If, as we have argued, television provides surrogate experience with recognised characters who are seen as an extended kin, television should also be able to provide surrogate experience, without danger, of fear-inducing objects (Bandura 1972). Bandura and Menlove (1968) showed children who were unusually frightened of real-life dogs either (1) a series of films of a boy playing with a dog, or (2) a series of films showing dogs of various sizes and fearfulness, or (3) a series of films in which no dogs were seen. When they had seen the films children were introduced to real-life dogs and it was found children who had seen the dogs on film were no longer frightened, while those children who had not seen dogs on film were still fearful of real-life dogs. While some interpret these results to suggest that children over time become immune to the horrors of real-life violence because they have seen violence so often on television, these results strongly suggest that contact with people, places and things on television are in many ways as effective as real-life contact. This latter argument has been, of course, one of the main themes of this book.

THE WORK OF BERKOWITZ: TELEVISED AGGRESSION PROMPTS STUDENTS TO BE AGGRESSIVE

During the past decade the most vigorous attack on televised aggression has come from Berkowitz who has consistently argued that viewers become more aggressive after they have seen violence on television. He maintains that the sight of aggression on television 'primes' aggressive drive in the viewer (or shifts latent aggressive drive from low to high gear) so that viewers will be more aggressive after the film if they can. Viewers, according to Berkowitz (1962), are most likely to give vent to the aggressive drive elicited by aggressive films if they find themselves in situations similar to those seen in the films. Some viewers, however, especially those who believe aggression is morally wrong, will inhibit and not give expression to the aggressive drive primed by the televised violence. Similarly a person can inhibit aroused aggressive drive if the environment will not permit him to be aggressive. For example, a child may see aggressive films in a home where aggression is not permitted. Berkowitz maintains that the results from a number of experiments, including the balloon-popping Mussen and Rutherford (Chapter 2), support his theoretical position.

The typical experiment is described by Berkowitz (1964) in *Scientific American*. A 'naïve' male college student is introduced to another male college student (who in reality is Berkowitz's accomplice) and they are both told that they are to take part in an experiment designed to study physiological reactions during various tasks. While they both complete such tasks as simple intelligence tests and their blood pressure is measured, the accomplice sets out to frustrate the student by insulting him – 'You're certainly taking a long time with that'. When the task is finished and the student suitably insulted, the two men are told that they are to watch a film. Quite often at this juncture the men are told different stories about what has happened to the hero in the early part of the film. The two men then watch seven minutes from the film *Champion* in which Kirk Douglas, a boxer, receives a severe beating, in the process of which he appears to lose his title.

In order to measure the effects that the film has had on the student, he is separated from the accomplice and told that the accomplice has designed a floor plan for a dwelling and the student is to judge this plan. The student has before him at this time an electric shock device which he is told is wired to the accomplice. If he thinks the plan is highly creative he is told to give one shock (a somewhat questionable procedure) and the worse he thinks the plan is, the greater and longer the shocks he is to administer. Naturally all the students are given the same floor plan and the electric shock device is not wired to the accomplice but to a recording machine which logs the number and duration of the shocks administered.

In general, Berkowitz finds that students who have seen the *Champion* film administer more shocks of greater duration than students who have seen films about canal boats or no films at all.

Justified versus unjustified filmed aggression

Berkowitz concludes that people who watch violence on the television screen are, therefore, more likely to be aggressive in real-life. However, like Bandura, he argues that certain types of filmed aggression are more likely than others to induce aggressive behaviour. Berkowitz and Rawlings (1963) repeated the experiment described above but told half the students that Kirk Douglas was a scoundrel about to receive his just deserts, and the other half that Kirk Douglas was the hero. The former film clip they label 'justified' aggression and the latter unjustified. Students who saw 'justified' aggression gave more shocks to the accomplice than students who saw 'unjustified' aggression. Likewise, by varying what students were told, about Douglas, Hoyt (1967) attempted to discover which motives legitimised aggression. Students who were first frustrated by receiving electric shocks were again told either (1) that Douglas was to avenge himself for an unfair beating received in the past, or (2) that

Douglas was in a kill or be killed position, or (3) a combination of both. Students administered most shocks where they thought Douglas was motivated by revenge – much as the students wished to revenge themselves of the unfair number of electric shocks they had received before film viewing.

Targets for aroused aggression

Berkowitz is determined to get mileage out of his experimental design. This time around it is used to see whether 'a person who sees a brutal fight may not himself display any detectable aggression immediately afterwards . . . unless he encounters stimuli having some association with the fight' – the words of the master. Thus it is that the insulting student is variously labelled as a 'boxer' or a 'speech major', or in later experiments as Kirk or Bob (Berkowitz and Geen, 1966). They find more shocks are given to the accomplice if he is labelled a boxer rather than a speech major, and if he is 'casually but pointedly' told that the accomplice has the same name as the victim, rather than the victor, in the film. One or two deviations from this pattern of results are explained away in terms of 'stimulus generalisation based on the apparent "Irishness" of some of the names employed'. However Berkowitz *et al.* conclude that the aggressive drive elicited by the *Champion* is more likely to find expression if a target appears who is associated with the victim of the filmed aggression.

Summary of Berkowitz's experiments

Results from a formidable number of experiments by Berkowitz and his colleagues may be briefly summarised as follows:

1. Overall, exposure to media violence rouses aggressive drive in viewers. However, these aggressive feelings can be held in check.

2. Viewers who see filmed aggression which they consider justified, rather than unjustified, are subsequently more aggressive. Few inhibitions against aggressive behaviour seem to be roused by exposure to justified aggression on film.

3. Media violence rouses aggressive drive in angered rather than non-angered viewers – presumably angered viewers have fewer inhibitions against subsequent aggressive behaviour than non-angered viewers.

4. Viewers with access to a target for their aggression will not inhibit their aggressive behaviour if that target is associated with the victim and not with the agent of the aggression seen on film.

A CRITIQUE OF THE PREVAILING ZEITGEIST OF ACADEMIC
OPINION: HIGH ORDER QUESTIONS ARE ANSWERED BY LOW
ORDER EXPERIMENTS

While numerous variations have been made upon these two experimental paradigms which lend support to the Bandura/Berkowitz positions, many criticisms can be made of these experiments. The principal criticism concerns the generality of research findings – can one extrapolate from these findings to the reactions of children in natural viewing situations? The problem of the generality of research findings refers to the degree to which the results of an experiment can be directly applied to situations occurring in real life. For most purposes the question of generality centres on four main points:

1. The representativeness of the research setting, i.e., viewing films alone in a laboratory.

2. The representativeness of the samples of people studied – mainly middle-class nursery school children and psychology undergraduates.

3. The representativeness of the films seen – the bozo doll attack and *Champion* (Are these the sorts of film which give cause for concern?), and

4. The representativeness of the method used to assess aggressive behaviour, i.e., would we be concerned if film portrayals of aggression only prompted students to give dummy electric shocks to others, or if children only attacked inflatable dolls?

The representativeness of Bandura-like experiments

While Bandura considers that 'experiments are not designed to reproduce the stimulus events that occur in real-life situations and they would be superfluous if they were', we have seen that he is confident that children do imitate the aggression seen on television in real-life (*Look*, 1963). We must, therefore, ask whether children behave in his experiments as they would behave outside the psychological laboratory. If one examines Bandura-like experiments in detail, one must ask the very commonsense question, 'What else can one do to a self-righting bozo doll except hit it?' Similarly what do very small children think of the laboratory setting into which they are placed? First, they see a film of a man hitting a bozo doll and then they are placed in an identical room also containing a bozo doll. What have become known as 'demand characteristics' must play a part here insofar as the very young child is usually anxious to please the experimenter and does what he expects the experimenter wants him to do – one four-year-old girl was heard to say on her *first* visit to a Bandura-like laboratory, 'Look, Mummy there's the doll we have to hit'.

Meyerson (1966) chose to make a Bandura-type experiment less obvious insofar as children after film-viewing were placed either in a room very similar to the one seen in the film, or a dissimilar one. Children imitated the aggressive film actor less when placed in a room dissimilar to the one seen in the film. Similarly Kniveton and Stephenson (1970) find that children who are allowed to play in the room containing the bozo doll *before* they see the film imitate the bozo attack much less after viewing (5 per cent of play time) than children who are brought in the room for the first time after seeing the film (26 per cent); and that one week later these latter children only imitate during 10 per cent of play time. It should also be remembered that four-year-olds are often reluctant to leave their mothers, so much so that in Kniveton's study 40 per cent of mothers had to remain in the room during the course of the experiment, which possibly accounts for the small amount of imitation recorded. However, in my own studies, where children watch media violence in small groups I have rarely found more than 5 per cent imitation after viewing.

Moreover, Bandura needs to establish that children learn completely 'novel' behaviour from an adult on film. Patterson *et al.* (1967) rightly point out that children who have never seen Bandura's films will attack a bozo doll by hitting it on the head with a mallet if a mallet and doll are provided. Thus, we cannot be absolutely sure that they learn these aggressive acts from the film or whether the film merely reminds them of an already established behaviour pattern. Nor, more importantly, should we forget that the bozo attack is not representative of media violence at large. Finally, we should note that Bandura works exclusively with middle-class nursery school children from the university campus. This fact alone must severely curtail the possible generality of findings, especially if one bears in mind that middle-class children are generally more anxious to please the experimenter than are working-class children. Kniveton and Stephenson have found considerable differences between middle-class and working-class children in their responses to televised aggression.

Problems of suggestibility in Berkowitz-type experiments

Detailed examination of Berkowitz's experimental paradigm reveals that his students *thought* they were watching justified film aggression and *thought* they were giving shocks to an accomplice. It would seem reasonable to ask what else the students *thought* when they took part in the experiment. Participating students generally 'earned' credits towards their psychology degrees and one wonders what they *thought* they ought to do to please the experimenter in order to obtain these credits. Surely these students talked about the experiment amongst themselves and since they were Berkowitz's own students they must have known what he expected. One's impression is that once both Bandura and Berkowitz had established their experimental designs (such as insult – *Champion* – electric shocks) they experimented with every permutation of this design rather than replicating their experiments with different measures, different films, different subjects and with considerably more attention paid to the long-term effects of filmed violence.

Indeed Berkowitz tacitly assumes that the cinema and television are equivalent since he generally shows his students the *Champion* projected as in a cinema. As we have noted darkness is more likely to lead to identity loss and greater involvement in the film seen which would tend to make students more suggestible. Moreover, why has Berkowitz used *Champion* so exclusively? It seems a particularly inappropriate film since it features a well known actor who, students are supposed to believe, is alternatively a hero or a villain. While the events seen in *Champion* are fictional, the film is very similar to real-life boxing which necessarily complicates any firm interpretation of results obtained.

More recent research by Tannenbaum (1972) has called into question the mainstream of Berkowitz's findings. Working within the same experimental paradigm as Berkowitz, Tannenbaum finds that it is not aggression *per se* which activates electric shocking but action on the screen. Tannenbaum argues that fast-moving action on the screen activates shocking even when the subject matter is not ostensibly aggressive since it arouses the viewer physiologically. These latter findings very much call into question the validity of Berkowitz's electric shock measure which has been assumed to be related to aggressive behaviour. While Bandura does point out that there is *no* correlation between the amount of imitative aggression shown off in the laboratory and the child's aggressive behaviour in everyday life, nowhere can I find reported any figures relating the propensity to give electric shocks to the actual real-life aggressiveness of the televiewer, or for that matter even of any student.

POSSIBLE USES FOR TELEVISED AGGRESSION

While it is possible to indict the experimental evidence which in turn has indicted televised aggression at a methodological level, it is more important to remember that these investigators have not asked whether viewers can find uses for televised aggression. They have merely assumed that televised violence injects violence into the viewer. I asked a group of adolescent boys as part of a study to be reported in the concluding chapter, 'What television programmes show you people helping each other?' since I was interested in the relationships portrayed in television programmes. A quarter of boys listed war films, westerns and detective serials, while another quarter listed family serials. Clearly those programmes castigated for the violence they portray also show models of co-operative behaviour which presumably Bandura would maintain will be imitated.

Virtually the only theoretical position which takes account of the uses that viewers find for televised aggression is the cathartic school, who argue that boys act out their aggressive impulses while tele-viewing aggression. Results suggesting cathartic reactions are almost inevitably found in field studies where research is conducted with a variety of different types of filmed aggression in more natural conditions. Experiments in natural field settings, such as those by Noble, and Feshbach and Singer, in marked contrast to laboratory studies, find that more aggressive boys are less aggressive after televiewing aggression, while other boys rarely behave much differently after seeing aggression on the small screen.

It is fair to say that the Berkowitz experiment was originally designed to disprove results from an early experiment in which Feshbach (1961) argued for catharsis. He found that a group of frustrated students who saw an exciting prize fight film wrote fewer aggressive words in a word association test than either frustrated students who saw a neutral film about the spread of rumours, or than non-frustrated students who saw the prize fight. He argued that the sight of a prize fight on film helped to clear out the aggressive feelings of frustrated students. In other words aggressive films may have a cathartic effect for aggressive viewers; may in fact help to clean out or purge the viewer of his aggressive feelings. The argument between Berkowitz and Feshbach has continued ever since. Feshbach alone dissents from the prevailing climate of academic opinion regarding the likely effects of filmed aggression. One convert to the prevailing climate of opinion, and who as we shall see has since become one of its outspoken members, is Seigel (1956) who was originally convinced that catharsis was a viable response to televised aggression. She showed 24 boys and girls aged between three and five years both ten-minutes of *Woody Woodpecker* in which 'raw aggression and relentless hostility' dominated every scene and a more peaceful cartoon featuring the *Little Red Hen*. Children, who watched in pairs, were then observed at play through one-way mirrors in a nursery school room containing a variety of toys not seen in the films. In this field study conducted in comparatively natural conditions children were neither more anxious (i.e., tense, stiff and sucking their thumbs) nor more aggressive (i.e., had been hostile to another child or a toy) after they had seen *Woody Woodpecker* rather than the *Little Red Hen*. While it appeared that cartoon aggression has little effect on child viewers she finds, in marked contrast to Bandura, that children whom their teachers said were aggressive were more hostile after viewing regardless of which film was seen.

ANXIETY RESPONSES TO TELEVISED AGGRESSION

In spite of the fact that both Himmelweit *et al.* and Schramm *et al.* report that children have bad dreams and appear frightened by realistic, rather than stylistic aggression portrayed in a stereotyped way, and by the sight of knives and violence filmed at close range, anxiety responses to televised aggression have not interested experimental psychologists. Indeed, it is only recently that Hyman (1973) has suggested that violence on the television screen may induce compassion for the victim. In many ways, it would seem preferable that children become acquainted with the violence which seems such an integral part of our society via their television sets, rather than in the streets where they live. The problem has been how to assess whether or not the sight of violence on the screen makes young children anxious.

I was concerned to try and discover how children respond to the sorts of violence they see in the news immediately after seeing their children's programmes. Noble (1970a) showed 24 six-year-old middle- and working-class children both a puppet film (*Patrick and Putrick* described in Chapter 5) and war documentary film which did not show the victim's pain. Groups of four children watched these films in different orders and their play was observed both before and immediately after viewing. We were primarily interested in whether or not realistic war newsreel would make children anxious. Freud (1933) has argued that when children become anxious they regress in their play and Barker, Dembo and Lewin (1941) demonstrated that six-year-old children, when made anxious by frustration, played like four-and-a-half-year-olds. They found that the degree of imagination shown in play decreased significantly after frustration and Wright (1943) similarly found that frustrated children talked much less often to each other after frustration.

We therefore assessed, for each minute of play after film-viewing, the degree of imagination (that is, creativeness), elaborateness and complexity shown in play by each child. We used the method employed by Barker *et al.* which rated examination of a toy least imaginative, followed in turn by conventional use of a toy, use of a toy in conjunction with another, and most imaginative play was said to have taken place where the toy was incorporated within a drama enacted by the children (respectively scored 1, 2, 3 and 4).

The scale seems valid since more intelligent children played more imaginatively than less intelligent children.

Children played significantly more imaginatively after they had seen the puppet film or when they had seen no film rather than after they had seen the war documentary. These results suggest that realistic violence, unlike *Woody Woodpecker*, makes children anxious which in turn causes them to play less imaginatively. But we found anxiety was not typical of all children. Six-year-old middle-class children played with a mental age of four and a half years when they had seen the war film, while six-year-old working-class children played with a mental age of six years and three months after the war film. Although other investigators claim that televised aggression affects all children in the same way, it appears that only middle-class children are disturbed by the sight of realistically filmed aggression – possibly because they have been told that all aggression is immoral. Working-class children, on the other hand, seem to play *more* imaginatively after seeing filmed aggression.

Moreover, we found that children who had seen the war film talked less amongst themselves (during 4 of the 20 minutes) than after they had seen the puppet film (during 6 of the 20 minutes) and talked most of all when they had seen no film (8 of the 20 minutes). Certainly the most striking feature of children's play after the war film was the silence. But apart from anxiety responses, it seems that children have to clear out the memory of events seen in a film, whether aggressive or not, before they can once again talk to one another. This latter finding very strongly suggests that we are so involved when watching films that we temporarily forget where we are, as indeed was argued in Chapter 3.

We have already suggested that the influence of televised aggression may be considerably more subtle than either Bandura or Berkowitz would allow. In Chapter 3, we argued that viewers relate what they have seen on television to what they see in life: 'When one enters a new situation one attempts to relate it to old ones by familiar signs' (Foote, 1951). Thus, rather than imitating the actors, we thought children would play with toys which were similar to the objects seen in the films. For this purpose children were given a wide range of toys to play with after film-viewing, some of which were related to the puppet film (dough, pastry and hammers); some of which related to the war film (actionmen dolls, toy guns and toy aeroplanes) and some of which were related to neither film (balloons, paper and crayons). After they had seen the puppet film, children played with puppet-related toys during 40 per cent of the time and war-related toys during 13 per cent of the time. After they had seen the war film, children played with war-related toys during 21 per cent of time and with puppet-related toys during 40 per cent of time.

Thus, while the puppet film did not inspire children to play with puppet-related toys, the war film did seem to activate the child's interest in war toys. Even so it should be noted that even after the war film children played with non-war-related toys four times as frequently as with war-related toys. Thus, regardless of the films children found puppets more interesting to play with than war toys. This finding may well prove the most representative as regards the effects of televised aggression. Instead of imitating aggressive actors, which occurred in this field setting during less than 5 per cent of play time, it appears rather that war films give children ideas both what to play with and indeed how to play with these toys in a stereotyped way. That the puppet film did not induce play with puppet-related toys need not surprise us, since this film was comparatively unusual to the viewing children and one suspects that repeated exposure, such as in advertisements, is necessary to firmly establish ideas about what to play with in children's heads.

Summary of the possible effects of filmed aggression in natural conditions

1. Aggressive films can cause the viewing child anxiety (both in terms of less creative play and a decreased amount of social interaction) rather than prompt aggressive drive (no child was hostile to another child after film-viewing) or prompt imitative aggression (no child imitated the soldiers seen in the war films).

2. Only certain types of aggressive films – most likely newsreel material – cause anxiety to the child viewer.

⟋ 3. Only certain types of children (middle- not working-class) are likely to become anxious when aggression is viewed. If anything, aggressive films induce more imaginative play amongst working-class children.

4. Children may reflect, by what I call 'contiguous relearning', the stimuli seen in the film in subsequent play – which is likely to be stereotyped.

5. Middle-class children were more responsive to the films seen than working-class children – perhaps middle-class children are more anxious to please the experimenter.

CATHARSIS: A DEFINITIVE STUDY

In a mammoth field study conducted in natural settings Feshbach and Singer (1971) evaluated the effects of prolonged viewing of televised aggression amongst 625 adolescent boys living in three private residential schools for middle-class boys and in four 'boys' homes' providing supervision, guidance and treatment for boys lacking proper home care. In each school boys were randomly assigned to watch a minimum of six hours a week for six consecutive weeks of either televised aggression depicting fighting, shooting or other forms of physical violence or non-aggressive programmes such as comedy, animal adventures and quizzes drawn from regular television fare offered during the evening or weekend hours. Boys were allowed to watch more than the assigned 36 hours of television as long as all programmes were from the assigned diet.

Various personality and attitude measures were given both before and after the six-week period of the experiment. Most important, however, was the behaviour rating scale which was completed daily for each boy throughout the six-week period. The house parent, supervisor, proctor or teacher most familiar with the daily activities of each boy was asked to assess him on each of 26 behaviours, 19 of which were related to aggressive acts. As is usual in field studies, the authors encountered many headaches; not all questionnaires were legible, boys got sick, some withdrew from the experiment and in three institutions they faced a rebellion because *Batman* was not in the non-aggressive diet. The experimenters were forced to allow these boys to watch *Batman*; but at least these authors catalogue their errors.

They found that the majority of differences between boys in the aggressive and the non-aggressive televiewing groups were insignificant. But they found that boys who watched *non*-aggressive programmes were more aggressive in their social relations with other boys than were boys who televiewed aggression. As we would predict from results obtained by Noble (1970a), this finding was not true of all seven institutions. It appeared only in the four homes for mainly working-class boys in need of proper care, namely boys who are most at risk (insofar as few of them would go on to college, half of whom were from minority ethnic groups and most of whom were more aggressive than the average adolescent). These boys were more aggressive to their peers, but not to their teachers, *only* when they viewed the non-aggressive diet. Deprived of their ration of televised aggression these boys did more pushing and shoving, had more fights, shouted angrily at each other and were more destructive of property than boys who watched the aggressive television programmes. These are results which strongly suggest that boys most at risk use televised aggression in order to control their own aggressive impulses; that watching televised aggression purges them of their aggressive feelings. While Feshbach recognises that it is impossible to control variables as effectively in the field as in the laboratory, nonetheless these findings clearly contradict the weight of evidence from the laboratory setting.*

* Wells' (1971) replication of Feshbach need not concern us since he only samples tuition-paying, middle-class boys.

Reactions to Feshbach's findings

Siegel (*Woody Woodpecker*), a member of both the US Surgeon General's Committee on Television and Social Behaviour and a consultant for the American National Commission on the Causes and Prevention of Violence (ANCCPV), reveals the current bias when reviewing Feshbach and Singer's findings. She (1973) writes, 'Most of us find these results less compelling than their authors do. For one thing they simply fly in the face of the dominant trend in the various other relevant experiments', and she discounts catharsis because of the possibility of 'systematic error' haphazardly introduced into their ambitious field research. She reveals that she and her fellow committee members regard televised aggression as simply 'unending dreary hours of commercial brutality'. Moreover, Feshbach has also to contend with the ANCCPV verdict on his research 'Catharsis of aggression amongst institutionalised boys, fact or artifact?'. Clearly the likely effects of televised aggression has left the arena of social science, and has regrettably entered politics. I leave the reader to make his own judgement of the 'various other relevant experiments', by which is meant Bandura and Berkowitz.

A rejoinder to Siegel

It is clear in which way Siegel tips the scales in the balance of probabilities. It is hoped that results obtained by Noble with working-class children, who played more imaginatively after a war rather than a puppet film, lend some weight to Feshbach's side of the scales. Moreover, both Ancona (1963) and Croce (1963) provide evidence in favour of catharsis. Ancona gave McClelland's 'Need for Achievement Test' both before and after frustrated students had seen either *Guns of Navarone* or a neutral film. Frustrated students' need for achievement was less after the *Guns of Navarone* than before viewing. Similarly Croce finds that frustrated students showed less 'need for power' after, rather than before, seeing *Ivan the Terrible*.

Moreover, there appears to be considerable confusion as to what is filmed aggression. For some it is an adult hitting a bozo doll, for others a prize fight, and for Feshbach and Singer it is westerns and war shows. Few investigators, if any, seem to be concerned that different types of filmed aggression will have different effects on different types of children.

A comparison between the effects of different types of filmed aggression

I do not claim to be a connoisseur of the cinema but I would hate to see the western disappear from our screens in the light of the evidence so far presented, since the western to me represents a stylised portrayal of violence ideally suited to children. As we have noted it was not aggression portrayed in a ritualistic and stereotyped way which caused children to have bad dreams but rather realistically filmed aggression and aggression involving the use of daggers and sharp instruments, rather than guns. I was concerned, therefore, to compare different forms of filmed aggression in an experimental and scientific way. It seemed reasonable to suppose that stylistic violence, which I defined as ritualistic, stereotyped and obviously set in historical times, would disturb children less than realistic violence filmed in modern times. But I also wanted to explain why knives should disturb children more than guns. Aggression involving knives is usually filmed so that both the aggressor and the victim are seen. The viewer does not always see the victim of aggression involving guns. The ethologist Lorenz (1963) argues that weapons such as guns distance the victim from the aggressor and consequently 'screen the killer against the stimulus situation which would otherwise activate his killing inhibitions'. In other words the sight of the victim's pain disturbs us so much that we can no longer hurt him. Indeed Hartmann (1969) found that filmed detail of the victim's pain and suffering resulted in less aggressiveness, again in terms of the number of electric shocks administered, than did the sight of hitting alone – at least with non-angered delinquents. Lorenz believes man is essential a slow-kill animal but weapons have disturbed the natural order of things and have turned him into a fast-kill animal no longer having to look at his victim. How else, he argues, can a pilot who cannot slap his own daughter drop bombs on hundreds of children?

Once again a field study approach was used, which meant that we went to schools, the children both viewed and played together afterwards in groups, and no special materials were provided since children played in their own school classroom. However, it did not prove easy to find a school which would let me show the victims of filmed violence nor would television companies lend me videotapes, and consequently I had to rely on hired films projected as in the cinema. Nor, I should add, did I conduct the study without some worries about what would be the likely responses of six-year-olds.

Forty-eight children from a working-class school, 40 per cent of whom were immigrants, were divided into four groups of twelve children. Each group saw a different type of filmed aggression and observers scored half an hour of each child's play at minute intervals for the degree of imagination shown as in the previous study, for the amount and type of social interaction, for destructive and hostile play, and for the amount of time film themes were reflected in play. One group of children watched realistically filmed aggression with sight of the victim – the brutal machine-gunning sequence from *Ashes and Diamonds*; another group watched realistically filmed aggression without sight of the victim – *War* documentary film; a third group watched stylistically filmed aggression with sight of the victim – the scene chosen was a witch being burnt from *Days of Wrath*; and a fourth group watched stylistically filmed aggression without sight of the victim – the *Battle of Agincourt* from *Henry V*.

Results, which are summarised in Table 7, clearly show that different types of filmed aggression have different effects on child viewers. As can be seen, children showed anxiety in play, since they played less imaginatively, after seeing any of the aggressive films except the *Battle of Agincourt* which in fact caused children to play more imaginatively than before viewing.

TABLE 7

DEGREE OF IMAGINATION SHOWN IN PLAY AFTER SEEING VARIOUS TYPES OF AGGRESSIVE FILMS (HIGH SCORE IS MORE IMAGINATIVE); NUMBER OF MINUTES OF DESTRUCTIVE PLAY, AND PERCENTAGE OF TIME SPENT IN SOCIAL INTERACTION (NOBLE, 1973)

	Realistic	Stylistic	Control before viewing
	Ashes and Diamonds	*Days of Wrath*	
Victim seen	50·5	53·3	
	1·83 minutes	0·33 minutes	
	36%	38%	65·6
			0·33 minutes
	War documentary	*Battle of Agincourt*	59%
Victim unseen	57·7	73·9	
	0·75 minutes	0·25 minutes	
	30%	68%	

Children were most disturbed, because they played least imaginatively, when they saw the victim in *Ashes and Diamonds* and *Days of Wrath*. Similarly, children seem more disturbed by realistic rather than stylistic aggression. Children were most disturbed after *Ashes and Diamonds* when they saw the victim in realistically filmed aggression. However, stylistic aggression without sight of the victim (*Battle of Agincourt*) seems to have inspired more imaginative play than before viewing. We may suggest that this type of filmed aggression has a cathartic effect.

Bearing Berkowitz's results in mind, we also examined the amount of time children spent in destructive play where they either hit each other or destroyed their play objects. As can be seen in Table 7, children most often destroyed play objects after they had seen realistically filmed aggression. It seems that Berkowitz is correct when he asserts that the nearer the filmed violence is to the child's own life the more likely it is children will be aggressive. However it should be noted that less than 3 per cent of play time was spent in destructive play. It would appear that much of the confusion regarding the likely effects of televised aggression can be clarified if we are clear as to the type of filmed aggression seen by the children. An obvious point which seems to have been overlooked in the past.

Similarly, as we can see in Table 7, children not only play more imaginatively after *Battle of Agincourt*, they also play together more often than after any other film or before watching the films, which tends to reinforce the idea of catharsis. Realistically filmed aggression caused children to play together less than did stylistically filmed aggression. Results suggest that realistically filmed aggression not only disturbs child viewers, it also tends to make them aggressive. However, children played equally together whether or not the victim was seen, since these differences were due to chance factors.

When we examined the minute by minute records describing exactly what children had done in the 30-minute play periods we were able to see how often they either imitated an aggressive actor, or imitated him in drawings; how often children reflected aggressive themes in their play or drawings and how often children reflected the scenes they had seen in the films in their play and drawings. We were therefore able to compare the amount of imitation (which Bandura argues results from seeing filmed aggression) with the amount of aggressive drive shown (which Berkowitz argues results from seeing filmed aggression) with the frequency with which children reflect film related themes in play (which I have argued results from seeing filmed aggression). Only 5 per cent of the playtime was spent in any way imitating aggressive film actors either in actions or drawings. Only 8 per cent of playtime was spent reflecting film related themes in play, while 19 per cent of playtime was spent reflecting aggressive themes. Just to place these results in context we also found that children spent as much time reflecting either Christmas themes in their play (8 per cent) or moon-landing themes in their play (7 per cent) as they did reflecting themes they had just seen in the aggressive films. *Days of Wrath* and *War* documentary films induced the greatest reflection of aggressive themes, 34 and 25 per cent of time respectively. I can only conclude that this is because both films showed fires, which tend to obsess young children. Aggressive themes were least reflected after *Agincourt*, only 2 per cent of time, and slightly more after *Ashes and Diamonds* (15 per cent). Once again results are consistent with the idea of catharsis after *Agincourt* since in free play before viewing aggressive themes were reflected during 6 per cent of playtime.

It is hoped that results obtained in this study, in spite of its many faults, indicate that both Bandura and Berkowitz have over-estimated the likelihood that children will imitate aggressive film heroes or be prompted to aggression. That more time is spent reflecting aggressive themes in fantasy (19 per cent) than in imitation (5 per cent) or reflecting situations seen in the film (8 per cent), I fear reflects on the very general nature of Berkowitz's theory, rather than on any theoretical strength. The more vague the postulate – and the idea that aggressive films prompt people to be aggressive is essentially vague – the more likely you are to prove that theory. Catharsis, we should add, is much more difficult to prove.

Finally in the light of the frequent criticism of the short-term nature of most of these studies, I attempted to record both the number and type of playground fights initiated by children who had seen the aggressive films over a one-week period. Compared to a control week in which these 48 children became involved in two fights serious enough to warrant teacher's attention and 14 less serious fights, children who had seen the aggressive films were involved in 33 fights, 14 of which were serious. Statistical analysis showed that these results were due to chance factors. However, statistical analysis did show that children who had seen the victim in filmed aggression had more serious fights in the playground over the week period than in the control period. The teachers also reported that fights had broken out between these children both in the lunch queue and in the classroom in the days after they had seen the aggression showing the victim. While it is clear that one cannot be sure that these fights resulted from watching the films, these children were unable immediately after viewing to draw and make objects similar to those seen in the films. Children who had seen aggression filmed without sight of the victim reflected film-related objects in play immediately after viewing during 14 per cent of the time, while children who had seen the victim reflected the film-related objects in their play during only 2 per cent of time. Further research is clearly necessary to see whether children remain aggressive if they are unable to 'work through' in play the horrific scenes they have just seen on film.

Summary of the comparative effects of different types of filmed aggression

1. Only certain types of aggressive film have adverse effects on child viewers. Neither aggressive drive nor imitation is prompted in all children by all aggressive films.

2. Stylistic aggression without sight of the victim may have cathartic effects in terms of more social interaction in more creative play after, rather than before, viewing.

3. Both realistic aggression and aggression filmed with sight of the victim seems to make children anxious.

4. Aggression filmed with sight of the victim may prime aggressive drive in the child viewer but aggressive feelings may not show themselves until the days after viewing. Reflecting film-related themes may in itself be cathartic.

AN EXPERIMENT DESIGNED TO QUALIFY THOSE TYPES OF AGGRESSIVE FILMS WHICH INDUCE IMITATION

In natural conditions imitation does not seem to occur whenever aggressive film heroes are seen. Noble and Martin (1974) set out to discover whether televised sports programmes led to imitation, and if so, what happened when the home team won and alternatively when the home team lost. Bearing in mind the differences found by Feshbach and Singer between aggressive and non-aggressive boys we thought it likely that there would be some interesting differences between these two types of boy when they had seen their team either win or loose. We also hoped to be able to say something about the likely ramifications of crowd violence at sports meetings.

Again a field study design was decided upon whereby groups of Irish boys televiewed a wrestling match between Ireland and England in their own schools, and where their free and unstructured play was recorded on videotape for later analysis. Teachers were asked for the names of boys who most frequently fought both in class and in the playground, boys who told stories featuring weapons of war, and boys who solved everyday classroom problems by fighting or shouting. Thirty-two boys who were mentioned in two or three of these categories were selected and called aggressive, while another 32 boys not mentioned in these categories were also selected but deemed non-aggressive. Eight groups consisting either of eight aggressive or eight non-aggressive boys aged between six and nine years were videotaped at play before seeing any television pro-gramme. Twenty-minutes of each boy's play were assessed for the degree of imagination shown (constructiveness), the amount of conflict and fighting between boys, and for behaviour in any way similar to the televised wrestling they were to see later. One group of aggressive boys and one group of non-aggressive boys then watched each of the following types of televised wrestling staged especially for this study, each featuring the same two wrestlers and the same number of falls.

In the first condition the Irish wrestler clearly beat the English wrestler, respectively identified by a shamrock and a union jack on their vests and by a dubbed commentary. In a second condition the Englishman defeated the Irishman and in a third condition the result was declared a draw and neither wrestler was dominant. Each of the bouts lasted eight-minutes and in addition one group of aggressive and one group of non-aggressive boys watched eight-minutes television about the island of Bali. Immediately after televiewing, boys' play was video-recorded for twenty-minutes and later scored for imagination, imitation of the wrestlers' holds and postures, and for aggression directed at other boys.

As can be seen in Table 8, none of the boys' play was anything like the wrestlers' before they had watched the television programme. Moreover, as can be seen in the table, none of the aggressive boys imitated the wrestlers when the home wrestler won, and none of the non-aggressive boys imitated the wrestlers when the home wrestler lost. Clearly for different types of boy different outcomes result in widely varying amounts of imitation. It would seem that when the home team wins aggressive boys are cleansed of aggressive feelings and do not imitate what they have seen (0 sec.), nor fight amongst themselves (5·6 secs.) whereas non-aggressive boys are prompted to imitate (213 secs.) and fight amongst themselves (137 secs.). The sight of the home team winning shows non-aggressive boys that their side's aggression is rewarded and thus legitimates aggression in a neo-realistic surrounding. But when the home team loses, aggressive boys imitate what they have seen (310 secs.) and fight amongst themselves (141 secs.) most probably because they share the frustration of defeat. Non-aggressive boys, on the other hand, do not imitate (0 sec.) nor fight dramatically amongst themselves (50 secs.) because they see that the home team's aggression is not rewarded. In the event of a draw, as can be seen in Table 8, non-aggressive boys are prompted to both imitate and fight amongst themselves considerably more than aggressive boys. In fact a draw results in the greatest amount of both imitation and aggression – but only for non-aggressive boys.

We may concur with Bandura, therefore, when he maintains that boys imitate the actions only of those they see succeed and in his remark that boys who imitated most in his experiments were not those who were most aggressive in school. We should, however, add a number of qualifications to his findings and point out that the amount of imitation shown depends on both the type of television programme seen and on the initial aggressiveness of the child viewer. If, in any way, we have created in microcosm the conditions of the spectators at a sports game, we should add that no matter what the outcome somebody in the crowd is later likely to behave aggressively.

We did not expect in this experiment any results indicating catharsis in the sense that viewers would be less aggressive and perhaps more imaginative after viewing because the aggression seen was neo-realistic, like Berkowitz's *Champion* film, but more importantly because the pain of the actors was shown in high focus. We noted in the previous experiment that the pain of the victim made children

Children in front of the small screen

TABLE 8

SUMMARY OF THE AMOUNT OF IMITATION, THE AMOUNT OF AGGRESSION
DIRECTED AT OTHER BOYS AND THE DEGREE OF IMAGINATION SHOWN BY
AGGRESSIVE AND NON-AGGRESSIVE BOYS BOTH BEFORE AND AFTER THEY
HAD SEEN VARIOUS OUTCOMES TO A WRESTLING MATCH

1. Amount of imitation (*in seconds*)

	Irish win		*Irish lose*		*Draw*		*Bali programme*	
	Before	After	Before	After	Before	After	Before	After
Aggressive boys	0	0	0	310	0	54	0	0
Non-aggressive boys	0	213	0	0	0	486	0	0

2. Amount of fighting (*in seconds*)

	Before	After	Before	After	Before	After	Before	After
Aggressive boys	4	6	61	141	54	105	1	10
	+2		+80		+51		+9	
Non-aggressive boys	10	137	0	50	0	227	5	7
	+127		+50		+227		+2	

3. Degree of imagination*

	Before	After	Before	After	Before	After	Before	After
Aggressive boys	41	36	28	4	25	14	41	31
	−5		−24		−11		−10	
Non-aggressive boys	28	11	45	29	42	1	48	36
	−17		−16		−41		−12	

anxious. However, as can be seen in Table 8 comparing play before
televiewing with play afterwards, the minimum increase in fighting
(just 2 seconds) and the minimum decrease in imaginativeness
(−5 points) occurred when aggressive boys had seen the home team
win. This increase and decrease respectively were less than occurred
before and after boys saw the television programme about Bali.
Compared to this control film, aggressive boys showed more anxiety
in play only after the draw and when they saw their home wrestler
lose. The picture is different for the non-aggressive boys. They
showed signs of greater anxiety in their play after seeing all the
wrestling matches – especially after the draw which was when the
greatest increase in fighting was observed, when the greatest amount
of imitation was seen and when maximum anxiety was shown in
play. In the previous experiment we noted that boys fought more
often in their playground when they had been unable to reflect in

* Scored each minute as No play with any toy (0), examination of toy (1),
conventional use of a toy (2), use of a toy in conjunction with another (3), toy
used as part of imaginative play (4).

play what they had seen in the films. Similarly here, where the television programmes ended indeterminately (the draw), boys not only fought amongst themselves most often but also most often imitated what they had seen, and played with minimal imagination. Two months later when we again video-recorded 20 minutes of play of these same boys in identical conditions, but without showing them the wrestling programmes, only 16 seconds of imitation and only $8\frac{1}{2}$ minutes of fighting were seen in over 2·7 hours of recorded play.

Summary of the effects of different outcomes of televised aggression on aggressive and non-aggressive boys

1. Amongst aggressive boys, the sight of the home team winning induces no imitation, practically no fighting and no anxiety is seen in their play.
2. When the home team loses, aggressive boys imitate what they have seen, fight most often and show the greatest amount of anxiety in their play.
3. Amongst non-aggressive boys, the sight of either the home team winning but more especially of a draw induces considerable imitation, a considerable amount of fighting and most anxiety is seen in their play.
4. When the home team loses, non-aggressive boys are not prompted to imitation, nor to fighting amongst themselves and only a small amount of anxiety is seen in their play.
5. The amount of imitation shown after seeing televised sport clearly depends on both outcome and type of child viewer. In general terms non-aggressive boys imitate film heroes more often, fight more often, and show more anxiety than do aggressive boys who have seen television sport.
6. The effects of the television programmes were confined to immediately after viewing. Two months later you would not have guessed that the boys had seen the wrestling programmes.

AN EXPERIMENT DESIGNED TO RECONCILE BERKOWITZ
AND FESHBACH

Throughout this chapter we have tried to show that much of the confusion relating to the effects of televised aggression is due to the way different investigators use different films and measure children's behaviour after viewing in different ways. There would seem to me to be a much smaller difference between Feshbach and Berkowitz than might appear at first sight. They could both be right if they are talking about the effects of different forms of filmed aggression on different types of viewer. We have tried to demonstrate that stylistic aggression in which the victim's pain is not seen may well be cathartic. We have also argued that realistically filmed aggression results in conflict. We must now allow for the differences between Berkowitz's students and Feshbach's boys in remand homes. It would seem likely that Berkowitz's students are largely from middle-class backgrounds unlikely to be in trouble with the law, while the boys in the remand homes sampled by Feshbach are from working-class backgrounds and in trouble with the law. We have already noted that children from different social classes vary in their response to televised aggression. These factors might be sufficient to explain why these investigators obtained directly contradictory results.

We therefore designed a study to try and reconcile the contradictory findings of Berkowitz and Feshbach, which would very simply involve showing both stylistic aggression (Feshbach) and more realistic aggression (Berkowitz) to both non-aggressive boys (Berkowitz) and to 'aggressive' boys (Feshbach) and observing the outcome. Once again a field study was designed so that results might be relevant to everyday real-life situations. With this intent in mind Noble and Mulcahy (1974) video-recorded television programmes portraying both realistic and stylistic aggression and showed these programmes to groups of children on a television set in their own school classroom and observed them at play after viewing. In order to sample both aggressive and non-aggressive boys we asked the teacher who had taught 48 six-and-a-half-year-old boys for two and a half years to say which boys were most often involved in serious fights in the playground, which boys conflicted most often in class, which boys usually described conflict and weapons when asked to tell or write stories and which boys solved everyday problems in class by either physical or verbal aggression. Twenty-four boys were eventually selected and put into two groups each consisting of six aggressive boys – who were mentioned in three or four of the categories listed above and six non-aggressive boys who were mentioned in none or one of the categories. Boys were selected from a school attended by both working- and middle-class children.

Each group of twelve boys initially played for twenty minutes in their classroom while observers, who did not know which boys were aggressive, rated their play for the degree of imagination (constructiveness) shown, the amount of conflict between boys, and for the amount of social interaction between boys. One group of boys then saw fifteen minutes of stylistically televised aggression recorded from the weekly western film, in which aggression was stereotyped and obviously set in an historical context. Boys' play was again observed for twenty minutes immediately after viewing. The other group of twelve boys watched fifteen minutes of more realistically televised aggression showing the victim's pain, recorded from a professional wrestling programme. This programme is not typically available in Ireland and boys frequently asked us whether or not people were hurt in the programme. It was thought that this programme was very similar to Berkowitz's *Champion* film since they both show close-ups of people fighting and seemingly hurting one another. Boys' play was observed for twenty minutes after viewing. Each group of boys then returned to watch the television programme they had not seen and their play after viewing was assessed a third time.

Results obtained in this experiment are summarised in Table 9, which shows the degree of imagination shown in play by both aggressive and non-aggressive boys both before and after seeing the two different types of televised aggression. As can be seen aggressive boys played more imaginatively after seeing the western than before seeing any programme, or after seeing the wrestling programme. Non-aggressive boys, on the other hand, played less imaginatively after seeing either the western or the wrestling than before seeing any programme. These results indicate that televised aggression makes non-aggressive boys anxious but stylistically televised aggression enables aggressive boys to play more imaginatively than before viewing, or in other words has a cathartic effect, in that stylistic aggression helps to free aggressive boys for more imaginative play. Indeed the only time aggressive boys play as imaginatively as non-aggressive boys play before viewing, is when they have seen stylistically televised aggression.

We have previously noted that children talk together less after, rather than before, film viewing. As can be seen in Table 9, all boys talked and played together less often after they had seen the aggressive television programmes. However, as we might expect, aggressive television programmes affect non-aggressive boys (a reduction of nearly 6 minutes) more dramatically than aggressive boys (a reduction of 3 minutes). Indeed the least decrease in social interaction, compared to before viewing, was after aggressive boys had seen the western, which is consistent with the cathartic response also noted in this experimental condition. Once again televised aggression seems to affect non-aggressive boys more adversely than aggressive boys.

While results so far reported lend support to Feshbach and Singer, results concerning the amount of conflict shown by boys lend support to Berkowitz's findings. Boys conflicted significantly more often after they had seen the wrestling (which is like the *Champion*) than after they had seen the western. The greatest increase in conflict (nearly four minutes) occurred when non-aggressive boys had seen the wrestling. Boys did not conflict significantly more often after they had seen the western than before viewing. Amongst aggressive

TABLE 9

SUMMARY OF THE DEGREE OF IMAGINATION SHOWN; THE AMOUNT OF
TALKING AND PLAYING TOGETHER; AND THE AMOUNT OF AGGRESSION
DIRECTED AT OTHER BOYS; BY AGGRESSIVE AND NON-AGGRESSIVE BOYS
BOTH BEFORE AND AFTER SEEING WRESTLING AND A WESTERN

1. Constructiveness scores (*high score is more imaginative*)

Boys' predisposition to aggressive behaviour in school	Experimental condition		
	Control before televiewing	Realistically televised aggression. Wrestling	Stylistically televised aggression. Western
Aggressive	36·6	36·0	43·5
Non-aggressive	46·3	37·2	37·7

2. Social interaction (*in minutes*)

Aggressive	13·6	10·0	11·3
Non-aggressive	16·9	10·9	9·7

3. Interpersonal conflict (*in minutes*)

Aggressive	1·8	3·4	2·8
Non-aggressive	1·6	5·3	1·9

boys conflict only increased marginally after they had seen the western which is again consistent with the cathartic increase in the degree of imagination shown in play.

Since this experiment was designed to simulate real-life conditions as far as possible we can generalise with some confidence to the probable effects of televised aggression in everyday life. However we must also note that because the experiment was not conducted within the confines of the laboratory, the distinctions we have drawn between both types of child viewer and types of aggressive film seen can be questioned. Putting possible criticisms aside for one moment it would seem that we have in this experiment replicated the findings of both Berkowitz, and Feshbach and Singer. Feshbach and Singer report a decrease in angry exchanges amongst more aggressive boys when they saw cowboy, police and war shows over a six-week period. We find that more aggressive boys play more imaginatively after seeing a western and do not conflict significantly more often nor interact less often than before viewing. It seems possible that boys playing more imaginatively may more frequently step towards one another – which is the literal meaning of ag-gression. A definition of aggression only in terms of harm intent would seem too constraining. The ethological concept that aggressive displays reduce destructive violence by means of ritualistic interactions may be more appropriate as regards the likely effects of stylistic aggression on aggressive boys.

Hopefully results presented here help to rebuke Siegel who discounts Feshbach and Singer's findings simply because they fly in the face of the dominant trend in the various other relevant experiments. It would seem that too limited a sample of both types of televised aggression and types of viewer have been taken in the 'various other relevant experiments'. If it is also remembered that the wrestling is similar to *Champion*, results obtained with non-aggressive boys replicate Berkowitz's findings with college students who are presumably not aggressive enough to invite police interest. The greatest increase in conflict occurred after non-aggressive boys had seen the wrestling, which suggests that 'legitimate' aggression in neofamiliar surroundings lowers the inhibitions of non-aggressive children and prompts them to show off aggressive actions. We should not, therefore, be surprised that realistically televised aggression, whether sport or news, prompts children to violence. If society continually generates newsworthy violence, our public actions not only disturb non-aggressive boys with well socialised constraints against aggressive acts, but also incites them to the violence which news and sport portray as the social norm.

Summary of the effects of different types of televised aggression on aggressive and non-aggressive boys

1. Berkowitz's theory that televised aggression prompts viewers to be aggressive would seem to hold true only for sport or realistically televised aggression, and then only for viewers who are initially non-aggressive.

2. Catharsis seems to occur only when aggressive boys have seen stylistically televised aggression, or sport where the home team wins, and then as Feshbach suggests, only amongst more aggressive boys.

3. Experimental studies and designs (such as those employed by Feshbach and Noble) which allow the necessary element of experimental control in more natural everyday media-viewing situations, suggest that the media have positive effects in such circumstances. For this author this conclusion holds good in spite of the results obtained by Berkowitz and Bandura.

CONCLUSIONS

When designing the experiments described in this chapter I have always asked myself the following question – 'Do we want to know with certainty what will happen in a highly specific set of circumstances, or do we want to know what is more or less likely to happen when media violence is seen "in natural, everyday viewing situations"?' I have no doubt that I want to know the answer to the latter, rather than the former question. Inevitably, studies of the latter variety will be less scientific than the former, since there are always more alternative explanations of results obtained in field rather than in laboratory studies. But as we have seen the whole tradition of conducting meaningful research in psychological laboratories has today been called into question chiefly because of the artificial demands which constrain 'subjects' in laboratories.

My aim in writing this chapter has not, however, been to suggest that we see even more violence on our television screens than is already available. Instead I would prefer to see a greater variety of aggressive portrayals, particularly those showing the realistic consequences of aggression. It is encouraging to note that both the BBC and ITA have changed their policy with regard to the portrayal of violence in children's programmes from one where the consequences of violence were never shown, to one which allows children, even if they become anxious, to see the realistic consequences of aggression. At least now children will not always think that aggression is clean and fun, but will be aware of the damage it causes. We have noted, and indeed argued, that the aggression which will have the greatest detrimental impact on children is the realistic aggression seen in newsreel material. Such aggression helps to define the real world as aggressive for the child viewer watching from afar. Censorship of newsreel aggression presents television authorities with their greatest challenge and most difficult political decisions. Nevertheless I cannot help but feel that televised aggression is really a scapegoat, rather than the cause of the violence which besets modern industrial societies, amply documented by Bronfenbrenner (1974). Unfortunately, research in the Bandura and Berkowitz tradition provides ammunition for those who wish to blame televised violence for the increase in aggressive crime which troubles us today. I maintain that violence is an inevitable result of the change in social organisation from what we have called village to industrial societies in Chapter 1.

Catharsis

Throughout this book we have asked the question 'What do viewers do with television?' Catharsis is the only explanation which poses the question of the effects of televised aggression in 'uses' terms. Hopefully we have by now demonstrated that catharsis is more than a figment of Feshbach's imagination, and that under certain fairly well defined conditions it does actually occur even though Siegel might not wish it. The fascinating question still remains as to why westerns should be cathartic for aggressive boys, in that they play more imaginatively after seeing stylistic aggression. It is perhaps easier to understand why aggressive boys do not fight nor imitate when they have seen the home team win. In this case their sympathy is clearly with the home team, and a win by them is a win for the watching boy, so much so that it seems to purge them of their aggressiveness while viewing.

Why should this be the case after a western? The clue, I believe, lies in the term cowboy which describes a boyish play-like activity. Regrettably children have to learn of the existence of violence both in our history and our society. They also have to experiment with aggression as they grow up. As I see it the most important function of play is to gain some experience of an activity, whether it be father, nurse or mother in fantasy as an indirect practice for possible real-life events which will occur later. As Bandura points out, and as we have seen, children are natural mimics of what they see and thus it can be argued that they gain experience of aggression by playing with it, and the form with which they most often experiment are the roles of cowboy or soldier. In both roles, moreover, they also enact comradeship under stress which Siegel tends to overlook in her description of televised aggression as 'unending dreary hours of commercial brutality'. Aggressive boys seem to join in such games most probably via identification, and cleanse themselves while viewing of any aggression bottled up inside them while participating in the western in imagination.

Nor should we forget that the western is recognised by many as an 'art' form, while Martin sees them as mythical portrayals of the Oedipal conflict in which the son fights the father in order to possess the attractive girl who symbolically represents the mother. This seems to be a far from adequate explanation of the symbols. If we take the view that myths are 'charters for social action' or, put another way, metaphoric expressions of prevailing values, we are perhaps helped to a more adequate explanation. There seem to be two recurrent themes in the western both of which depict symbolically prevailing values, namely 'good against evil' and 'man's fight with nature'. The latter I take to be a pictorial view of Darwin's concept of the survival of the fittest. Our children do ask, 'How did man become civilised like this?' and 'What was he like before?'. And whereas until the scientific age Genesis served to explain man's condition, we now tacitly accept Darwin's view of man emerging from the primal horde of apes. The western literally provides our young with a visual sense of white man's history, in which only the fittest survive. Survival of the fittest has become the charter of our age; it is the prevailing value children encounter both in school and when they leave it. Perhaps in some perverse way the western pre-pares our children to encounter this ethic. But the western also contains remnants of the older morality plays, the struggle between good and evil. In a typical western the sheriff is asked, 'Is there any law down there?', to which the answer is 'Not much'. Where else do children see men without law, and where else do they see the good prevail in the long run?* Regrettably, they do see men without law in the news in Northern Ireland, for example, and here there are too few goodies and no certainty that good will prevail. Which would you rather they watch and accept as the prevailing charter for social action?

* It might not be speculative to argue that our children stand in the same relationship to the 'wild west' and war films as before Christ, Greek children stood to the battle of Troy and Odysseus's wanderings. Both myths, perhaps better called legends since they each have a base in historical fact, define the hero and acceptable codes of conduct in trying situations. Suffice it to say the wild west is considerably less gory than the genocide practised at Troy even if the Gods did warn and later extract retribution (nemesis) for such offences against the natural order (hubris). Gerbner (1971) reasons that 'dramatic violence, free from the constraints of reality, calculates the risks of life and the pecking order of society for symbolic purposes'. In other words dramatic violence, whether on television or not, is communication not violence.

8

Televiewing and deviant behaviour

Throughout this book we have adopted the approach known as 'uses and gratifications' (Katz, 1959), and concentrated on what people do with the mass media, rather than what the mass media does to people. To imagine simply that television is but a hypodermic injector of violence is to obscure the way that television is used by its audience members. As we saw in the last chapter the dominant approach of the psychologist has been to argue that television is a school for violence in that it continually shows models of aggressive behaviour that the child will copy, or primes viewers to behave aggressively after viewing. We have suggested that this approach results from the albeit unconscious televiewing style of the middle-class American researcher swept along in the *zeitgeist* of public opinion. Working-class and aggressive children do not appear to use television for relaxation as do middle-class children, but rather as a short-term source of stimulation and excitement which, as we have tried experimentally to demonstrate, helps to drain off aggressive impulses and keep them from real-life expression.

In this chapter I shall extend this latter argument even further, and argue that delinquents, far from learning their criminality from the small screen, retreat to television because of a lack of adequate real-life social relationships. In the village, we argued, the child came to a realistic appraisal of self because the extended kin unit, representing society in microcosm, provided him with mirror perspectives of self which inevitably socialised the child to fit into the wider social context. Delinquents, I shall argue, first and foremost receive either contradictory mirror images of self from a restricted group of kin members, or alternatively so few mirror images of self are available from such a confined number of people that the delinquent never acquires a satisfactory self-image. In such a case delinquents turn to the mass media for alternative significant others with whom to interact, as in the village they would have turned to uncles and aunts for substitute family relationships.

Like the child in the concrete operations stage, early researchers
virtually assumed that children become violent simply because they
watch violence in the mass media. For example, Blumer and Hauser
(1933) claimed that 10 per cent of delinquent boys and 25 per cent
of delinquent girls had been shown how to commit crimes, or had
seen portrayed in the cinema 'romantic' criminals who obtained
wealth by illegal actions. A second Payne Fund study by Cressey
and Thrasher (1933) likewise reported that delinquent boys who
played truant also frequently attended the cinema. Similarly Hoult
(1949) reports that delinquents read twice as many 'harmful' comics
as carefully matched non-delinquent boys. However, a more recent
study by Berninghausen and Faunce (1964) failed to discover a
difference between delinquents and matched controls in the number
of 'sensational books' read.

In a further attempt to demonstrate that there is a relationship
between real-life violence and diets of media aggression, notwith-
standing the fact that even if such a relationship is observed it
proves little, Pfuhl (1961) surveyed nearly 800 fourteen- to seventeen-
year-old adolescents and correlated self-reported delinquent acts,
such as playing truant, with their media preferences. More 'delinquent' girls and boys went to the cinema more often, saw more
crime films and read more crime comics than less 'delinquent'
adolescents.

TELEVISION TEACHING CRIME TECHNIQUES

In the days of the cinema, as we have seen, films were said to have
taught crime techniques to their audiences. Since we have argued
that television teaches people how to behave socially, I cannot deny
that viewers learn how to commit crime from the dramatic professionals who display their skills on the small screen. While young
criminals often publicly report that, 'I learnt it from the telly', the
only field study which systematically tests this hypothesis did not
prove that television was an effective teacher. Several versions of a
television programme were prepared and transmitted in some of
which a man breaks into charity boxes to steal cash. Milgram (1973)
checks that viewers have seen a version of the programme and sends
them off to receive a free gift where they find themselves alone with
a charity box. While a satisfactory number of viewers break into
the box, such thefts are no more characteristic of those who have

'seen it on the telly' than of those who saw the programme without the crime.

CULMINATION OF A RESEARCH TRADITION: A CRITIQUE OF ERON

Just how far the hypodermic image of televised aggression may be pursued, we may judge from the much reported research of Eron (1963) and (1972). He set out to discover whether children who watched aggressive television programmes were more aggressive in real life than children who watched less aggressive programmes. He began by classifying television programmes for the amount of antisocial aggression portrayed. Surprisingly, *Lone Ranger* and *Perry Mason* were deemed non-aggressive and *Have Gun will Travel* and *77 Sunset Strip* were deemed violent. He then asked 700 mothers and 522 fathers to list the three television programmes which were the favourites of their eight-year-old children. Having ascertained the aggressive diet of the eight-year-olds, he attempted to relate this diet to everyday aggressive behaviour, both in the short and longer term. But prior to endorsing the relationship we can predict he will 'discover', it is worth examining in detail Eron's measure of everyday aggressive behaviour. Children were asked at school to name any boy in their class who 'does not obey the teacher?; starts a fight over nothing?; gets very mad at a bully?; will always fight back if someone hits them first; is rude to the teacher?; takes other boys things without asking?; gives dirty looks and sticks his tongue out at other boys?; swears when another boy annoys them?; makes up stories and lies to get other boys into trouble? and pushes back if someone pushes him first?' As can be seen the questions hardly measure what might be called delinquent behaviour – nor does Eron list these questions in the report of his study.

However, Eron finds that boys rated as 'aggressive' by their schoolmates more often prefer to view 'violent' television programmes than boys rated as less 'aggressive'. He concludes that there is a definite relationship between televiewing habits and real-life, aggressive behaviour, and writes 'buttressed by manipulative laboratory studies such as Bandura *et al.* (1963) we can speculate with some confidence that televiewing does affect real-life behaviour and that the modelling variable is a crucial one'. For this writer it is difficult to see how most of the acts of aggression in the classroom could have been copied from the television characters in the aggressive programmes. There is no mention whatsoever of the possible uses to which the boys' favourite television programmes might have been put. Yet while Eron (1972) claims that his results hold good some years later, we still know remarkably little about the tele-viewing style of delinquents.*

One of the first studies funded by the Television Research Committee was designed to explore the televiewing habits of delinquents in England to see what, if any, were television's effects relating to deviancy. Halloran, Brown and Chaney (1970) arranged for 281 males and 53 females aged between ten and twenty, who had been placed on probabtion by the juvenile courts in the Midlands, to be interviewed by their probation officers about their televiewing habits. Halloran *et al.* then interviewed a matched sample of working-class adolescents, although quite what they were looking for is not clear since they state on page 83 that 'no specific hypotheses were set up'.

Viewing times and programme preferences

Somewhat surprisingly both probationers and controls watched *some* television for about five hours a day. When, one might ask, do they find time to be delinquent if boys view for about 36 hours a week and girls 32 hours a week? Nor did probationers differ from controls in programme preferences, since they both chose the same television shows as their favourites. Moreover, no less than 81 per cent of male probationers, when asked by their probation officers, said they watched television in order to learn something, which was equivalent to the percentage of controls (89 per cent) who also replied yes. Nor did probationers (23 per cent) any more than controls (24 per cent) view television in order to relax.

If delinquents watched no more television than controls and if both groups liked the same programmes, were there any differences between samples? In the case of boys, delinquents (42 per cent) said they liked exciting programmes more often than controls (35 per cent). 'Exciting' in this instance means mystery, police, crime, westerns, thrillers, aggressive, war and murder programmes. Yet no differences were found between the two samples when their preferences for aggressive, murder and war films were examined – these were chosen by only 13 per cent of delinquents as their favourite compared with 10 per cent of controls. As far as informational programmes were concerned, delinquent boys (8 per cent) less often

* This follow-up study which so impressed the Surgeon-General's Committee is not only questionable in the first instance but claims to discover a relationship between mother-nominated preference for violent programmes at eight years and peer-evaluated aggressiveness ten years later. These latter ratings, however, were retrospective and thus somewhat suspect.

than controls (13 per cent) said they most liked 'educational and cultural programmes' defined as news, politics, talking, religious, hobbies and classical music.

IDENTIFICATION WITH MEDIA HEROES

In essence, therefore, the only differences to emerge between delinquents and matched controls is a slightly greater preference for exciting programmes and a lesser preference for informational programmes. More important, to my mind, are the similarities between probationers and their matched controls, particularly as regards their favourite ten programmes. We have suggested that the delinquent may use television to get back to the society from which he is alienated. While Halloran *et al.* report that probationers, according to their teachers and probation officers, got on with people of their own sex as well as controls, the overwhelming mass of evidence from the field of delinquency studies suggests that delinquents experience very poor relationships with their families, particularly with their fathers (Glueck and Glueck, 1943; Masters and Tong, 1968). Might delinquents show a preference, therefore, for those television programmes which allow for recognition and para-social interaction with more normal families? Indeed, probationers rated *Coronation Street* as their third most popular programme and *Crossroads* (a programme of like ilk) as their fifth most popular programme, whereas controls rated *Coronation Street* as their fifth favourite programme and *Crossroads* as second favourite. If we bear in mind that *Coronation Street* is the longer running and more established of these two, it is possible that probationers enjoy at least surrogate interaction with the characters they feel they know in this programme.

Moreover when asked, 'Is there any one on television that you would like to be, if you were not yourself and had the chance to be anyone else?', fewer probationers were inclined to identify with television characters (65 per cent) than controls (78 per cent), which suggests that probationers do not seek to lose their identities when televiewing, but may rather use television to interact with recognised characters. This could explain why probationers said they admired a hero for his skill and prowess (11 per cent) more often than controls (3 per cent) as a reason why they liked particular programmes. Recognisers, as we have seen, play opposite those characters they feel they know, and whose qualities they are able to describe.

Conversations about television programmes

We have argued that one motive for pseudo-social interaction with recognised television characters is a lack of adequate real-life social

F

contacts. Thus we may expect that delinquents might indeed talk less about television programmes they had seen than controls. Halloran *et al.* found in the first instance that fewer delinquents (66 per cent) than controls (80 per cent) watched television in order to talk about it later with their friends. In this respect they differ significantly from their working-class counterparts who clearly use viewed television programmes as a talking point to establish communality with their colleagues. This tendency was much less marked for middle-class respondents, only half of whom used television in this way. Moreover, when specifically asked how often they discussed television programmes with fathers, mothers, 'some other member of the family' and friends, probationers reported significantly less talking than controls. If one bears in mind that probationers did not talk less often to siblings nor girl friends than controls, a picture emerges not of cognitive poverty, as the authors suggest, but rather of inadequte personal relationships with parents and adults within probationers' families. It thus seems highly likely that television may be used by probationers as a means of establishing contact with adults with whom their real life contact is inadequate.

The cognitive poverty hypothesis

Halloran *et al.* conclude that delinquent boys may be cognitively impoverished as regards televiewing since, because they do not discuss television programmes with other people, they are unable critically to review the programmes they have seen. Thus the probationers' preference for television heroes because of their 'skill and prowess' may rub off into real life, as was found by Bailyn (1959) who reports that 'rebellious independent' boys liked programmes featuring aggressive heroes. Likewise Lovibond (1967) discovered that a preference for crime and violence programmes amongst eleven- and twelve-year-olds in Australia predicted a more fascist attitude – in that such children admired the use of force to dominate and exploit the weak. Cognitively impoverished probationers unable to distance themselves from those television programmes seen may also in Schramm *et al.* terms 'confuse the rules of the real world and transfer violence from television to real life'. Instead of relying on these rather vague formulations of a tentative hypothesis, I decided in the first instance to explore in depth the way delinquents saw televised aggression and secondly to investigate televiewing style with reference to family relationships.

Delinquents' discrimination between different forms of televised aggression

Generally speaking, social scientists are too inclined to use measuring techniques which put words into people's mouths, and then to imagine that people have actually used the psychologist's words to describe their environment. We have already noted this tendency in questions relating to identification. One technique which allows us to plot out the cognitive map whereby people classify televised aggression is the repertory grid – which attempts to discover those verbal labels a person uses and more importantly how a person's verbal labels interrelate. In order to elicit the verbal labels used by delinquent boys when describing those exciting programmes which Halloran *et al.* report they like more than non-delinquents, I interviewed 37 recently convicted delinquent boys aged between twelve and fifteen years who were in a classifying school, en route to an approved school. It was thought these boys might recently have viewed television in a family context as would 30 control boys who were matched for age, social class and intelligence and selected from a large secondary modern school in Leicester. It might be expected that twelve- to fifteen-year-olds, beyond the pale of probation, might be at risk as regards televiewing violence.

Each boy was individually interviewed and shown photographs from eight television programmes, namely, *The Saint*, *The Avengers*, *News* (Vietnam war pictures), *Dr Who*, *The Virginian*, *Big Bread Winner Hog*, *Z Cars* and *Mission Impossible*. Discussion with both control and delinquent boys revealed that these programmes were their favourites with the possible exceptions of *Dr Who* and the *News*, which were selected because they respectively show imaginative and real fighting. Boys were asked to identify the programmes from which the pictures came and asked whether they had seen fighting in that programme. Programmes with which boys were not familiar or in which they had not seen fighting were eliminated and similar programmes substituted. Each boy was given three photographs from three different programmes and asked in order to elicit the verbal categories used to give structure to the television environment, 'In what way is *fighting* in two of the programmes the same but different from the third?' Each boy's own verbal descriptions were then noted by this author on the squared paper which constitutes the repertory grid. As can be seen in Table 10, which is the grid completed for a disturbed twelve-year-old, similarities were noted in the left-hand side and differences on the right. Thus, for this boy some television characters are good fighters and some not so good; some wait for people and shoot – others do not wait before shooting. This procedure was repeated eight times until all the television programmes recognised had been compared with at least two other programmes. As can be seen in the table this boy mentioned five ways in which television fighting differed, since at times he could not answer and at other times repeated himself.

TABLE 10

THE REPERTORY GRID COMPLETED FOR A DISTURBED TWELVE-YEAR-OLD
DELINQUENT BOY AS REGARDS FIGHTING HE HAD SEEN ON TELEVISION
(NOBLE, 1971A)

	Similarity between two of three programmes	Dr. Who	Avengers	News	Virginian	Saint	Z Cars	Hog	Mission Impossible	Difference between one of three programmes
									Programmes	
	Good fighters		√		√	√	√	√	√	Not such good fighters
	Waits for people and shoots	?			√			√		Does not wait before shooting
I	With police	?		√	√	√	√		?	Not with police
	Uses a gun on people		√		√	√	?	√	√	Only uses a gun on prisoners
	Uses a gun		√	√	√	√	√	√	√	Does not use a gun
	Lifelike		√	A	√	√	√	√	√	Not lifelike
	Stops crime	?	√		√	√	√		√	Starts crime
II	Could happen			√	√	√				Could not happen
	Clean	√	√			√	√		√	Dirty
	Good reasons		√			√	√		√	Bad reasons
	Acted	√			√	B			√	For real

I Similarities/Differences elicited during sorting procedures.
II Similarities/Differences supplied by the investigator.

    Comments (A) Not lifelike – 'hit 'em when not done ow't,'
               'Kill them, put them against a wall and shoot them.'
          (B) For real – 'sticks up everybody nearly, jumps on them and
               kills them.'
               (Are they really dead?) Yes (when the programme is over
               do people get up again?) No: really dead.

√ Indicates the similarity (left-hand side of grid) is relevant for a particular
   programme.
? Indicates that neither similarity nor difference is relevant for a particular
   programme.
Blank Indicates the difference (right-hand side of grid) is relevant for a particular programme.

This done, each boy was asked for each programme in turn
whether the fighting had been done by good fighters or not such
good fighters, and whether or not people waited before they shot.
If the boys thought the fighters were good a tick was placed under
that programme in the first line of verbal categories, if not such a
good fighter applied the square was left blank, and if he was not
sure a question mark inserted. Thus for the boy's grid in Table 10,
there were good fighters wherever there are ticks – namely *The
Avengers, The Virginian, The Saint, Z Cars, Big Bread Winner Hog*

and *Mission Impossible*; and not such good fighters where there are blanks – namely *Dr Who* and the *News*. Boys were also asked questions during this stage to prevent boredom; some of the answers elicited are listed in the table.

I also provided some verbal labels, if they were not mentioned spontaneously, in order to find out whether or not delinquents transferred violence from television to the real world. I asked each boy whether the fighting he had seen in each programme was acted (as in a school play) or for real (had to go to hospital); was lifelike (people do fight like that in Leicester, for example) or not lifelike (nobody really fights like that), and whether or not such fighting could happen. As can be seen in Table 10, this boy thought people were really killed in *The Saint*, but the fighting in the *News* was not lifelike since 'Hit 'em when not done owt' and 'Kill them, put them against a wall and shoot 'em, that's not lifelike'. Moreover, since some writers consider that viewers are subsequently more aggressive when they have seen justified, rather than unjustified aggression, I asked boys whether they thought the fighting in each programme was for good or bad reasons, and whether such fighting stopped crime or started it. I argued that if delinquents imitate the fighting of aggressive television heroes, they would probably see greater justification for that fighting than controls. The boy, whose grid is reproduced in Table 10, thought that all fighting was to stop crime except in the *News* and *Hog*, and he was unsure why people fought in *Dr Who*.

Dimensions perceived by delinquents in televised aggression

Delinquents showed few signs of cognitive poverty when talking about their favourite programme in this way. Taken overall, the verbal labels used to describe the differences between the fighting seen in the eight selected television programmes fell into six categories, and delinquents as frequently as controls drew five of these six distinctions. These were that some fighting involved weapons (*The Saint*) and some did not (*Z Cars*); there was more fighting in *The Saint*, *The Avengers*, *The Virginian* and less in *Z Cars* and *Dr Who*; there was justification for the fighting seen in *The Avengers*, *Z Cars* and *Mission Impossible* but little justification for fighting in *News*, *Big Bread Winner Hog* and *Dr Who*; that some fighting was for real (*News*) while in other programmes it was acted (particularly *Dr Who*); and some fighting was in other times (*Dr Who* and *The Virginian*) whereas other fighting was in the present day (*The Saint*, *News* and *Big Bread Winner Hog*).

The only difference between delinquents and controls was that controls mentioned that some heroes fought alone, especially *The*

Saint, whereas other heroes fought with friends especially in *Z Cars* and in the *News*. If this latter discrimination indicates that delinquents do not perceive that individuals can co-operate even to be aggressive, there is perhaps no reason to be surprised since we have argued that many delinquents are socially isolated. While delinquents mentioned a significantly lower number of differences than controls (3·9 and 4·7 respectively), does this indicate cognitive poverty? Does it mean that delinquents perceive all types of televised aggression in a homogeneous and undifferentiated manner?

Delinquents' cognitive maps of televised aggression

Repertory grid procedures allow one to examine the inter-relationships amongst the types of similarities and differences between fighting in the selected television programmes. If cognitively impoverished, delinquents may be expected to provide fewer similarities and differences, as we have seen, but further they may be expected to provide a set of verbal labels to describe television programmes which are very strongly associated. Although in such a case different verbal labels are mentioned, each label is used in a similar way to every other label. This point may be made clear if an example is provided. If we examine the pattern of ticks and blanks for the verbal label 'good fighters – not such good fighters', does an identical pattern of ticks and blanks occur again for any other verbal label? It does, it occurs for the verbal label 'lifelike – not lifelike'. This boy thinks the fighting in *Dr Who* and *News* is not lifelike (blanks), but he also thinks *Dr Who* and the soldiers in the *News* are not good fighters (blanks). Thus for *this* boy good fighters are also those who are lifelike. Similarly, for *this* boy good fighters are those who use guns since fighting in all programmes except *Dr Who* (blank) involves guns and fighting in all the programmes except *Dr Who* and *News* (blanks) is good fighting. However, if we further pursue this cognitive map analysis, good fighters are not those who wait before shooting, since there is little agreement between the two horizontal patterns of ticks and blanks for these programmes (only 3/8 good fighters wait before shooting; compared with 8/8 good fighters who are also lifelike). By comparing each line of ticks and blanks with every other line we can find out whether boys perceive televised aggression in an undifferentiated and homogeneous way (all horizontal lines of ticks and blanks fairly similar) or in a complex and differentiated way (each horizontal line of ticks and blanks different from every other). Thus we can find out whether cognitive maps are complex or simple.

It was found, when this analysis was completed, that delinquents, if anything, were more likely to provide verbal labels which were independent of each other (35 per cent of all labels related to all others) than were controls (37 per cent of all labels related to all others). Thus while delinquent boys may be less able than controls to describe why they like or dislike a programme, or say how fighting in some programmes is different from others, delinquents are no less able than controls to discriminate between the types of aggression they see on television. In other words, while controls use more words to describe televised violence, the words they use repeat themselves in meaning, while delinquents use fewer words but each word has a precise and specific meaning.

While at the classifying school, delinquents are assessed by psychologists so that they may receive the most suitable schooling. Amongst other assessments made, the psychologists assess each boy for aggressiveness in terms of likely behaviour aimed at the hurt or injury of people. Amongst the 37 boys interviewed, two were assessed as severely aggressive – in that they had caused grievous bodily harm and 11 were assessed as mildly aggressive. In addition to the psychologists' assessment, Eron's (1963) Guess Who questionnaire was given to the delinquent boys. While boys had only known each other for about two weeks, they had lived together during this time. Only half the boys mentioned on more than five occasions by their fellow delinquents were assessed by the psychologists as aggressive. Nor when the cognitive maps of aggressive delinquents, whether assessed by psychologists or by Eron's technique, were compared with non-aggressive delinquents (most of whom were committed for theft) were any differences discernible. In each case 35 per cent of all labels were related to all others.

Confusions between the reality and fantasy of television fighting

So far it would appear that delinquents are not among those older children who confuse the rules of the fantasy world with the real world. When asked, 34 per cent of aggressive delinquents, 30 per cent of non-aggressive delinquents and 20 per cent of controls thought the fighting in fictional programmes was real rather than acted, but these differences are due to chance factors. But, as we have argued, confusion between the reality and fantasy of television programmes indicates viewer involvement, and thus it would appear that one-third of delinquents and one-fifth of controls were in some degree involved in the eight selected television programmes. Many younger boys believed that people were sufficiently hurt in such fighting to have to go to hospital, but no boys aged fifteen or more thought the fighting in fictional programmes was real. A few boys, moreover, maintained that violence in the *News* was acted, and the reason given by the boy in Table 10 is typical. The extent of this confusion was also surprising, since 14 per cent of delinquents and 17 per cent of controls said the fighting seen in the *News* was not lifelike. But perhaps to delinquents who have had more contact with the police, the news programmes were more lifelike than for controls with less contact with police. Bearing in mind the results from the previous chapter which suggest that viewers become anxious when they see realistically televised violence, we can perhaps assume that delinquents no less than controls have to operate some sort of defence mechanism to screen themselves from realistically filmed aggression. Nor, finally, did delinquents whether aggressive (70 per cent) or non-aggressive (65 per cent), any more than controls (65 per cent) perceive justification for the fighting they had seen on television.

Summary

The results presented here are not in accord with Eron, who contends that televiewing aggression affects real-life behaviour. Aggressive delinquents in this study, assessed by means of Eron's scale, were found to be no different from either non-aggressive delinquents or controls as regards the complexity of their classification of televised fighting, nor did they believe fantasy aggression was more real, nor did they perceive more justification for televised aggression. If delinquents are as capable as controls in delineating realistic from acted filmed aggression and justified from unjustified aggression, are delinquents also likely to imitate such aggression? The evidence presented here suggests that the attempt to explain delinquency in terms of either cognitive poverty with regard to televiewing or the imitation of television models is not yet proved. Whilst delinquents seem in most instances as capable of using aggressive television portrayals as controls, could it not be argued that televiewing, even by deviant individuals, can serve useful functions without fear of direct imitation? Exactly what uses can delinquent boys find for television?

DELINQUENTS' IDENTIFICATION WITH MEDIA HEROES

We have seen that delinquents do not perceive that people can co-operate even to be aggressive. We have seen that they think televised fighting is marginally more real than do control boys. These factors suggest a slightly higher degree of involvement with television programmes which we could perhaps predict if delinquents are raised without adequate social anchorage. The case history of the boy whose grid we have examined reveals that his mother co-habits with the lodger; the boy's father, when he returned, regularly and severely beat him; and that on frequent occasions he has had to sleep in the coal-shed. It is highly probable that this boy will spend the rest of his life in state institutions. My only surprise is that some citizens wish to blame television for his deviancy.

DELINQUENTS' SOCIAL ANCHORAGE

If brought up like the boy cited above it is perhaps not surprising that delinquents differ in their televiewing style from non-delinquents. A number of writers have commented on the lack of adequate social relationships in the families of deviant individuals; for example, Glaser (1956) writes that the family is 'the principal non-criminal reference group' and that 'criminal identification may occur through positive reference to criminal roles portrayed in the mass media'. If delinquents are raised in non-warm families we may predict that their self-concept is not rounded out because of a lack of suitable mirrors. Such boys may turn to the media to locate the significant others who are lacking in their environment. In order to try to test this hypothesis the repertory grid technique was again employed with the same sample of delinquent and non-delinquent boys we have already described. On this occasion the test was used first to discover what boys thought of males they knew in life, and secondly what they thought of the television heroes in the programmes we have already cited with the exception of the *News*.

Repertory grid used for identification and self-concept

Each boy was presented with photographs of *The Saint*, a hero who broke the law; *Barlow*, a hero who enforces the law; *Dr Who*, a hero acting in fantasy setting; *The Virginian*, a hero acting in an historical setting; and *Steed* (from *The Avengers*), a hero in the counter-espionage tradition. Boys were asked to name these heroes and if unable to name a character correctly, a hero of like type was substituted. Similarly, boys were asked to tell me the first names of their fathers, or father substitute and their two best friends. These names were written on cards as were the captions 'Me-now' and 'Me – as I would like to be'. In each case I read the captions to the boys and presenting a mixture of three of these cards and photographs of television heroes, asked the boys, 'In what ways are two of these similar but different from the third?' As before the resulting similarities and differences were recorded on repertory grids. Boys frequently repeated answers or could not reply, but after ten sets of three captions and photos were presented, delinquents recorded an average of 6 similarities to non-delinquents 5·4 similarities.

If as we have argued, inadequate social relationships cause the delinquent to turn to television for surrogate interaction with significant others, we may expect delinquents more than controls to say that their favourite television heroes do not enact a part on the screen but behave in that way both on and off the screen. As we have seen, involvement with television heroes leads to a confusion of the reality and fantasy of their media performance. Boys were asked, if not spontaneously mentioned, whether television heroes were actors (as in a school play) or for real (behaved like that all the time), and whether the heroes were lifelike (I have met people who behave like that) or not lifelike (I have never met anyone who behaves like that). Boys were also asked whether people they knew, including themselves and television heroes, started fights or did not start fights and whether they did good or bad things.

In order to discover what boys thought about themselves, about television heroes and about people they knew, they were asked in turn to assess each of these people according to the similarities and differences previously mentioned; similarities were recorded as ticks, differences as blanks and in rare cases where neither applied as question marks. An example of a completed repertory grid can be seen in Table 11. This boy had perceived six pairs of similarities and differences between television heroes and people that he knew. He was then asked whether *Dr Who* used a gun or not (the first verbal label on the grid). As can be seen he did not consider that *Dr Who* used a gun (since there is a blank under *Dr Who*). By way of contrast, this boy said *The Saint*, *Steed* and both his best friends did use guns. There is a tick under each of these names indicating that each of these characters used a gun. As can also be seen this boy wanted a gun – he has replied for 'Me – as I would like to be' that he would like to use a gun.

We have suggested that delinquents are socially isolated, which we may expect to be reflected in poor identification with males known to them in real life. The grid technique provides a relatively indirect method by which identification can be assessed. Boys were first asked how they perceived themselves namely 'Me – now' and secondly how they would like to be perceived namely 'Me – as I would like to be.' These perceptions of self were then compared for each boy with his perceptions of father and best friends. Clearly boys were not asked whether self-concepts or fathers and best friends were acted or for real. Simply put, the ticks, blanks and question marks which appear in the vertical column below 'Me – now' were compared with the ticks, blanks and question marks which appear below father, and then with those which appear below best friends. In Table 11 the matching score between Me and Father was 8 similarities, with best friend 4 similarities, with next best friend 7 similarities – out of a total possible of 11 (13 pairs of similarities minus 'acted – for real' and 'lifelike – not lifelike').

TABLE 11

THE REPERTORY GRID COMPLETED FOR A DISTURBED TWELVE-YEAR-OLD
DELINQUENT BOY AS REGARDS IDENTIFICATION WITH MEDIA HEROES AND
PEOPLE KNOWN TO THE CHILD (NOBLE, 1971B)

Television Heroes, Father, Self and Best Friends

	Similarity between two of three people	Dr Who	Father, David	Steed (Avengers)	Best friend, Georgi	Saint	Me – as I would like to be	Barlow (Softly, Softly)	Next best friend, Malcolm	Virginian	Me – now	Difference between one of three people
	Have guns			√	√	√	√	√	√	√		Never use guns
	Plain clothes		√		√	√	√	√	√		√	Stage clothes
	Good fighters			√	√	√	√	√		√		Not such good fighters
I	Likes best			√	√	√	√	√	√	√A		Not like so much
	Always fighting			√	√	√	√	√		√	√	Does not fight so much
	Waits for criminals and shoots			√	√B		√	√		√		Does not shoot criminals
	Acted			√		√		C		√		For real
	Like			√	√	√	√	√	√	√	√	Dislike
	Tough	√	√	√	√	√	√	√	√	√	√	Weak
	Lifelike			√		√		√		√		Not lifelike
II	Starts fights	√	√D	√	√	√	√	√				Does not start fights
	Does good things				√	√	√	√	√	√		Does bad things
	Fast		√	√		√	√	√		√	√	Slow

I Similarities/Differences elicited during sorting procedures.

II Similarities/Differences supplied by the Investigator.

A Likes best of all.

B 'Georgi waits for me with a shotgun. I wear a tin vest and (he) shoots at me when I come round the corner.'

C 'He wrote *Softly, Softly* himself, and he is a policeman when he is not on the telly.'

D 'Well, he hits me' (confirmed from record sheet).

√ Indicates the similarity (left-hand side of the grid) is relevant for a particular person.

? Indicates that neither similarity nor difference is relevant for a particular person.

Blank Indicates the difference (right-hand side of grid) is relevant for a particular person.

It was also possible to assess whether or not each boy wished to be like his father or his two best friends. Such an assessment was made by comparing the boy's perception of 'Me – as I would like to be' with his perceptions of Father and Best Friends. In Table 11, the boy did not wish to be very much like his father (only 4 matches out of a total of 11) but he did want to be very like his best friend Georgi (10 matches out of 11) and did not wish to be like his second best friend, Malcolm, (5 matches). It was therefore possible to compare delinquent and control boys with regard to the extent that they perceived themselves as like people they knew.

If as we have argued, delinquents suffer from breaks in mirror reflections of self by important people in their families, their self-concept is likely to be more inconsistent than the self-concept of non-delinquent boys with access to a balanced range of mirror reflections of self. An attempt to assess the consistency of self-concept was made by comparing both delinquents' and controls' assessment of real self (Me – now) with ideal self (Me – as I would like to be). The boy whose grid appears in Table 11 would seem to have a poorly integrated self-concept since the match between 'Me – now' and 'Me – as I would like to be', is 5 out of a total possible of 11.

In the case of the delinquent boy whose grid we are examining, he did not wish to be like significant males known to him in real life, which has perhaps resulted in an inconsistent self-concept. Is there any way we can test whether he better relates to media heroes than to people known to him? In order to examine boys' identification with media heroes, each boy's conception of self was compared with his conception of media heroes. As can be seen in Table 11, this boy perceived 5 out of 11 possible similarities between 'Me – now' and *Dr Who*, 4/11 for *Steed*, 6/11 for *The Saint*, 5/11 for *Barlow* and 5/11 for *The Virginian*. In other words, there were 5 corresponding ticks, blanks or question marks between the vertical column under the 'Me – now' and the vertical column under *Dr Who*, 6 corresponding ticks, blanks and question marks with *The Saint* and so on. This procedure was repeated for ideal self-assessments, namely 'Me – as I would like to be'. For the boy in Table 11 the matching scores between 'Me – as I would like to be' and television heroes were respectively *Dr Who* 1/11, *Steed* 10/11, *Barlow* 11/11 and *The Virginian* 9/11. It is apparent that although this boy did not perceive himself as like television heroes he did indicate that he would like to be like many television heroes. For example, between 'Me – now' and *Barlow* there were only 5 out of 11 possible similarities, whereas for 'Me – as I would like to be' and *Barlow* there are 11 out of 11 possible similarities, more similarities than for father or best friends.

Delinquents' relationships with males known to them in real life

Is the example we have studied typical of delinquent boys? Having analysed both delinquent and control boys' grids in the way outlined above it was found, as expected, that delinquents were significantly less able than controls to relate to their fathers and best friends. The match between 'Me – now' and Father and Best Friends for delinquents was 60 per cent and for controls 68 per cent. Statistical analysis showed that a difference of this magnitude – nearly 10 per cent – would be expected, by chance, only five times in a hundred. More importantly delinquents wanted to be even less like their fathers and best friends, a match of 56 per cent, than controls 66 per cent (match between 'Me – as I would like to be' and Father and Best Friends). A difference which statistically would not occur by chance more than once in a hundred times. Moreover, delinquents more than controls wanted to be even less like their fathers and Best Friends (56 per cent – roughly chance level) than they already perceived themselves (60 per cent). Does this inability to relate by mirror processes to people known to them in life, as we have argued, result in a fragmented self-concept?

Fragmentation of delinquents' self-concept

Comparing real self percepts (Me – now) with ideal self percepts (Me – as I would like to be), there was, as expected, a greater discrepancy between the two for delinquents (a match of 56 per cent) than for control boys (a match of 63 per cent). This larger gap between self and ideal self may perhaps explain why delinquent boys are deviant. If they set themselves unrealistic goals, they may be motivated to try to close the gap by deviant means. Other researchers have noted that neurotic patients have a larger discrepancy in self-concept than normals and when undergoing psychotherapy the gap between ideal self and real self percepts progressively closes (Butler, 1960; and Dymond, 1954). Given a comparative inability to relate to people known to them in real life, which seems to have resulted in a fragmented self-concept, is there any evidence that these boys turn to television to seek out significant others with whom they can relate?

Delinquents' relationship with media heroes

As might be expected, the matching scores between 'Me – now' and television heroes were at levels which would be expected by chance – namely 50 per cent. Delinquents achieved a 47 per cent matching score while non-delinquents achieved a 49 per cent matching score. Both groups of boys, however, wanted to be more like television heroes than they actually saw themselves – for both groups the matching scores between 'Me – as I would like to be' and television heroes was 63 per cent. Thus delinquent boys, less often than controls, perceived themselves like their fathers and best friends, and wanted to be even less like such significant males than controls. Control boys wanted to be most like Fathers and Best Friends (66 per cent) rather than television heroes (63 per cent). The converse was true of delinquent boys whose matching score with significant others in real life (56 per cent) was lower than with television heroes (63 per cent).

On the one hand, the highest matching score calculated for control boys was between 'Me – now' and Father and Best Friends (68 per cent); on the other hand, the highest matching score calculated for delinquent boys was between 'Me – as I would like to be' and television heroes (63 per cent). These results strongly suggest that delinquents turn to television for suitable males with whom to relate, when, and only when, there is a lack of suitable real-life males. If this is the case we may expect delinquents to be more involved with television heroes than controls, even though both groups seem to relate similarly to these heroes.

MEDIA DEFINITIONS OF THE 'REALITY' OF THE REAL WORLD

As we have argued in previous chapters, involvement with television characters results when viewers recognise television characters and feel they know them, and thus deny that they merely enact their roles on the television screen. Half the delinquents thought that the male television heroes were real and lifelike as compared with only 31 per cent of controls. While delinquents may be relatively unable to relate to people in their immediate environment, delinquent boys related to television heroes as capably as controls and indeed seemed to have made their television heroes as real as people known to them in life. Nor did delinquents confine their relationship to television heroes who broke the law; they related themselves more positively to the policeman *Barlow* (62 per cent) than to the law breaking *Hog* (50 per cent – chance).

It seems reasonable to suppose that boys deprived of adequate personal relationships may attend to television not only to compensate for abortive and ineffective social relationships but also to attempt to re-establish effective interpersonal contacts. It appears likely that delinquent boys interact, albeit only one way interaction, with law-upholding heroes in the hope that they may one day be able to interact with people they respect. While the delinquent cannot influence the way in which a television character will behave, as he might be able to in real-life interaction, it seems likely that they turn to television for a relationship which makes few demands of them. This may indeed be the only type of relationship with which they are able to cope, particularly if their real-life relationships are of the type described in the case history of our delinquent boy.

The influence of the media on deviancy is therefore complex and not without its redeeming features, but nevertheless television may aggravate deviancy by defining the affluent life style enjoyed by television heroes as normal for real life. Several delinquent boys, when comparing television heroes with people they knew, often mentioned that they were 'posh', had good cars, expensive clothes and highly desirable material possessions. Neither they, nor people they knew, possessed such objects. Such comments suggest that delinquents felt deprived, relative to the heroes they see on television. Given that these boys could not adequately relate to people known to them, but could relate via the illusion of intimacy to television heroes, who constituted something of an alternative point of reference, delinquent boys may come to accept the affluent life style of the hero as a depiction of a reality which may be feasible for them. It is in this respect, as argued in Chapter 1, that the media are most potent, since they seem to define the 'life-style' which denotes membership of the larger society which television makes visible. Sherif and Sherif (1964) maintain that the Texas adolescents they studied wanted to own motor cars, which most of the teenagers they saw on television possessed. The encouragement of unrealistic consumption patterns as normal, whether by advertising or by programmes indirectly selling a way of life, would seem to be the most disturbing aspect of the relationship between the media and deviant behaviour. As Merton (1957) comments deviant behaviour may occur at a societal level 'when there is an acute disjunction between the cultural norms and goals and the socially structured capabilities of members of the group to act in accord with them'. (You cannot always get what you want.) Television's glamour programmes may encourage such disjunctions, and unlike psychotherapy which seeks to reduce the conflict between real and ideal self, may aggravate such conflicts which will result in further alienation amongst delinquents whose membership of society is at best marginal.

SUMMARY AND COMMENT

I may be accused in these studies of trying to answer questions of a higher order by means of studying televiewing styles at a lower order. While not proofs, these studies were the nearest I could get with the tools available to the social scientist, and more importantly with intellectual honesty, to the problems of deviancy and television. I tried to let delinquent boys speak their own language about televiewing, but it should be remembered that the repertory grid, while flexible and indirect, can lure users into errors in reasoning. I have tried, therefore, throughout this book to cite enough detail of studies to allow the reader to make his own judgements. Nor should it be forgotten that very few delinquents are aggressive to the point of causing grievous bodily harm and a criminal record denotes being caught, rather than being deviant. Boys who are caught may have acquired a stigmatised self-concept and may not choose to be honest with investigators like myself. Nor was the whole range of television heroes sampled; the studies need repeating with television characters from family serials who do not achieve success glamorously.

These points aside, it would appear that, first and foremost, delinquents do not receive adequate mirror reflections of self from the significant males in their restricted kin groupings. Delinquents acquire a self-concept which is fragmented. To alleviate the tension experienced, we have suggested that delinquents turn to television for surrogate significant males and indeed they believe that these televised male characters are real, rather than actors portraying a part. Relationships enjoyed with television characters are undemanding, and cannot of course provide that essential feedback concerning self-image which should be provided by real-life significant others. But, then, where else except on television, can boys with inadequate social anchorage regularly meet and interact with something resembling an extended kin grouping in a society where the individual has become isolated from community groupings, and in the case of many delinquent boys, isolated from even that most basic of all socialising units, the family?

9

Producers: Gatekeepers to the wider society

Throughout this book we have ascribed a positive role to television in the types of industrial societies in which we live. To a point I can agree with McLuhan that the medium is the message insofar as televiewing does not necessarily involve the viewer in identity loss, but clearly only some programmes are likely to fulfil television's function in mass societies. We have suggested that television when art allows the viewer to experience those emotions the artist wishes to communicate, and we have suggested that television by dint of its regularly appearing characters and personas, has those functions once fulfilled by extended kin members. Moreover, we have suggested that television is uniquely suited to make the wider society visible to increasingly isolated audience members. These functions, in large part, are fulfilled by the content of the programmes we view.

Who, though, decides on programme content? Who are the gatekeepers to the wider society? Whose are those names we see in the credits? What is their conception of a child? Are they aware of the unique qualities younger children bring to the small screen, which we have tried to describe in Chapter 5. For the main part, this chapter will be given over to studies of the producers of children's programmes, in particular the way they view their child audiences and the way in which naïve producers acquire the current values of their established counterparts. These questions necessarily involve the study of the production process and of television producers themselves. We shall begin, therefore, with a case study of a 'classic' children's favourite, *Blue Peter*, and later examine how producers' conceptions of children's reponses to this programme correspond with the child's actual responses.

STUDIES OF MASS COMMUNICATORS

One can study programme content either as social scientists by counting the number of left-handed rapes by non-Anglo-Saxon protestants in a given amount of time;* or through the eyes of the viewer as we have attempted in this book, or by studying television

* Gerbner (1969) comes close to this at times.

producers to find out why they chose to screen certain programmes. Taking this latter way, few would suggest that producers set out to make our children delinquent. Nor do producers work in a vacuum; their products inevitably reflect the values and customs of the production agencies for which they work. As McQuail (1969) has pointed out, the study of communicators within their institutions has only recently attracted research attention. White (1950), for example, found that newspaper editors only printed one-tenth of material which came to them via the wires of the large press agencies and relied on highly personal judgements. Such gate-keepers relied on highly personal judgements of what was deemed newsworthy.

In addition to personal judgements, Breed (1955) demonstrated how the novice reporter became socialised into the prevailing ethic of the newspaper. He discovered, when interviewing 120 newsmen in middle-sized American newspapers, that they were encouraged to conform to newspaper policy by means of sanctions exerted by the work group which resulted in reporting that 'supports the existing power relationship in society, usually class interests and property protection'. But perhaps more important than either the organisational structure or the individual preferences of television producers is the audience that the communicator has in mind when making a television programme. Pool and Shulman (1959) suggest that a newsman writes his story for an imaginary audience either of critics or supporters. Who then are the imaginary audiences that producers of children's television have in mind when making their programmes?

TARGET AUDIENCES OF CHILDREN'S TELEVISION PRODUCERS

The European Broadcasting Union commissioned a report on children's programming conducted by Halloran and Elliott (1969) who sent questionnaires asking about children's programming policies to broadcasting organisations in Europe. They discovered that there was no consensus view as to what was a child, let alone what were the needs of child television audiences. In some countries children were not regarded as televiewers until five years, in others not until seven years, but, taken overall, children between eight and ten years were provided with more television programmes made specifically for them than children in other age groups. The BBC made special programmes for children aged up to twelve years, while the state-run French broadcasting authority made specialised programmes for adolescents which 'should gradually lead young people towards a greater cultural and social awareness'.

When programme types were examined in relation to the needs of children of different ages, most institutions reported that they provided more non-entertainment programmes for the twelve- to fifteen-year-old age range and that generally children under seven years were regarded as audiences for light entertainment and variety. These findings suggest, although the survey was far from complete, that children's programmes are predominantly scaled down adult programmes; progressively scaled down and entertainment-orientated for the younger child. Moreover, since children's broadcasting occupied some 10 per cent of broadcasting time but was only allocated 5 per cent of the budget, one might suppose that children's departments, where they exist, are the Cinderellas of the television companies. All television producers have to consider and operate within very tight budgetary constraints.

In order to investigate further what producers think of their child audiences, the European Broadcasting Union, at the instigation of Halloran and Stevens, decided to study television producers' reactions to the very popular children's programme, *Blue Peter*. I was asked to conduct the study and report on it to the European Broadcasting Union's workshop which producers from all over Europe were to attend. The objectives of the exercise were first to examine the intentions of the *Blue Peter* producers, secondly to evaluate these intentions by means of interviewing children after a specific programme had been transmitted, and thirdly to ask the television producers assembled at the workshop to predict and evaluate likely children's responses.

THE PRODUCTION OF BLUE PETER

Blue Peter is a magazine programme for children aged between five and twelve years transmitted by the BBC, which attracts audiences of between five and eight million viewers for the two half-hour programmes presented each week. The programme was the responsibility of one senior editor, Biddy Baxter, and two editors, Edward Barnes and Rosemary Gill, who were kind enough to spare several hours of their time to talk to me, show me scripts, and allowed me to watch several rehearsal sessions during which I observed the progress from raw to finished product. Three professional personas are employed to face the cameras and to present all the material scripted for the programme. The senior editor was finally responsible for the show, while one editor was in charge of outside film recordings and the other responsible for 'items' to be transmitted live from the studio. They were backed up by two to three scriptwriters and other production assistants. Three women were specifically employed to answer the letters the children are encouraged to write to the programme, which then amounted to nearly a thousand a week.

Once scripted, the programme moves to the studio where it is rehearsed several times over, timed, and control over the finished visual product passes to a director who is responsible for the technical camera work, although the script usually contains specific instructions on how items are to be shot virtually second by second. Directors are not specifically allocated to the programme; and may change from broadcast to broadcast It is reported that some more artistically minded directors have ruined some children's programmes by insisting on oblique camera shots. The final decisions that I witnessed as regards camera technique were taken collectively by the editors and the director in the control box.

The objectives of Blue Peter

The producers' objective was to entertain and educate simultaneously. The senior editor began working at the BBC in schools educational broadcasting. In order to attract and hold the interest of the widest possible range of viewers, the programme presents a wide variety of specific items within a magazine format, in the producers' words 'to interest and entertain children by showing them what is fascinating in the world around them'. Moreover, the producers insisted that the programme was not merely for passive viewing; considerable ingenuity was exercised to ensure that the child viewer at home was encouraged to become actively involved with materials presented in the programme. Thus the children were weekly shown how to make a simple object, usually from easily available and inexpensive materials, for which printed instructions are available if the child writes to the programme after viewing. These objects are rarely thought out by the personas. Children's efforts are rewarded in a variety of ways if they send objects to the studio. The highest reward appeared to be the inclusion in the programme of the object made, followed in turn by a *Blue Peter* badge which the personas wear conspicuously in each programme. Successive good efforts deserve different *Blue Peter* badges. Having read some of the children's mail it became apparent that children find few outlets for creative expression, and the programme had quite rightly tapped on area of children's needs.

Moreover, the *Blue Peter* charity appeals have by now become nationally famous. Once again the goal is for children to collect easily available items such as postage stamps, wool and bottle tops to raise money for charitable causes. The programme keeps children in contact with both the progress in achieving the desired target and the way the money is spent. 'Items' are screened in later programmes which show the children the fruits of their labours. Once again the post-box demonstrates that this objective meets a very real need for the children in a mass society.

The illusion of intimacy

In order to convey information, the producers felt that children should first feel familiar with the programme. In their words: 'The set, which is adaptable to the needs of the programme, is basically a set of open shelves with toys and ornaments on them against a plain cyclorama'. The first and last item in each programme is filmed with these shelves as a backdrop, so that younger viewers in particular recognise the programme both when it starts and finishes transmittion. Moreover, the same three compères are employed weekly and come together in front of these props at the beginning and end of each programme. 'This is the familiar setting into which any item can be put. Children feel secure with the familiar faces, and are then ready to take any surprise offered'. Familiarity is also encouraged by the frequent references to *Blue Peter* books, tractors and other objects during the course of each programme. Similarly *Blue Peter* animals make regular appearances to show children 'what it is like to own a pet'.

To encourage the illusion of intimacy further, one of the personas acts as an ambassador for each item presented live in the studio and for items pre-recorded on film. When guests appear in the programme they are usually seen in conjunction with a persona and are rarely allowed to address the camera directly. Thus the personas' heads are usually seen in close-up, and guests in much smaller scale. Moreover, it was intended that children think the programme live and unrehearsed. Considerable efforts were made to make the programme seem informal. However it is now admitted 'the production secretary types all the words for Val, John and Peter' (the personas). The illusion encouraged by the producers is that of the face-to-face group, which we have argued is television's unique power. A power, I might add, not recognised in so many of the purely 'educational' programmes transmitted.

The personas' roles

We have seen some of the techniques used to encourage the illusion of intimacy which fosters a sense of security for the viewing child. Just how closely television programmes simulate the extended kin may be judged from the roles allotted to the compères. John is to be thought of as an elder brother who is active, outdoor, prepared to 'have a go' and make mistakes. Peter's role is that of father, literally com-père, unflappable, steady, stable and should anything go wrong (and the animals frequently do not behave as scripted), Peter has to smooth an air of calm and act as though nothing untoward has happened. In order to complete the family unit, Val is to be seen as an elder sister or the older girl next door. She is fashion conscious, and frequently shows the children how to make things. The extended kin function of television at its best, and *Blue Peter* in spite of its critics is near the best, is thus clearly uppermost in the producers' minds. Moreover, the programme is very carefully scripted so that no one persona is dominant. The three have complementary roles and are to be seen as such. Nevertheless, the illusion of intimacy was so potent that the *Blue Peter* books, published annually as part of the tradition, were in fact written by the producers but published with the personas as both authors and receivers of royalties. In this and other aspects there have now been changes.

Selection and presentation of items

We have described the vehicle in which programme content is carried. Magazine programmes, which by their nature attract large audiences by dint of a variety of content, require a standardised and packaged format if they are to achieve an identity. So-called 'items' are culled largely from newspapers – which is an interesting example of the way one media feeds upon another. 'Stories, music and clips from recently released films are included. Topical events of a non-political nature are reflected. In each programme, hobbies and something interesting to make are demonstrated. Competitions are also included. Children are shown what is fascinating in the world around them.' The demands of the 'package', however, determine the eventual order in which items will be presented. The bulk of 'items' are transmitted live from the studio but the highlight of most programmes is considered to be the items which have been previously recorded on film outside the studio. The producers were emphatic that no film item should be used to start or end the programme since it would deter from the sense of familiarity which is an integral part of the programme's composition.

When I was finally able to pin the producers down as to their likely target audience, an admission they rightly found difficult for a magazine programme, they concurred that the programme was written for a seven-year-old. Film items were considered fare for older viewers because they satisfied a need for adventure. Thus, film items were usually sandwiched between studio items and placed near the middle of the programme in the running order. Needless to say, film items always feature one of the compères, but they have the very real intent of trying to demonstrate the human face behind

various occupational and social roles. John has demonstrated on
film, by actually becoming for a day a waiter, a parachutist and a
circus clown, what is involved in such social roles both behind the
scenes and 'on stage' where we more normally view them. Similarly
Blue Peter takes an annual trip abroad which is filmed to give
children what Aldiss maintains is television's correct function,
namely – an impression of how people in other countries live and
work.

Producers were very concerned to maintain a 'balance' between the
various items presented. Equal use has to be made of each compère
so that the team image is maintained and usually personas take
turns to present items. No two film items would ever follow one
another as a careful intuitive appraisal is made of each item as
regards its speed of presentation, length and excitement. Balance
is maintained by varying the order in which long and short, fast
and slow, and exciting and less exciting items, are presented. I rarely
saw a running order changed once scripted, although occasionally
short 'filler' items were removed altogether if the programme
threatened to run over time.

Children's evaluation of producers' intentions

In order to discover the effectiveness of producers' intentions it was
decided to interview children the day after they had seen a *Blue Peter*
programme in their own homes, since we thought children would
be unable to talk about *Blue Peter* in a vacuum. Clearly we evaluated
but a single programme in what is essentially a series, which somewhat worried the producers, and created logistic problems of a high
order. However, while producers knew that the *Blue Peter* transmitted on 29th January, 1968 was to be subject to scrutiny no
attempt was made to produce a special programme. In the event
this programme began with the title superimposed upon the model
traction engines seen later in the programme (0·5 min); John and
Peter then examined the traction engines for 3 minutes before
proceeding to plough a field with them in the studio (another 3
min.); Valerie joined John and Peter with an old print of a traction
engine and they talked about the Blue Peter tractors in Africa (1
minute); John was then seen on pre-recorded film as a circus clown
in which we saw him make up, learn to fall and appear in front of
the audience (4·5 mins.); back to the studio where Valerie showed
the children how to decorate a coathanger so that it looks like a
clown (3·5 mins.); John and Peter appeared with Backing Britain
tee shirts (Union Jack upside-down and made in Portugal, 2 mins.);
children then viewed a short film clip about ospreys showing their
feeding habits (1·5 mins.); after which Valerie introduced a Scotsman

with a live osprey in the studio (4 mins.); the personas then closed
the programme. Photographs which were taken during the re-
hearsals were used to show to children when they were asked about
the programme.

In order to discover what children thought of producer intentions
we asked questions designed to answer the following: Firstly, how
well can children recall a television programme seen the night before?
Secondly, as well as being entertained, do children learn anything,
especially about everyday social roles from the programme? Thirdly,
do children remember or try to make the object constructed in the
programme? Fourthly, do children recognise the roles of the three
personas? Fifthly, do children feel secure when viewing *Blue Peter*?
Sixthly, do they see the programme as spontaneous or as a rehearsed, polished product? Seventhly, do children feel that different
camera shots are necessary in a children's programme? Eighthly, do
children think a correct balance is achieved between the various
items seen in the programme? And finally, how do children of
different ages respond to the variety of items seen, and are the
developmental trends outlined in Chapter 5 evident? We were therefore able to ask questions of children which span the theoretical
ideas outlined in several chapters of this book.

All the children in a primary and a junior school were asked to
watch BBC television from 4.30 to 6 pm on Monday, 29th January.
They were not told that *Blue Peter* was the programme in which
we were interested, and also viewed *Jackanory* and *Tales from
Europe*. Twelve children at each of the ages from five to eleven
years were randomly selected the day after the programme was
seen and individually interviewed by trained interviewers in their
schools. The sample was not totally representative of children in
Britain since our goal was to explore in depth, rather than width,
children's reaction to producers' intentions.

Children's recall of Blue Peter

First, interviewers checked that children had seen the programme and
in order to try to elicit honest answers were told that we had talked
to many children about *Blue Peter*, some of whom had said they
liked it while others did not like the programme. Each child was
then asked what happened last night in *Blue Peter*, which thing
came first, which second and so on? Predictably, as we have seen
in Chapter 5, five- and and six-year-olds remembered only 18 per
cent of the items seen, while seven- and eight-year-olds remembered
46 per cent of items and nine- to eleven-year-olds recalled 43 per
cent of items. The producers' intent of writing for an imaginary
seven-year-old seems well vindicated since these children best re-

called the programme, and in the correct order. However, as we might expect, only nine-year-old and older children recalled the linkage items such as the tee shirt.

The two items best recalled by children were the making the clown sequence and the film of John as a circus clown – which were recalled by three-quarters of the children interviewed; linkage items such as the old print and tee shirt were recalled by 8 and 15 per cent of children respectively. The fact that making the clown and clown film items were so well recalled suggest that the producers' emphasis on leaving the studio and looking at the world outside, and their emphasis on the construction of objects which can be made by children are well justified. We asked each child how they could make the clown coathanger. This sequence lasted $3\frac{1}{2}$ minutes and involved the demonstration of some 15 separate steps – the first 12 of which were shown visually and the last 3, due to lack of time, only verbally. Surprisingly, children on the day after transmission recalled an average of 31 per cent of the steps demonstrated. Indeed the steps presented only verbally were recalled by a quarter of the children interviewed. As expected, children aged nine and more recalled 42 per cent of steps, children aged seven and eight 29 per cent and five- and six-year-olds 15 per cent. While only 40 per cent of children thought the coathanger worth making, and only 3 per cent had tried to make it, these recall figures for instructions given the day before (each step lasting about 14 seconds) are surprisingly high, especially if one compares them with, say, the success of programmed instruction. It would seem that children do learn in the context of entertainment because, unlike school, they are motivated to enjoy what they see. It says something for the freshness of *Blue Peter* that the producers provide materials which allow the child to explore 'worlds' outside his area of knowledge on film and also within his range of capabilities by making a simple object.

Learning while being entertained

We have already seen something of television's power in teaching skills that have only been demonstrated once before camera. We also asked the children whether *Blue Peter* had taught them anything. Six out of ten replied 'Yes', and this in schools catering for both middle- and working-class children. Some children listed facts about traction engines – that they were fired by steam and used to plough fields prior to the pneumatic type. Others told us about ospreys, which they said were rare sea eagles, living on fish and in danger of extinction. Once again short televised presentations had imparted the sort of knowledge taught in school. But the most interesting answers were those about circus clowns. We have already argued that television's unique power is its ability to penetrate behind scenes and make visible the human face lying behind the social exterior of roles. Children stressed to us that clowns had to learn to fall, to juggle and to make up. Similarly, children commented that clowns are not always happy and they have to learn to do their job. Such knowledge which is not orientated to the school curriculum is perhaps best acquired via the medium of television. *Blue Peter* has an honourable record in its attempts to present both national and occupational roles in a realistic and non-stereotyped manner and still manages to attract eight million viewers – a figure of which *Panorama* might be jealous.

Moreover, it appeared that different items in the magazine format appealed to children of different ages. We expected that younger viewers would most prefer those items presented from the studio, since they help the young child to feel secure. Indeed five- and six-year-olds most liked the coathanger and traction engine sequences while older children preferred the clown film which seems to have satisfied their need for adventure. Further probing revealed that 40 per cent of children most liked an item because it was funny, while a quarter of children liked an item because it taught them something new and one in five children liked an item because it was interesting. The two essential ingredients of popularity would appear to be humour (John usually acts the fool in the filmed sequences) and information. It is probably worth stressing that learning can indeed be fun, and that children, as in the village, learn best by watching and doing, rather than by being instructed in institutions whose sole function is perceived as teaching.

We found that as children grew older they progressively came to reply on a combination of both words and pictures to help them understand what they were viewing. Younger children emphatically said that it was the pictures which they understood. At five and six years, 60 per cent of children thought the pictures most important in helping them understand, which fell to 50 per cent for seven- and eight-year-olds and to 40 per cent for nine- to eleven-year-olds. It would seem that children can learn before they can read, and moreover that younger children do indeed learn by watching and that words are of secondary importance – which if true has implications for educational broadcasting.

The illusion of intimacy

We have noted that the *Blue Peter* presenters enact roles which resemble those of extended family members. We asked children who had presented the programme and as noted in Chapter 5, five-year-olds could not accurately recall the names nor descriptions of the presenters. However, we then presented children with a photo-graph of the three presenters and asked them 'Is John like anyone you know? and Why?' John is supposed to enact the part of an elder brother for the child viewer. A quarter of the children had recognised his role and said that John was like an elder brother, an uncle or a friend. Some children said that both John and the person they knew had similar accents, but more children saw John as naughty – the sort who puts mud in inkwells. John is thus seen as being fairly close in age and interests to the viewing children. Peter, on the other hand, was at the time of the study new to the programme and had then to find the poise he so capably displays today. Only 15 per cent of children recognised Peter as like someone they knew, but all the five-year-old boys interviewed said that Peter was the person they liked best. These boys saw Peter as 'like daddy' and seemed to respond to his unflappable father-like image. Older children said of him, 'He is not really happy – but he tries hard to be' and did not recognise him at all. In view of the fact that the first and almost inevitable choice is for female presenters for younger children's programmes, we should note the popularity of a father-like figure especially for young boy viewers.

Valerie is to be seen as like an elder sister or elder sister's girl friend. A quarter of the children recognised her as like someone they knew but not as an elder sister, since the majority saw her as an 'aunty' and a few as 'mummy'. Half of the younger children recognised Valerie in this way because she either looked the same or more frequently behaved the same as real-life aunties. If it is re-membered that an aunty is someone with whom the child may take liberties not allowed by the parents, that an aunty is almost someone with a licence to spoil the child, these results are of considerable interest. They suggest that the child's relationship with Valerie is far less formal than it would be with a member of the immediate family and that Valerie in particular would seem to enact the role of an extended kin member, which, as we have argued in Chapter 1, is one of television's unique functions. Perhaps we should mention that the BBC nickname of 'Aunty' may not be inappropriate.

Moreover as previously noted in Chapter 3, girls recognised the personas as like people they knew more often than boys – 50 and 36 per cent respectively. As found in Chapter 3, some 40 per cent of children did seem to recognise the presenters as like people they knew and virtually as members of an extended family. The producers were, however, concerned that the personas should present inter-locking roles, in which they were largely successful since no two compères presented the same image to the children. Indeed, when children were asked to evaluate compères, all the three were seen as very similar – they were all seen as young, friendly, happy, nice, helpful and both easy to watch and easy to understand. That compères were seen as so similar suggests that they are perceived and evaluated as a team, rather than as one dominant persona with helpers. Predictably John was the most popular compère (47 per cent), followed by Valerie (35 per cent) with the novice Peter coming in a poor third (18 per cent). Once again personas were popular because they either made things (30 per cent), or went outside and did daring things (17 per cent) which suggests that *Blue Peter's* emphasis on activity and outside film items is well vindicated.

Security while viewing

Producers were concerned that the younger child should feel secure while viewing. Accordingly, children were presented with two photographs from the traction engine sequence, two from John as a circus clown, one of Valerie making the clown coathanger, one of Peter and John with the Backing Britain tee shirts, and one depicting all three personas with the osprey. Children were asked, 'Where do you think they make *Blue Peter* and which of these photographs were taken in the *Blue Peter* Studio?' As expected, only children aged seven years and older (89 per cent correct; five to six years 41 per cent correct) were able to say accurately that all the photographs except John as a circus clown were taken in the studio. Older children recognised the studio because four-fifths of them recognised the studio props, as was anticipated by the producers. When interviewers probed children's answers, two-thirds of the five- and six-year-olds thought both the traction engine and osprey sequences had been filmed outside the studio since they said, 'The osprey might peck you and fly off its nest', and the traction engine 'might blow up'. These answers seem to indicate that younger children recognised the studio as a safe familiar place since items considered dangerous were thought to have been filmed outside the studio. Indeed, one five-year-old said that *Blue Peter* was made 'at home', and four-fifths of the children who preferred studio items to outside film items did so because the studio was familiar. One ten-year-old girl when asked 'Why do you like familiar items best?' replied 'Because they are safe'. These answers strongly suggest, as we have argued in Chapter 1, that it is by means of repeated viewing that children come to feel they know both the people and the places they see on television. A fact, of course, recognised by the producers of *Coronation Street* and *Sesame Street*. Most children believe that the cast members really do live on *Sesame Street* as one boy said, 'You know where I live, you're there every day'.

However it should be noted that children appear to outgrow a need for security while viewing. While five- and six-year-olds preferred those items transmitted live from the studio, older children preferred items previously recorded on film, because they were unusual. In part, the magazine format allows the producers to satisfy a wide variety of children in the audience by means of the balance struck between different types of item.

Spontaneity

So far we have vindicated producer intentions. There was one area, however, where their techniques did not match the mood of the child viewers. Producers were concerned that children saw the programme as spontaneous in which the personas made up their words as they went along. Children were not fooled. We asked them, 'Did Val, John and Peter make up their words as they went along or did someone write the words for them which they had to learn like a school play?' One-third of the children thought they made up their words because they say 'er, but two-thirds of the children said the programme was scripted because the personas never hesitated and because of 'all those credits at the end'. Children also showed us that they understood the rules of camera etiquette. They said, 'When one compère speaks all the others look at him', and, 'John in his film did not talk as much just to you as he did in the studio'. Children particularly mentioned that only the compères spoke to them and that studio guests did not speak just to them. The remarkable characteristic of children's answers was the degree of sophistication shown even by young children in their understanding of television's techniques. The producers no longer attempt to give the impression that the programme is spontaneous.

Film literacy

As we have seen throughout this book, children who have been brought up with television display a remarkable understanding of this new medium even at very young ages. It is almost as though they have learnt to 'read' this new medium simply by watching. We wanted to discover children's reactions to the various types of camera shot commonly employed in television programmes. Forty-two children,* who were representative of the larger sample, were presented with three photographs of the osprey in the studio – one a close-up shot of the osprey, one a medium range shot of the osprey and his handler and one a long shot of the osprey, his handler and the three personas. Children were asked which photograph they liked most, liked least and why. Three-fifths of the children most preferred the close-up because they could see the detail, and a fifth each preferred the long shot and the medium shot. While

* Time did not permit us to ask all the children these questions.

younger children preferred the long shot to the close-up, older children preferred the close-up to the long shot. Five- and six-year-olds said, 'I want to see the people and not just the bird' which would again seem to indicate that the young child needs to be able to locate what he sees in a familiar context. As we have suggested in Chapter 1 a large part of television's appeal is composed of the familiarity of its content which enables viewers to feel that they know the people and places they see regularly.

While viewers seem to prefer familiar contexts and personas, the children we interviewed were in no doubt that they preferred a variety of camera shots to the static camera work of those home movies to which friends subject us. We asked children whether they would prefer to see the programme filmed from just one angle as in the long-shot photograph or whether they would prefer that 'the pictures should get bigger and smaller and move around the room after people'. Ninety per cent of children said they preferred a variety of pictures, since the use of different angles made the programme appear as more lifelike, and both people and objects were seen more clearly from a variety of perspectives. Only one child said, 'I cannot find what I was looking at when the pictures change'. However five- and six-year-olds again differed from their elder counterparts in so far as they did not appreciate the close-up technique as much as older children, nor, as we shall see later, as television producers. But they all preferred variety – in the words of one seven-year-old boy: 'I should like to start with a picture of the whole studio and all the people in it, then I would like to look at all the various things in the studio in detail.'

Balance between items

We have seen how producers give structure and unity to *Blue Peter*, which is essentially a collection of heterogeneous items. It is in the distillation of an identity for the programme that producers' intentions are both most elaborate and most necessary, since without structure the programme would be destined for oblivion. Producers several times stressed the need for a balance to be maintained between items in the running order. We attempted to assess the child's concept of balance by presenting him with seven photographs representing the sequences seen in the programme and asking him to select a running order 'as if you were in charge of the programme'. Children were also asked why they placed the photographs in the order chosen and whether they thought each item was fast or slow, long or short and exciting or dull – these being the dimensions used by the producers.

Six out of every ten children chose the running order used in the programme, but 40 per cent of children chose a second running order which was of considerable interest. These latter children preferred to start with the traction engine with people sequence, followed in turn by the traction engine alone, the osprey item, the close-up of the clown, long shot of the clown, Val making the clown coathanger, and closing with the tee shirt sequence. Once again it appeared that the child's need for security while viewing was paramount in the way they ordered items. Children seemed to need that the programme opened with sight of the familiar personas, rather than a picture of traction engines over which credits could be superimposed. Children chose to follow the traction engine sequence with the osprey item, which as we have already noted, was thought by younger children to have been filmed outside the studio, and which they found a little frightening. Children seemed to prefer to both start and end with items clearly recognised as filmed in the studio and with sight of the three personas. It would seem that children, no less than producers, were keenly aware of the need for a structure to give shape to the magazine format.

When we examined the reasons given by children why the items were placed in the order they had chosen, we found that 17 per cent placed an item first because it was good or funny while 4 per cent placed the least interesting item in first place. Sequences were placed second in order because they too were good and interesting (21 per cent) or because they followed logically from the first item (20 per cent). Children would have started with the sequence which they thought was shortest, and fastest but which was also exciting. The second item would have been slower, longer and the most exciting. Items were placed third, fourth, fifth and sixth in the running order because they either followed logically from previous items (20 per cent), they were good (10 per cent) or funny (8 per cent). Children said the third sequence should be slow, exciting and the longest item, which was to be followed by a fast, short item which was less exciting. The fifth and sixth sequences would then be slow, less exciting but long and short respectively. Moreover, children were as concerned with the final sequence as they were with the initial sequence. Items were placed last because they were most interesting (16 per cent) or alternatively because they were least interesting (13 per cent), but children agreed that this item should be slow and short. The dimensions used by the producers would seem, therefore, to be relevant for children, who also seemed to want to be 'hooked' by an initial short exciting sequence and their interest maintained by the most exciting item. In many respects children seemed no less sophisticated than producers in their ability to organise sequences within a gestalt, or a mosaic of picture images, which in some way is greater than the mere sum of the parts.

Somewhat elaborate analyses were conducted to compare children of different ages and these are reported elsewhere (Noble, 1970b). However, we wanted to discover which groups of items seemed to the children to go naturally together in the running order. Children associated the traction engine, the tee shirt and the osprey sequences. This cluster most probably represents informational items presented live from the studio. A second cluster was one concerning clowns – namely John as a circus clown and Val making the clown coathanger. Children also perceived very strong similarities between the traction engine photographs. It would appear that children perceive similarities between items in terms of content.

Summary of children's reactions to Blue Peter

By and large the producers' intentions were well perceived by children. Perhaps we should not be too suprised in this respect since these producers have kept an audience of between five and eight million child viewers over a period of several years. It is worth summarising results at this juncture since we still have to compare children's reactions with the predictions of producers of children's television programmes which hopefully will reveal the 'imaginary child audiences' which producers have in mind when they screen their programmes.

First – In natural conditions children recalled 30 per cent of the selected *Blue Peter* programme the day after viewing.

Secondly – in natural conditions children recalled 30 per cent of the steps demonstrated to make the clown coathanger.

Thirdly – children most like those items which show them how to make things and maintain their interest in the programme after viewing and those items which present the human face of occupational roles.

Fourthly – while children found the programme entertaining nevertheless 60 per cent of children said they had learnt something from the programme, especially about the realistic aspects of everyday social roles.

Fifthly – the children perceived the personas as something of an extended kin with whom they felt at ease. John was perceived as an elder brother, Valerie as an aunty and Peter as like a father. Moreover, children saw the personas' roles as interlocking and answers suggested that the personas has created the illusion of intimacy.

Sixthly – as intended by producers, younger children in particular recognised the studio as a safe and familiar place, while older children preferred exciting film sequences mediated by a persona.

Seventhly – while producers expected children to perceive the programme as spontaneous, the children thought the programme too polished to be spontaneous.

Eighthly – children overwhelmingly demanded variety in the way their programmes were filmed. Younger children, though, preferred to see items in the context of the familiar setting and personas, and unlike older children, preferred longer shots to close-ups.

Ninthly – children ordered the items in *Blue Peter* so as to maintain interest throughout the programme. The producers' criteria of assessment, namely excitement, speed and length were appreciated by children, many of whom recorded the programme so that it both started and ended with sequences clearly perceived as safe studio items presented by all three compères.

PRODUCERS' PREDICTIONS OF CHILDREN'S RESPONSES TO BLUE PETER

Three intelligent and sensitive producers communicate bi-weekly with between five and eight million children. John, Peter and Valerie are as well known to the children as are members of their own extended kin, and moreover these personas are elder brothers and aunties which the child viewers share in common. This is the age of mass communications, only television has this unique power to communicate effectively between a small select few to the majority of the nation's children. So who are the communicators who act as gatekeepers to the wider society? And what do they imagine to be the nature of their child audiences? How do children out there impress their needs and desires upon the people who talk to them twice weekly? Is it a salutory fact that audience research is more concerned with who views than with why they view? The communicators are in danger of communicating in a vacuum without adequate feedback as to the effectiveness of their work. They rely merely on the number who switch both on and off to know whether communication has been achieved. As yet the role of the mass communication researcher as a mediator between the audience and the communicator has hardly developed.

I must however thank the *Blue Peter* producers for revealing some of their secrets to me and to the European Broadcasting Union. Whether or not this type of exercise will be repeated is questionable, since sitting in the front row taking copious notes was the novice producer who is now the editor of *Blue Peter*'s main and imitative rival, *Magpie*. Mass communications is a competitive business, although why it should be so is another question. Suffice it to say that the power of being able to talk to so many people at once can be most lucrative.

Bearing in mind Halloran and Elliott's finding that television

G

organisations regarded young children as an audience for entertainment and variety, we wanted as the third stage of this research project, to discover what imaginary audiences television producers had in mind when making programmes for children. Gathered in London for the European Broadcasting Union's workshop exercise were 42 producers of children's programmes from several European countries and from educational networks in America. These producers, the term is used here in its widest sense, were responsible for a whole range of children's programmes including those for adolescents and pre-schoolers in France, Germany, Belgium and Scandinavian countries. They were shown a videotape of the selected *Blue Peter* programme and asked to predict children's reactions on a lengthy questionnaire in either English or French, unaware that children's reactions had already been assessed.

Differences in recall

We thought it would be interesting to discover what producers felt children would recall the day after transmission. They were asked how many of the 15 steps required to make the clown coathanger would be recalled, first by five- and six-year-olds, secondly by seven- and eight-year-olds, and thirdly by nine-, ten- and eleven-year-olds. Producers estimated that five- and six-year-olds would recall an average of 4·6 steps, seven- and eight-year-olds 7·6 steps, and nine- to eleven-year-olds 10·7 steps. These estimates are consistently double the number actually recalled by the children (five to six years, 2·3 seven and eight years 4·4; nine to eleven years 6·3 steps). There would seem to be a tendency for producers to overestimate consistently the capacities of young child viewers, which suggests that they may present too much information in programmes designed for young children, especially for the five- and six-year-old child. Producers seem to have a conception of the young child as a miniature adult, which as we have seen in Chapter 5 is not the case.

Producers' and children's preferences for programme items

Producers' imaginary child audiences are somewhat better able than real audiences to recall television programmes the day after viewing. What though of preference for programme sequences? Producers were asked which sequences in the programme they most liked and these preferences were examined in relation to the children's preferences. Producers and children alike were unanimous that John as a circus clown was the most attractive sequence since it was chosen as most popular by 40 per cent of children and producers alike. However producers (30 per cent), more often than children, liked the osprey sequence (17 per cent), while children (17 per cent) preferred the clown coathanger sequence more often than producers (8 per cent). Producers were somewhat critical of this item, arguing *inter alia* that it was not worthy of the child's labour. This is hardly surprising since producers were not at the time of viewing conversant with the *Blue Peter* tradition in this respect. But mere differences in preference for items tells us little as to how producers as a group make judgements.

We asked both producers and children which sequences they thought were most *visually* effective. Producers and children agreed that John as a circus clown was visually the most exciting. Producers, however, thought the osprey sequence (35 per cent) considerably more visually effective than did children (15 per cent). Conversely children thought both the traction engine and coathanger sequences (40 per cent) considerably more effective than did the producers (10 per cent). It would seem, therefore, that both producers and children most like those items which they consider visually effective and dislike those items which they consider are presented verbally. Producers and children did not though agree as to the visual effectiveness of the items seen in *Blue Peter*. Clearly there is a need for further research to discover why such discrepancies arise and if possible to determine the characteristics of a good visual item for both producers and children alike.

Producers' views on the illusion of intimacy

Producers were asked what sort of image the three personas presented to children. Producers clearly saw John as adventurous and nearly half of them said that John would appear as an older brother to child viewers. Similarly, producers thought Valerie would be seen as mother-like (25 per cent) or as like an elder sister (33 per cent). Peter, however, they did not rate highly; they said he is too aloof and unfriendly and only one-tenth of producers suggested that he would appear as a father figure. Producers were therefore able to predict the way in which children would recognise the personas, namely John as an elder brother, Valerie as something akin to an aunty and Peter somewhat vague. Thus, whether or not children and producers could agree as to a 'good' visual item, producers understood the para-social interaction process which we have argued is television's unique involvement mechanism. It is important to note that producers did see the roles of the personas in terms of extended kin members.

More specifically, producers were asked which persona would be best liked by child viewers of different ages. Once again producers' skill in this type of assessment was evident since they predicted virtually without mistake the preferences of nine- to eleven-year-olds. They said John would be most liked by 65 per cent of these children (he was most liked by 61 per cent); Valerie would be most liked by 28 per cent (she was most liked by 27 per cent of these children) and Peter would be most liked by 11 per cent (he was most liked by 8 per cent of these children). It appears that to be a television producer one must be able to estimate the popularity of the persona virtually without error, which strongly suggests that it is the 'face men' rather more than content, which determine whether or not a television series will work. Moreover, as we have argued, these face men are accepted by the viewers as virtual members of their extended kin.

Once again, though, results indicate that producers did not fully comprehend the reactions of the five- and six-year-old. Half of these children said that Peter was their favourite compère, while the rest preferred Valerie. Producers overwhelmingly predicted that Valerie would prove the most popular persona for five- and six-year-olds because of her maternal image, while one-third of producers thought John would prove most popular with the younger children. If, as we have argued, young children in industrial societies see little of their fathers, it is not perhaps surprising that young children seek out something akin to a surrogate father, a com-père, on television when given the opportunity. Moreover, that it is the extended kin image of the persona which most interests producers was reflected in their comments at the conclusion of the EBU workshop. 'We decided that too many young people are subject to maternal and feminine contact; from mothers at home to women teachers in school, and that television programmes offer an opportunity for a male personality to be seen and *to exert a masculine influence on the child viewer*' (my italics).

However, producers did not perceive the three compères as members of a team playing interlocking roles. It may be recalled that children perceived the three personas in a homogeneous and similar way. Producers, however, thought that John was a significantly better and more active compère than either Valerie or Peter. In this respect producers, perhaps because they were not familiar with the programme, tended to see one persona as dominant, which children did not. As we shall see, this discrepancy in part explains why producers were not often able to predict how the children would react to the various items in the programme. No doubt, however, producers' opinions have changed following the advent of the two-man news presentations in which newsreaders now display complementary roles.

Producers' predictions of children's security needs

Although producers tended to rely on one persona to the exclusion of others, producers were able to predict that young children would prefer studio to film items and vice versa. Three-quarters of the producers thought that a correct balance had been achieved between studio and film items. Producers agreed with the *Blue Peter* producers that the studio items satisfied a child's need for a secure base and that items transmitted live from the studio made for more intimate contact with the child. However, some evidence which places these results in the wider context of the total production process was found. Many producers pointed out that studio items were cheaper to produce than film items and that the 'proper' mode of television production is from the studio, rather than filmed on location. While producers correctly predicted that younger children, more often than older ones, would prefer studio items because of the secure base, many producers stated that children would be unaware of the difference between studio and filmed items, but, as we have seen, this held good only for five- and six-year-olds.

Spontaneity

Although the producers knew that the *Blue Peter* programme they saw was scripted (they were given scripts at the workshop), they said that children would not see the programme as spontaneous. Once again producers were able to understand how children would respond to *Blue Peter*. Similarly, both producers and children agreed that animals were featured prominently in the programme to show children how to care for pets and because children are attracted to animals. Both children and producers agreed that the inclusion of animals in the programme would make children kinder and more sympathetic to animals in real life. That the producers did not perceive the animals as growing up with the programme is hardly surprising since they saw only one programme from a whole series. Children, on the other hand, frequently asked us about the animals they had seen in the past in *Blue Peter*. One six-year-old claimed that he had learnt to keep goldfish from the programme as he said, 'You keep them in bowls and sprinkle pepper on the top.' Once again the *Blue Peter* producers have capitalised on the fact that children and the programme grow up together, much as children and extended kin would have done in the village.

Television production techniques

Children's answers gave some, but not unequivocal, support to the idea that what might be called film or television literacy develops with age. However, even the younger children appear to have more understanding and appreciation of the medium than most people might think. In this respect producers were asked more detailed questions than children and this, as might be expected, resulted in a wide and varied response. Initially producers were asked whether close-up, medium close-up, and long shot had been used in *Blue Peter* to optimal effect. Most of the producers thought close-up techniques had not been used as often as they would like. Indeed one producer went so far as to say, 'Television is close-up because it creates a momentary sense of familiarity with the programme'. Close-up is clearly the portrayal of the talking head, the technique most inclined to create the illusion of intimacy and to give the viewer the impression that the televised persona speaks just to them.

Producers thought that neither long shot nor medium close-up were likely to attract the child's interest, and that these techniques made the programme both difficult to watch and understand. Once again producers' preferences for close-up technique matched the preferences of children aged seven and older. Producers seemed relatively unaware that five- and six-year-olds preferred longer shots because they could see the people and put what they saw in perspective. A few producers expressed sympathy with this point of view but generally speaking they seemed more concerned with detail rather than with people, perspectives or wider settings. Even bearing in mind the fact that many of these producers did not make programmes for the five- and six-year-olds there was, as noted several times before, a lack of understanding of the very young child's response to the small screen.

Ordering of items in the programme

The same method as used with the children was employed to discover how the producers would have ordered the same items in the selected *Blue Peter* programme. It was found that three-quarters of the producers chose the running order which was used in the programme (more often than the children). A second running order (but a very poor second) was to begin with John as the clown, followed in turn by the osprey, the tee shirt, the traction engine and to close with the making of the clown coathanger. Analysis revealed that producers most liked the clown (39 per cent) followed in turn by the osprey (30 per cent), the tee shirt (11 per cent), making the clown coathanger (8 per cent) and least liked the traction engine (7 per cent). The running order selected by the producers was therefore to place the item they most liked first in the running order, the item they liked second best second in the running order and so on.

Examination of the reasons why items were ordered in this way showed that 52 per cent of producers would have started with the most important or definite items. Fifteen per cent of the producers would have started with funny items, while only 11 per cent would have had a quiet easy starter. An item was placed second in the running order because it was funny (16 per cent), interesting (13 per cent) or a logical follow-on from a previous item (13 per cent). An item was placed third in the running order because it was interesting (14 per cent) activated practical work (10 per cent) or achieved a balance between male and female presenters (10 per cent). The fourth position in the running order was where the least interesting item was placed (15 per cent), or because an item was funny (15 per cent) or continued logically from the previous items (15 per cent). The final position in the running order was reserved for funny items (27 per cent) or the dullest items (14 per cent). Producers therefore placed the most interesting material at the beginning of the programme and the least interesting material at the end.

Children and producers did not seem to agree how a balance could be achieved between items in the *Blue Peter* programme. Producers were far less varied than children in their ordering of items. Given the choice, producers (75 per cent), more often than children (60 per cent) chose the running order used in the programme. Children were significantly different from producers in that they did not order items in terms of liking: children seemed to have ordered items for reasons other than those used by producers. Producers clearly ordered items to present the most interesting and striking item first. Children would have both started and ended with more interesting items. Producers would have started the programme with an item previously recorded on film. Children reserved the middle of the programme for such items, which then became a high spot in the programme. Children chose to both start and end with items transmitted live from the studio. These findings again indicate that children wished to start and finish in safe familiar surroundings and to have a climax in the middle.

It would appear that producers placed the most interesting material at the beginning of the programme in order to capture the largest possible audience. Other television producers frequently maintain that they have to 'hook' an audience very early in the programme. The audience, because of 'button apathy' (being too lazy to change stations), will continue to watch the rest of the programme, regardless of content. The results reported above tend to confirm that children's television producers also think about their child audiences in this way. It is worth noting that psychologists, such as Vernon (1953), have reported that audiences best recall the first half of a television programme. Psychologists argue that viewers remember these items merely because they are presented early in the programme – the serial order effect. Our results suggest that audiences may best recall the first half of a programme because this is where many producers deliberately present their most interesting material.

Children, as we have noted, would not have ordered the items in *Blue Peter* in this way. Moreover, it was also found that children perceived similarities between items in terms of content (i.e., all the clown items were associated in their running order). However, producers perceived a very strong association between the traction engine and John in the circus item. Both these items were presented by John and it would seem that producers saw similarities between items in terms of the compère who presented them. Producers also perceived an association between the clown coathanger and osprey items – both presented by Valerie. The tee shirt item, which was presented by all three personas, seemed to be independent of the other items. It appeared therefore that while children perceived similarities between items in terms of content, producers seem to have associated items in terms of personas. Children, it may be remembered, perceived the personas in a homogeneous and similar way, producers did not. These differences may explain why children saw similarities between items in terms of content and the producers in terms of personas. Producers' over-concern with personas seems to have dimmed their awareness of the child's apparent liking for a concrete material link between items.

SUMMARY AND COMMENT

While this research is limited to one particular, yet popular programme, it is apparent that producers and children did not concur in their appraisal of the selected *Blue Peter* programme. While the primary aim of the workshop exercise was to provide 'feedback' about a television programme to television producers, the results also tell us about the way children's television producers perceive programme content. It was suggested in the introduction of this chapter that three factors exerted influence on the producers' conceptions of programme content. These were:

1. The conception that producers have of the needs, interest and capabilities of their target audiences.

2. The personal values of producers.

3. The conformist pressures exerted by the work group or the ethos of the professional television producers on the individual programme-maker.

Target audiences

The research reported above suggests that the target audiences, as perceived by producers, are different from the real-life audience in the following respects:

1. Producers overestimated the capacities of child viewers. Children recalled only half the number of clown coathanger steps estimated by the producers.

2. While producers correctly predicted the older child's need for adventurous items on film, they seemed unaware of the unique needs of the five- and six-year-old viewer. These viewers preferred studio items presented by all three personas, maintained that 'dangerous' items were made outside the studio and recalled fewest of the clown coathanger steps.

3. These results suggest that the producers conceive of the five- and six-year-old child as a miniature adult. As we noted in Chapter 5, the reactions of five- and six-year-olds to television are somewhat unique.

However, producers were accurate in their conceptions of target audiences in the following respects:

4. Producers correctly perceived the roles that the personas presented to the children – those of elder brother, aunty and father.

5. Producers recognised that the children would not see the programme as spontaneous because it was too polished.

6. Producers correctly predicted how children would respond to the animals in the programme – in terms of interest and appreciation of animal welfare.

If correct, these results are surprising since it appears that producers understand what children like but not what they can understand. Psychologists, on the other hand, understand what children can comprehend but not what they will like. Co-operative research would benefit both producers and psychologists.

Conformist pressures exerted by the producers' work group

Sherif and Sherif (1956) have suggested that when small groups of individuals interact, shared attitudes and values become the personal attitudes and values of each individual in that group. While the results presented below could be interpreted in terms of the producers' personal values, I think they are better interpreted in terms of the socialising pressures exerted by his work group.

7. While producers ordered the items in the programme from most to least interesting, children would have ordered items to maintain interest and excitement throughout the programme. Children reserved the first and last positions in the running order for the most

interesting items. Producers, in general, choose their order so that the audience is compelled to start viewing, and then because of apathy will continue to view. It seems likely that television producers are told about 'button apathy' by members of their work group. The fact that many producers ordered items from most to least interesting suggests that this was not a personal decision but a value shared with other television producers. In this instance the socialising pressures of the work group may work against the child's best interests.

8. While both producers and children most liked items which they thought were well presented visually, children and producers did not agree about 'good' visual presentation. Again, the fact that producers to a large extent agreed with one another suggests that producers shared some common criteria for 'good' visual evaluation. Results again suggest that the social pressure of the work group may not give the child more enjoyment.

9. Many producers overestimated the popularity of close-up filming for child viewers – particularly the five- and six-year-olds. It seems likely that producers' values such as 'television is close-up' are indoctrinated either formally during training, or on the job. Once again such values are not necessarily appreciated by child audiences.

10. While producers saw similarities between items in terms of personas, children saw similarities in terms of content. When asked to order items in the programme, all but the five- and six-year-olds, who seemed to order items for reasons which were not readily comprehensible, ordered items so that they followed one another because their content was similar. As we have noted in Chapter 5, after the cognitive revolution the most primitive logic assumes primary importance for the seven- and eight-year-old child, even to the extent that two separate items about clowns were placed one after the other in the running order. Producers, in general, seemed unaware of these tendencies, choosing rather to order sequences in the programme in terms of the persona who presents them. We have noted that children saw the personas as a homogeneous group while producers saw the personas as being very different. It would seem likely that professional television producers lay stress on personalised presentations in programmes for young children. The high level of agreement noted between producers with regard to persona evaluation suggests that these were not personal values but were values shared with the work group. As noted above, such production techniques are not necessarily demanded by the child audience.

While the results above must be treated with caution – they do suggest that content can be understood in terms of producers' intentions. I would suggest content is better appreciated in this way than by counting the number and types of items seen in television programmes. Moreover, co-operation between researcher and producer may help to eliminate some of the discrepancies noted above, but more research is required in order to understand the production process itself – to examine how socialisation exerts influence on the individual producer.

The author is well aware of the limitations of this research. However, the purpose of the study was to investigate the difficult area of the intentions of television producers for which precise methodology can reveal the obvious rather than the interesting.

Finally some criticisms of *Blue Peter*: *Blue Peter* may be said to epitomise the best BBC production traditions. Too much praise may lead to even further stereotyping in television production. While none of the children we talked with thought that the compères 'talked down' to them, other ten-year-old working-class children have voiced this opinion, perhaps because working-class children need an extended family on television less than their more mobile middle-class counterparts. Working-class children described *Blue Peter* as 'wet and sissy'. They said the compères wore 'silly badges' and that the children who have appeared in the programme were 'snobby'. However, it must be pointed out that *Blue Peter* does receive some favourable mail from working-class children. Comments such as these suggest that there is a need for a greater variety of television programme for children. The public's notion of a 'children's hour' in this country implies a certain type of programme – the validity of which can and should be questioned.

CONCLUSION

Taken overall, we may conclude that producers do not fully comprehend the unique televiewing world of the very young child, which we have attempted to describe in Chapter 5. There would appear to be something of a gap between producers and their audiences insofar as mass communications only communicate in one direction. It is left to those viewers with energy enough to write and to small audience research departments to make viewer reaction known to the communicators. Moreover, as we have seen, producers tend to make programmes which will be applauded by their workmates and which conform to the ethos into which they are socialised. In spite of the primitive feedback they receive in terms of audience numbers this ethos may not always work in the best interests of the child viewer. How can the gap be filled, and mass communications made effective two-way processes? It would seem that the mass communicator researcher might be able to help but it should be the responsibility of the production agencies both to fund and conduct research which helps to fill the gap. It could be money well spent.

When researchers gain access into the hallowed halls of the mass communicators, we find the experience most rewarding. We discover *inter alia*, that producers intuitively sense that they can exert a masculine influence on the young child viewer; that they can by careful scripting and photographic techniques provide something akin to the extended family unit where it may be lacking in real life. Producers seem to feel in their bones that theirs is a medium which can compensate for some of the isolation experienced by the individual in industrial societies. They can, in the words of Kenneth Clark, make television an art form and by 'a combination of words and music, colour and movement extend human experience in a way words alone cannot'. Producers know that television uniquely simulates the way 'we talk about things sitting around the room after dinner'. Producers seem aware that by television they can create the mode of communication employed in the pre-industrial village, that 'television should retain the character of the spoken word, with the rhythms of ordinary speech' directed at that far-removed extended kin audience sitting at home and answering back.

10
Conclusions

We began this book by asking the fundamental question, 'Why should television be so popular?' Many answers were rejected before we came to agree with McLuhan that television in part constituted the global village. A theory is of little use unless it has explanatory power, and hopefully we have by now demonstrated that television has those functions previously ascribed to the extended kin group into which children were born. As is the case with most theories they must start from a relatively simple but somewhat obvious position which has been disregarded in the past. But as is also the case the theory must be developed to positions of increasing generality, from less and less particular circumstances to more and more general situations. It is to be hoped that the fundamental starting point remains in mind when criticism is levelled at such concepts as the global village, which out of context appear ridiculous.

A theory stands or falls on the validity of its assumptions. Space does not permit an elaborate recapitulation either of the theory outlined in Chapter 1 or of the conclusions drawn at the close of each chapter. We argued, first and foremost, that the self is defined by the reflections of the 'me' mirrored in the eyes of the stable extended kin group. We suggested that the individual becomes social since the extended kin represents society in microcosm and the roles the child will enact in the future are clearly visible to him. Television, we proposed, serves the same functions as the extended kin, especially in these days of mobility where families have become isolated self-supporting units. We have tried throughout this book to relate research findings to these hypotheses and will now report, by way of a conclusion, on studies designed to test the hypotheses set up in Chapter 1.

We need to show that we come to establish identity via the reflected images of self as seen in the reactions of a stable group of significant other people, and then to show that identity status determines televiewing style. The present study, which was conducted with male adolescents in a boarding school, was designed, first, to see whether identity was related to the mirror images of self reflected by both family and peers and, secondly, to explore in detail the uses made of television by boys differing both in friendship pattern and in the consistency of their identities.

THE ASSESSMENT OF INDIVIDUAL IDENTITY

A technique akin to one described in the delinquency study (Chapter 8) was used to measure identity defined in terms of self-concept. Fifty boys aged between thirteen and fifteen years, from two forms in a boarding school catering for somewhat privileged Irish boys, were asked both to describe aspects of themselves and the way in which they thought others perceived them on a variety of seven-point rating scales. Boys were asked to describe the way in which they thought significant other people saw them (the 'me's) and the way they saw themselves (the integrative I). Each aspect of self was assessed on sixteen scales of the type 'At home with the self – at odds with the self', 'Able to see the funny side of things – unable to see the funny side of things', 'Stable – changeable', 'Wise – foolish', 'In one piece – all broken up', and 'Happy – sad.' Thus, boys were asked to say both for an assessment of self as a social object (As my parents see *me*) or for an integrative 'I' concept (Myself as *I* am now) the degree to which either 'me' or 'I' was seen as happy or sad and stable or changeable. Boys were asked to put a tick, for example, under either very happy indeed, very happy, happy, neither happy nor sad, sad, very sad or very sad indeed for each aspect of self on each of the sixteen scales.

In order to assess how boys thought the significant others in their environment saw them, they were asked to complete the rating scale, first for adults – namely, 'As my parents see *me*', and 'As my teachers see *me*'; and, secondly, for peer evaluations – namely, 'As my class see *me*', 'As popular boys see *me*', and 'As others see *me*'. In addition, for each boy we attempted to assess the ideal social 'me', namely, 'As I would like others to see *me*'. The same method was used to assess aspects of the self as subject rather than object, the 'I' rather than the 'me'. Boys were asked to evaluate, first, the current 'I', namely 'Myself as *I* am now', secondly, the ideal 'I', namely, 'the real self inside me' and 'As *I* would like to be' and, thirdly, some historical aspects of self, namely 'The way *I* was reared at home', 'As *I* used to be in the past' and 'How *I* developed in the past'.

For each boy, therefore, we were able to see how the way he thought he was seen by teachers, parents and classmates actually corresponded to the way he saw himself. Moreover, we were able to see whether he thought he was seen as a different boy by his parents on his home 'stage' to the sort of boy as seen by his class on the school 'stage'. More academic readers will possibly recognise the influence of William James and Cooley in the thinking which underpins this methodology. Since the same scales were used throughout, it was comparatively easy to translate their somewhat nebulous concepts concerning the variety of social selves evident in any one person into numerical terms. In order to assess the degree of integration of the self-concept or identity, scores were calculated for each boy which described the degree of correspondence between the 'I' and 'me' concepts. Specifically, each boy's evaluation of 'Myself as *I* am now' was compared with his evaluation of how parents see me, how teachers see me, how the class sees me, how popular boys see me, and how others see me. Likewise, each boy's evaluation of ideal social me, 'As I would like others to see *me*', was compared with his evaluation of how parents, teachers, class, popular boys and others see me. Finally each boy's assessment of current integrative self, 'Myself as *I* am now', was compared with both ideal self – namely 'As I would like to be', the real self inside me and with historical aspects of the self – how I developed in the past, the way I was reared at home and 'As I used to be in the past'.

For each boy, therefore, it was possible to measure the integration of his identity, or put into numerical terms, a score describing the degree to which the way he thought he was seen by significant others actually corresponded to the way he saw himself.

THE ASSESSMENT OF SOCIAL ANCHORAGE

We can predict from the theory outlined in Chapter 1 that boys embedded within a stable group of mutual friends within the fixed community of the boarding school will have more stable identities than boys isolated by their classmates. While we may expect a boy's identity also to be shaped by home background, adolescents undergoing an identity crisis must to a fair degree be dependent on their peers for mirror reflections of self by which to establish identity. We therefore asked boys in each class to tell us the names of their best friends, boys they respected, boys they did not respect, boys they would take home, boys they would tell their problems to, boys they would take on holiday, boys they would choose as room-mates, boys that they would follow and boys who were the leaders of the class. From the answers given we were able to draw sociograms which described the friendship patterns in each class of boys.

THE DEVELOPMENT OF THE ADOLESCENT
IDENTITY CRISIS

As part of a larger study (Noble and Murphy, 1974) these data were collected from boys aged thirteen, fourteen, fifteen and sixteen years. It was found that identity was most integrated at thirteen years (average score of 80 – since scores ranged from 25 to 175 this represents an integration score of 47 per cent),* had become dramati-

* Calculated as $\dfrac{100-80}{150}\%$

cally less well integrated at fourteen years (average score of 107 – an integration score of 30 per cent), stayed at this level during the, fifteenth year (average score of 106 – an integration score of 30 per cent), and, most interestingly, became considerably more integrated during the sixteenth year as boys prepared to leave school (an average score of 90 – an integration score of 40 per cent). However, statistical analysis revealed that while age was an important determinant of the integration of a boy's identity, the number of reciprocal friendships in the class was a stronger and more reliable predictor. This latter finding lends considerable support to the assumption which under-pins this book, that identity is harnessed to the number of stable reflections of self available in the environment.

HOW MANY AND WHAT TYPE OF MIRROR REFLECTIONS ARE NECESSARY FOR A CONSISTENT IDENTITY?

If we take the degree to which each boy is accepted and respected by other boys in the class as indicating the number of mirrors available to him, or put another way, the degree of social anchorage, we can discover how idividual indentity is related to the social context in which a boy finds himself.

When various scores representing the integration of individual identity were correlated with the number of times a boy was chosen as someone that members of the class would choose to live with, the strongest and most significant relationship was with the integration score representing 'Myself as I am now' in relation to the way he thought he was seen by others ($r = +0.428$, $n = 26$).*

The next most significant and strong correlation was with the integration score representing the way the boy would like to be seen again in relation to the way he thought he was seen by others ($r = +0.392$). These findings mean that boys who are embedded in their peer groups see themselves in the same way that they think significant other adults and peers see them and vice-versa, that boys isolated from their peer groups do not see themselves in the same way as they think they are seen by others. Moreover, social anchorage could not be predicted merely from the integration score representing myself as I am now in relation to the way they thought only their peers, namely popular boys and other boys in the class, saw them ($r = +0.30$), nor from the way they thought only parents and teachers saw them ($r = +0.23$). These results bear out what was argued in Chapter 1, namely that it is in the balance of mirrored images coming back from a variety of people representing the wider

* All correlations are positive (+), indicating that boys with integrated identities have the largest number of friends and vice-versa.

society that individual identity is established, since social anchorage can only be predicted from an amalgam of the way boys think parents, teachers, and boys in the class see the 'me'.

The importance of the above findings can be judged relative to the strength of the co-relationships between social anchorage and the integration of identity representing 'Myself as I am now' in comparison with either historical or ideal aspects of identity. It was impossible to predict which boys would establish mutual friendships in the boarding school from the integration of identity score representing 'Myself as I am now' in relation to the way he thought he was reared at home and the way he thought he had developed in the past ($r = +0.28$), nor in comparison to the real self inside him and 'As he would like to be' ($r = +0.33$), nor from an amalgam of these measures ($r = +0.34$). It is of considerable interest to note that social anchorage is determined more by the way other people see the 'me' – the object, than by either historical or 'ideal' measures of identity – the subject. These results bear out much of what was said about the importance of mirror processes, rather than history or future, in the establishment of an identity for all occasions.

Identity integration and social anchorage

Detailed analysis of the sociograms revealed that each boy fell into one of three distinct categories: first, boys who were isolated in the class, namely, boys whom nobody chose to live with, whom nobody chose as a best friend, whom boys least respected and were least likely to follow; secondly, boys who were embedded in a net of reciprocal friendship, namely, boys who chose one another as best friends, boys whom they would confide in, but who were not the leaders of the class; and thirdly, boys who were the popular leaders, namely, those that the boys would follow but, importantly, would not choose to live with, confide in nor to take on holiday. According to the theory outlined in Chapter 1, boys embedded in a network of reciprocal friendship should have the most integrated self-concepts since they receive accurate reflections of self from their friends, who cannot be flatterers too. This in fact was the case, these boys did see themselves (the I) as they thought they were seen by others (the social 'me's as seen by parents, teachers, friends, class and popular boys). The mean integration score for those fifteen boys from the two forms who were embedded in a group of friends was 67; representing an integration score of 55 per cent.

As predicted, boys who were isolated from their peers, those whom nobody chose to live with, showed far less integration of identity. Their mean score was 85, representing an integration score of 43 per cent. Finally we must describe the integration of the identities of the boys who were popular leaders, who nevertheless were not chosen as best friends or room-mates. These boys' average integration score was 124, nearly double that of the boys integrated within a peer group, representing an integration score of 17 per cent. What is interesting about these popular leaders is that they choose to see themselves as the opposite of the way they think they are seen by significant others. In other words, these are boys who rebel against the image which parents, teachers and other boys in the class project upon them. Just as the boys embedded in the peer group accept the image of themselves as seen by others and make it their own, so these boys are equally aware of the image of themselves as seen by others but choose to reject this image by making themselves the opposite. In other studies this has been called negative identification, or use of a reference group in a negative sense. It must be stressed that both rebels and boys integrated within the peer group use the image of self as mirrored by significant others as a point of reference, but in different ways. The unpopular boy, isolated from his class, seems comparatively unaware of the way he is mirrored by others and is thus unsure about his identity since he is not able to see himself from varied and stable points of reference. Boys with integrated identities from now on will be called conformists, boys with identities which oppose the demands of significant others will be called rebels, and boys with identities which are not related either positively or negatively to the way they are seen by others will be called problem boys.

Rebel, conformist and problem boys' use of mirrors

As might be expected rebels, conformists and problem boys not only vary in the consistency of their identities but their current identity stands in differing relationship to both historical aspects of the self and to the reflection of the self as seen by significant others. Predictably 'rebels' say that 'Myself as I am now' is the reverse of the way I was reared at home while conformists see 'Myself as I am now' as very like the way they were reared at home. Both these groups of boys have used their families as mirrors to reflect and define the self, but while rebels reject their past rearing, conformists accept it. The current self of problem boys, though, bears no meaningful relationship to past selves at home which suggests that they have been unable to use their families as mirrors – these are boys who have experienced breaks in mirror reflection – hence their descriptive term 'problem'. Likewise rebels are aware that their current identity is unlike their ideal or real self, conformists see their current identities as like both real and ideal self, while the current identity of problem boys bears little meaningful relationship to either real or ideal self.

Similarly, when we examine 'Myself as I am now' in relation to the way boys think they are seen by significant others, we find rebels reject the definition of self projected upon them by parents and teachers and even more strongly reject the image of self projected on them by other members of the class. Rebels are clearly able to use mirror processes in the establishment of an identity but they immensely dislike other people's definitions of themselves. We can begin to see why rebels are chosen as leaders but not as roommates; since they 'look down' on their classmates, they are not the sort of boys to whom one tells one's problems. We should, however, note that even rebels seem to outgrow this phase during their sixteenth year. Conformists, as their name implies, accept the social 'me's they see reflected by parents, teachers and by boys in the class. These are adolescents who do not have to exaggerate their acts in a bid for leadership, and are therefore easier to live with and to whom boys can tell their problems without fear of immediate ridicule. The current self-concept of problem boys is not related either positively or negatively to the way parents, teachers or the class see them. These are boys who seem unable to use relationship to mirror the self and consequently they are isolated and as we shall see, unhappy and lonely.

The picture drawn here of the three types of boy will cast light on their respective televiewing styles. When we looked at the way boys said they would like to be seen by others, their ideal social identity, rebels as expected perversely chose an ideal social identity which was the exact opposite of the way they thought they were seen by parents and teachers. Many, but not all the rebels, chose an ideal social identity which corresponded to the way they were seen by class members and which was the antithesis of the values encouraged in this Franciscan school. The ideal social identity of conformists on the other hand corresponded to the way they thought they were seen by parents and teachers rather than to the way they thought they were seen by classmates. Rebels conform to peer group standards while conformists conform to parental standards. Needless to say, problem boys were unable to match their ideal social selves with the way they thought they were seen by parents or teachers nor by classmates. Nor, perhaps more worryingly, did problem boys' identities show signs of increasing integration at sixteen years when other boys seemed to outgrow the adolescent identity crisis.

TELEVIEWING STYLE, SOCIAL ANCHORAGE
AND IDENTITY

Proverbs, it is said, bear age and, 'He who would do well may view himself in them as in a looking-glass'. I hope that the research reported so far does vindicate the axiom of self as mirror which underpins this book. We must now attempt to demonstrate that television can help to alleviate adolescent identity problems. Viewed in terms of indentity and the ease with which boys can live with themselves, we may expect that both rebels and problem boys will more closely attend to television in order to alleviate identity strain than conformists who should exhibit a quite distinct televiewing style. Questionnaires designed to elicit the uses to which various programme types were put were completed by the fifty boys we have described above.

Viewing times

Boys were asked to list those programmes seen each day in the week before they completed the questionnaire. Each class of boys had its own colour television set in a special television room, and could receive programmes transmitted by the BBC, by Harlech and Ulster commercial television and RTE (the Irish State controlled channel financed in part by commercial advertising). Contrary to the much voiced notion that rebels escape by watching long hours of television, rebels in fact watched the least number of programmes (an average of 9·25) while both conformists and problems each watched an average of 11 programmes. Rebel adolescents have many interests outside the school perimeter and many interests apart from television.

Favourite programmes

Each boy was asked to rank order in terms of popularity each of the programmes he had seen in the previous week, since it was thought that the boys with differing types of identity would not watch vastly different amounts of television but would attend to different types of programme. Certain programmes were almost obligatory viewing regardless of identity and social anchorage. Football programmes were most frequently viewed by boys in all three groups (an average of slightly more than two programmes) and were ranked by problem boys as their favourite and by conformists and rebels as their second favourite. Likewise two exciting series programmes, such as *Cannon*, were viewed and were ranked by rebels and conformists as favourite and by problem boys as second favourite. Less popular, but equally obligatory, were popular music programmes watched by three out of four boys regardless of identity group and respectively ranked fifth, sixth and seventh by rebels, problems and conformists. Amongst boys who live together these three programme types provide a common talking point.

More interesting in relation to identity strain were boys' preferences for family serials, compère programmes, westerns and films. We have argued that family serials uniquely afford boys with a chance to interact with an alternative family or community. As might be expected, rebels despised even the alternative communities seen in the family serials. They watched them least of all (0·6) and ranked them as eighth favourite. Conformist boys watched them more often (0·9) and ranked them as sixth favourite while problem boys not only watched them twice as often (1·6) but ranked them as third favourite. As predicted in Chapter 1, the need for continuity in televiewing and sustained interaction with a regularly appearing group of people is paramount amongst boys who are isolated in school and whose identity has suffered from breaks in mirror reflection in the past. Likewise boys' need for pseudo-social interaction with personas was greatest amongst lonely problem boys who not only most often watched compère programmes (0·8) but also ranked them most favourably (seventh) – compared to rebels (0·2), ninth favourite and conformists (0·6), eighth favourite. Similarly the comparative immaturity of problem boys was reflected in their marked preference for children's programmes (0·9) and ranked fifth favourite compared to rebels and conformists (both watched 0·3 and ranked tenth favourite).

We have seen how problem boys alleviate identity strain in their televiewing preferences. Rebels have also to cope with an identity which is not socially approved and which we may reasonably expect them to lose when televiewing exciting series rather than family serials and children's programmes. Rebels not only watched more films (1·6) and westerns (1·0) in a typical week than either conformists (1·3 and 0·3) or problem boys (1·0 and 0·6);* they also rated both films and westerns more favourably (third and fourth) than conformists (fifth and eleventh) or problem boys (fourth and eighth). Boys who experience identity strain attend to both westerns and films, but these two programme types, which allow for vicarious identification, are most preferred by rebel boys who have a mirror image of self to reject. While problem boys also attend to these programme types, their identity strain is alleviated by para-social interaction with recognised people and characters – after all they

---

* Small differences in one week's viewing are considerable if multiplied by 52 to give a yearly quota, i.e. for westerns – rebels 52, conformists 16 and problems 32.

have no mirror image of self to either reject or accept. We thus have the curvilinear pattern of involvement described in Chapter 4 on escape.

Finally, we are able to comment on the televiewing style of conformists who embody the best Schramm *et al.* tradition of acceptance of school norms. Compared with the other groups, these boys watch and prefer news and documentary programme types, as well as, more interestingly, comedy. Conformists watch nearly twice as many news type programmes (1·1) as rebels (0·6) or problem boys (0·3) and rate them third favourite compared with rebels seventh and problem boys tenth preference. Comedy programmes, seen by these boys as primarily vehicles for showing the funny side of everyday relationships, are most popular with conformist boys (1·1 and fourth favourite) who, as we have seen, can cope with both parents, teachers and classmates. Rebels can cope with comedy to a degree (0·2 and sixth favourite) while problem boys can hardly laugh at all (0·2 and ninth favourite) at the sorts of relationships they have not been able to cope with in the past. Television, therefore, by its variety of content manages to satisfy the needs of each of these three types of boy. Boys unable to define who they are, whose self-image bears little meaningful relation to past selves in a family context are unable to project themselves in the future and do not mix well at school. These boys, the problems, seek out those programmes which allow for interaction with regularly appearing television personas and characters. Deprived of adequate family relationships in the past they attend closely to family serials on television not only to reduce alienation and isolation but also, as I hope we shall demonstrate, in order to learn how to cope with future relationships. Rebellious boys who reject those images of self they see projected by others and who also experience some identity strain seek out exciting programmes, which as we shall see, help them temporarily to lose their identities. Conformist boys, and this label is literal rather than derogatory, seek out news and documentary programmes – all too easily called reality materials – programmes, though, which broaden their horizons, and comedy programmes which show the funny side of everyday relationships. But we should not forget that we are describing a male middle-class adolescent sample; we would find similar types of identity stress in working-class and female samples and I am tolerably confident that television would satisfy the same needs but the types of programme viewed and ranked as favourite would differ. Finally we should note that in the boarding-school situation certain programme types were virtually obligatory viewing amongst boys regardless of identity strain; these programmes at least provide common ground amongst disparate individuals.

USES FOUND FOR DIFFERENT PROGRAMME TYPES

As we have seen in Chapter 4, programmes labelled as escapist, for example, are often put to uses not implied by that label. Throughout this book we have questioned the somewhat arbitrary way in which researchers have classified programme types and then assumed that their classification is correct. In the present study therefore we attempted to discover those television programmes boys watched which made them laugh, showed real life, annoyed them, taught them new things, made them frightened, told them about Ireland, made them happy, showed people in other countries, were watched to talk about with friends and showed them what they might do in the future. Boys were asked to list programme titles under each question and then to rank order all the programmes mentioned from most to least favourite. Viewed this way we were able to discover which of the functions listed above were best satisfied by different programme types. Some of the answers were obvious as, for example, comedy, which boys only watched to make them laugh and to make them happy. Other answers, however, revealed a variety of functions for programmes that one would not necessarily assume were used in those ways. Thus, if you asked which programme types most frequently tell you about Ireland, family serials were more frequently mentioned than news programmes, respectively 50 and 45 per cent. Likewise family serials (35 per cent) more often told boys about real life than the news (30 per cent), while even exciting series programmes were said by 17 per cent of boys to tell them about real life. These results lend support to the assertion in Chapter 1 that fictional television programmes do help to define life styles.

So far we have analysed functions by programme types. We can also analyse programme types by function by extracting every mention of a programme type and examining the number of functions it is said to satisfy. Several programme types had very specific functions. Films were used only to induce fear (68 per cent), which bears out what was said in Chapter 1 about the cinema, and to talk about with friends (32 per cent). Football was used mainly to talk about with friends (69 per cent) but was also used by these adolescents to show them what they might do in the future (31 per cent). Other programme types, however, had a great variety of functions. Boys found the greatest number of uses for the news, which in order of function were to show other countries (25 per cent), Ireland and new things (each 19 per cent), real life (15 per cent) but equally was annoying (15 per cent) and finally showed boys what they might do in the future (7 per cent). This method of analysis also highlights the similarities and differences between exciting series programmes and family serials. Family serials predominantly showed real life (31 per cent), but in Ireland (39 per cent), yet did not show boys what they might do in the future (11 per cent) and were found annoying (8 per cent). Series programmes also showed real life (21 per cent), but in other countries (21 per cent), yet managed to show boys what they might do in the future (21 per cent) and were talked about with friends (21 per cent).

Function of rebel, conformist and problem boys' favourite television programmes

We are now in a better position to understand why boys with differing identities showed comparatively distinct patterns of programme preferences. When boys were asked to rank the programmes they view for the above uses in order of preference, only conformist boys preferred programmes which made them happy (rank 2) to programmes which made them laugh (rank 5). Both rebels and problem boys more favourably ranked programmes which made them laugh (ranks 3 and 2 respectively) rather than programmes which made them happy (ranked 10 and 9 respectively). It would seem that only boys with intact identities can use televised comedy to make them happy, while boys suffering from identity strain alleviate the tension experienced by laughing at children's, cartoon and comedy programmes alike. Likewise we see the same difference between boys in the marked preference of conformist boys for programmes which frighten them (rank 1), which are ranked fourth by rebels and sixth by problems. Not only do these results strongly contradict the oft cited Rileys, they suggest that stable boys with intact identities most enjoy being scared a little by television while boys with least stable identitites are least able to cope with fear whether induced by television or not.

We have consistently argued that television does help to define real life and provides models for social learning which will be enacted in the future. All boys ranked those programmes which show them what they might do in the future very highly – it was the third most popular use which boys found for programmes cited under this list of uses – which suggests that television does show boys how to behave in the future. Which boys, though, most need to watch such programmes? Rebels, unlike conformists and problems, know what they don't want to be like in the future but have no clear idea as to future identity yet remain discontent with the present. Rebels (rank 2) use programmes which help to define themselves in future roles more often than either conformists or problem boys (each rank 4).

However, the fact remains that the most frequent use to which favourite programmes were put was to talk about them with friends.

Here again, we find clear-cut evidence that this function too is determined by identity. Both groups of boys who experience identity strain, problem boys and rebels, rank such programmes as first favourite in the list of uses, while conformist boys rank them third favourite. It is almost as though boys with identity strain, who are unsure how to present themselves to others, need a handy starting-point for conversations, and as argued in Chapter 1, common ground is provided by television programmes they know they will have both viewed. Conformist boys with stable identities need such common ground less than the others since they accept the projected definitions of self they see reflected by the others to whom they talk.

The way television provides common ground for talking between different people

The argument, so central to Chapter 1, that television provides common ground for discussion amongst disparate individuals clearly needs to be numerically described and tested. Television, by its variety of content, affords nearly all boys, regardless of self-image, with opportunities for discussion with both parents and friends alike. Each boy answered specific questions asking what programmes do you watch to talk about with friends and then to talk about with parents. Peer group needs were met by watching exciting series programmes (36 per cent), followed in turn by films (28 per cent), football (19 per cent) and popular music programmes (11 per cent). These programme types, moreover, are those which constitute obligatory viewing and for which there are few differences in preference between different types of boy, indicating the conformity pressures at work in a boarding school community. Quite different programme types, and a greater variety, were watched to talk about with their parents when at home. News programmes headed the list (30 per cent), followed in turn by comedy (19 per cent), and to a lesser degree films (11 per cent), exciting series (11 per cent), family serials (7 per cent), and persona shows (7 per cent). While there were no differences between boys in the average number of programmes (1·2) viewed to talk about with parents, only conformist boys' favourite programmes are those they talk about with their parents. Sixty per cent of rebels watched the news, which we know they dislike, to talk about with their parents. One can begin to see why they are rebels – since parental pressures seem to be orientated towards 'reality' materials on television with an eye to the boys' self-betterment. Among the conformist and problem boys comedy (30 per cent) was most frequently used for this purpose – one suspects for problem boys as a safety valve of laughter sparked by difficult relationships and for conformists and their parents in order to feel happy.

We can make the above statements with some confidence, since when boys were asked how often they talked to their family when at home about television programmes and given four choices – every day, every other day, once a week and hardly ever, results fell into a familiar pattern. Only one-third of boys suffering from identity strain, rebels and problem boys, talked to their families daily or every other day compared to three-quarters (73 per cent) of boys who accepted the parents' reflection of their self-image. No less than a half of rebels replied hardly ever; these are of course boys who have found an identity which resists parental reflection; while half the problem boys, whose identity is torn between different social stages, said they talked to their families about television only once a week. Perhaps these boys are problems because they are unable completely to reject or accept the social definition of self which is differently reflected by actors on different social stages with whom problem boys try to maintain contact.

THE SOCIAL LEARNING PROVIDED BY EVERYDAY TELEVISION PROGRAMMES

We proposed in Chapter 1 that television's important function is to show viewers how to behave in a variety of different situations. In other words television provides very necessary social learning in industrial societies where not all the social roles to be occupied in the future are clearly visible in the real-life family group. This is particularly true of boys in single-sex boarding schools in Eire who are not only deprived of the opportunity to interact with the opposite sex, but also fail to see parental models during adolescence and are presented rather with models of monastic excellence. We may expect, therefore, that these boys in particular will use television to instruct them about future social behaviour, especially relational acts. Boys were therefore asked which television programmes showed the following relations between: happy families, happy married couples, happy parents and children, people helping one another, and young people in love. Since we have also suggested that television can show boys what they have to do to be visibly teenagers, boys were also asked which programmes showed the following types of non-relational but self-image models: teenagers, popular boys, boys like the self and, lastly, successful young men which it was hoped would tap likely future behaviour. As with other questions of this type, boys were asked to list programmes which showed each of the above categories and then to rank the programmes listed in order of viewing preference.

Seen in the above way it becomes clear that many of the programme categorisations employed in the past by media researchers neglect important areas of content. For example, when we asked which programmes showed people helping each other, war and westerns (27 per cent) were mentioned most frequently and as often as family serials (27 per cent), and more often than news, comedy, religious and children's programmes (each 12 per cent). Likewise westerns (25 per cent) showed happy families. It is clear that those programmes which are most frequently castigated for showing nothing but commercial brutality in fact are the most salient source of models of co-operative behaviour which is presumably imitated.

We can also analyse these data to see which relationships and self-image models are seen in particular programme types by extracting every mention of comedy, for example, and counting the social behaviour types portrayed. Comedy is most frequently listed as showing happy marriages (42 per cent), followed in turn by happy families (25 per cent), happy parents and children (11 per cent) and of the non-relational self-image categories – teenagers (11 per cent) and popular boys (11 per cent). Comedy clearly shows relationships rather than self-image identification models. Similarly family serials exclusively portray relationships; they show people in love (38 per cent), happy families (24 per cent), helping (14 per cent)* and parents and children (10 per cent). Popular music programmes manage to combine portrayal of both relationships and self-image models. First and foremost, they show teenagers (40 per cent) and popular boys (25 per cent), but at the same time they also manage to show happy families (25 per cent) and parents and children (10 per cent). On the other hand, both football and exciting series programmes, in the view of these boys, show no relationships since football shows only successful young men (57 per cent) and popular boys (43 per cent) and does not show people helping each other (0 per cent), while exciting series show only successful young men (63 per cent) and boys like the self (37 per cent).

The social learning provided by everyday television programmes for boys with differing identities

We can now see that each boy's favourite programme types, football and exciting series, can be classified as showing boys like himself and successful young men. In other words, adolescent boys' favourite

* Percentages vary since 27 per cent of programmes listed as showing helping were family serials, whereas when the relations and self-image categories were counted for family serials alone, helping was only 14 per cent of total answers describing the relations shown in family serials.

programmes help them to define themselves both in the present and in the possible future. Popular music programmes – obligatory viewing – show teenagers and help the adolescent define his self-image as a member of the wider society. Here too we can see the relationship with identity strain since popular music programmes were rated fifth favourite by rebels, who are searching for an identity which opposes the demands of significant others, were rated sixth favourite by problem boys, who are merely searching for an identity, and were rated seventh favourite by conformists whose identities are embedded within the community but who nevertheless need to find a place in the wider society.

Central to the argument proposed in this book is that problem boys, who suffer from breaks in mirror reflection, would more closely attend to family serials in order to learn how to cope with those everyday relationships which they are unable to manage currently. We have noted that these boys most favourably evaluate family serials, which in fact show and instruct these boys in the yet to be acquired relational arts of marriage, parenthood, helping others and falling in love. Rebel boys, who equally suffer from identity strain, preferred films and westerns most. These programmes also show happy marriages, people in love, happy families, helping and happy parents and children, which suggests that rebels are only slightly less worried about the future than problem boys. Rebels' television diet offers them the same view of future relationships but from a different perspective. Conformist boys showed a marked preference for comedy and for news. News did not feature in answers to the questions concerning relationships but comedy most certainly did. Comedy no less than family serials and no more than films and westerns shows family, married, and parent–child relationships. The differing programme preferences of the three types of boy all show how to enter relationships in the future, although the instruction comes from different sources.

The importance of the social learning afforded by the media for boys with differing identities

When we examined the rank order into which the programmes listed as showing either relational or self-image models were placed, we find the usual differences between samples. Amongst problem boys, programmes which showed 'boys like themselves' were ranked as first favourite while both conformists and rebels ranked them ninth. Boys who do not receive a consistent mirror image of self from the people they live with would seem to have to attend to television in order to see boys like themselves in action. As we have noted before, both conformists and rebels do receive mirror images of self from the people they live with and they have no need to see boys like themselves in action on the television screen.

Not only are problem boys worried about their self-image they also seem worried about basic relationships. After boys like the self, problem boys most preferred to see successful relations especially in marriage and families. Rebels most preferred programmes that showed them teenagers, followed in turn by love (which was interpreted on this questionnaire as sex), and successful young men. Conformists most preferred to see successful young men, popular boys with teenagers and marriage equal third. Thus, while rebels showed a distinct preference for teenagers, conformist boys showed a preference for successful young men. We may interpret these results to suggest that problem boys prefer television programmes which help to clarify their self-image and instruct them in future relationships; rebels most prefer those programmes which help them define a teenage identity which cocks a snook at those adults who wish to impose an identity upon them and conformists seek out those television programmes which instruct them in the art of future success.

CONTINUITY IN TELEVIEWING

We have suggested that television is remarkably repetitive in that it affords viewers with an opportunity to interact with a regularly appearing group of people who come to form something of an extended kin especially for the isolated viewer at home. To a degree we have already seen that it is the problem boy who most seems to need continuous contact with a family on the television screen. In Chapter 3 we proposed that viewers who recognised television characters most frequently predicted how they would behave. Boys were therefore asked not only how well they could predict what would happen in various types of programme but also how disappointed they were if they had to miss a programme in a series and in a serial.

Well, how repetitive are television programmes? If we take the multi-functional news as a baseline we find that 2 per cent of boys say they are very good at predicting what will happen, 23 per cent are good, 34 per cent are not so good and 40 per cent say they are poor. It is worth noting that a quarter of the boys can predict even the news well. In order of ascent boys can next best predict (good and very good) classic serials (47 per cent), family serials (49 per cent), films in the cinema (52 per cent), films on television (73 per cent) and are best of all at predicting detective series – no less than 90 per cent. Once again this method of analysis, first, reveals that over half the viewers of these programme types know what is going to happen and, secondly, provide yet another way by which to classify television programmes. As argued in Chapter 1, films lose considerable impact in the sense that they keep you guessing, when relegated from the cinema to the small screen.

Moreover, boys responded in like manner both to detective series programmes and to films on television. A different pattern of answers emerged for the serial programmes in which most importantly the characterisations remain constant, in continuous interaction and where the theme is ongoing across episodes. These are programmes which provide a regularly appearing *group* of people akin to the village community described in Chapter 1. Films and series programmes, though, are self-contained episodes broken only by the advertisements in which either one or a small core of people appear regularly and who constantly present themselves on different social stages – akin to the urban man described in Chapter 1, with the exception that the boys always know the detective will succeed.

It appears that television is predictable, one might think to the point of nausea, but again we find that a very large proportion of boys are disappointed to miss episodes in either serials or series programmes. A quarter of boys (23 per cent) are very disappointed to miss an episode in an exciting series, a third are disappointed (38 per cent), a quarter are a little disappointed (26 per cent) and only 13 per cent are not concerned to miss them. Nine out of ten boys, it appears, want to watch a character regularly. The figures are no less impressive for family serials. A quarter of boys are very disappointed, a fifth (22 per cent) disappointed, nearly a third a little disappointed (28 per cent) and only a quarter (26 per cent) are not concerned to miss a programme. While we should not forget that boys can catch up on a missed episode in a serial by watching the next episode, which is clearly not possible for series programmes, three-quarters of the boys like to see the same characters interact regularly and develop over time. These figures, it is hoped, bear out the arguments of Chapters 1 and 3, and show that there is almost something of a compulsion in the way we view television's prime output.

Identity status and need for continuity in televiewing

We have argued in Chapter 1 that compulsive televiewing can help to alleviate identity conflicts. Boys who suffer from identity strain were much more disappointed to miss both series and serial programmes than boys with identities which embody the definition of self projected by others. No less than 82 per cent of rebels were either disappointed or very disappointed to miss a series programme portraying urban man, and nearly half of them (47 per cent) were similarly disappointed to miss an episode in a family serial. Problem boys were expected to be most disappointed to miss the regularly appearing community of characters in family serials because they are deprived of an extended kin in real life. These boys were indeed most disappointed (56 per cent) to miss an episode in a family serial and only marginally more disappointed to miss a series programme (60 per cent). Conformist boys, on the other hand, showed least disappointment – 40 per cent were disappointed to miss a series programme and only one-third disappointed to miss an episode from a family serial. Identity strain, therefore, seems to result in somewhat compulsive viewing where rebels seek out urban man successfully presenting self on a variety of stages, and problem boys with unclear identities seek out substitute social anchorage in the form of a regularly appearing community of characters with whom to interact; characters, moreover, that become as well known to them as distant relatives.

Nearly half the problem boys, who cannot predict how they should be seen by significant others, nevertheless say they are very good at predicting what will happen in family serials. Moreover, problem boys said they were twice as good at predicting what would happen in family and classic serials as in exciting series and films on television (48 and 23 per cent very good). Rebels, on the other hand, could predict films and series programmes better than serials (45 and 39 per cent very good). Conformists predicted serials (59 per cent) considerably better than films and series (36 per cent). Boys whose identities embody the definition of self projected by others are therefore best at predicting how the same characters will interact over time yet show little compulsion in their viewing. While they watch serials compulsively, problem boys with unclear identities are still learning how the community characters they know well will interact over time. These boys seem relatively unable to understand relationships in real life, and of course their hazy identities embody this fact. Rebels, who reject others' definitions of their identities dislike a realistic community of characters and are least inclined to predict how they will act, and yet perversely watch them with something bordering on compulsion. There is no doubt, though, that while the outcome of both series and films is fully known to rebels while viewing, they recognise urban man when they see him and watch his presentation of self on different social stages so intently that they hate to miss even a single episode.

RECOGNITION AND IDENTIFICATION

According to the theory outlined in Chapters 1 and 3, viewers who best predict outcome are those who recognise, that is, feel they know characters. We have seen above how prediction varies not only with the type of boy but also with the type of programme. Rebels have shown the same programme preferences as were found for delinquents in Chapter 8, that is, a distinct preference for the television hero who constantly presents himself in new and untried situations. Is this preference sustained because boys put themselves into exciting heroes' shoes, or is it rather that boys watch the hero like hawks and respond to him?

We first asked boys which television characters are like people you know in real life? Three-quarters of the boys listed at least one television character similar to someone known in real life, but characters from family serials so dominated the answers that this question only taps a limited area of the recognition process. Boys saw similarities between the characters in family serials and people both at home and in school. Nevertheless there were some interesting differences in the extent of recognition amongst different types of boy. All the conformist boys recognised characters and on average they recognised at least two television characters from the same programme as like people known to them in life. If, as we have argued in Chapter 4, boys suffering from breaks in mirror relationships use recognised television characters in order to practise interaction skills, we should expect problem boys next to recognise most frequently. This was the case since three-quarters of these boys did recognise an average of nearly two characters from the same programme (1·8). Least recognition was apparent amongst rebels, only half of whom recognised an average of one character (0·9).

It is quite normal, therefore, for boys with integrated identities to recognise television characters and, moreover, to recognise at least two such characters and watch them interact. Amongst problem boys, where adequate mirror reflections of self are lacking, we see that they recognise in the same way as conformist, rather than rebel boys. The televiewing style of the alienated and deprived boy shows signs that he seeks to redeem his identity by recognising at least two interacting characters on the television screen where significant others are lacking in real life. Rebel boys recognise the characters from family serials least of all but like the delinquents in Chapter 8, seek out one lone hero with whom to interact.

We have suggested (Chapter 3) that intent televiewers talk back to the celebrities seen on the small screen. In Chapter 4 we have argued that talking back to the set systematically varies according to social anchorage. Boys were therefore asked, 'How often do you find yourself talking back to people on television?' and given the choice of very often, often, not so often, never and never thought about this question. One-third of boys never talked back or had never thought about this question, 40 per cent talked back not so often, while one-fifth talked back often and one-tenth talked back very often. Boys reported that they talked back at newsreaders, at personas and quiz compères – namely, illusion of intimacy celebrities.

While the illusion of intimacy is no less potent than argued in Chapter 3, i.e., two-thirds of boys report that they answer characters or celebrities back on the screen, once again we find talking back is determined by identity status. Boys who talk half as often with their families about television, namely those boys suffering from identity strain, talk back to people on the set at least twice as often as conformist boys with integrated identities. As argued in Chapter 4, rebels who claim a large number of friends more often talk back (42 per cent very often and often) than problems (25 per cent) who have fewest friends who in turn talk back more often than conformists (13 per cent), who are embedded in a group of mutually chosen friends. These results reiterate the argument of Chapter 4; rebels will interact with anyone; even problem boys who suffer from communication difficulties interact with recognised television people, while conformists have least need to answer back.

Rebels who talked back most frequently were found predictably to identify least often with television characters. Boys were asked, 'Which television characters do things you might like to do?' and asked to name both the character and to specify what he did that was attractive. While answers were dominated by *Kung Fu*, only 58 per cent of rebels identified with an average of one character, as compared with 79 per cent of conformists who identified with 1·35 characters and three-quarters of problem boys who identified with nearly two (1·70) characters. Thus while rebels, in search of an identity, recognise a lone hero from an exciting series programme, they do not necessarily identify with him. Conformist boys, with stable identities, tend to identify rather than recognise; these were boys it may be remembered who most enjoyed being frightened. Taken overall, however, problem boys with unclear identities often choose to lose them via identification and yet equally often choose to flex their identities by answering recognised television characters back. The televiewing style of the alienated and deprived does indeed contain elements of an attempt to re-establish effective interpersonal relationships.

INVOLVEMENT AND IDENTITY LOSS

As we would predict from the arguments in Chapters 1, 3 and 4, alienated boys who seek adequate relational models from television where they are lacking in real life, may be expected to be more involved with television and hence choose true to life programmes or

H

make fantasy programmes appear truer to life than other boys. Boys were asked to list their three favourite programmes and to say whether each one was very true to life, true to life, fairly true to life, not so true to life, or not true to life. In spite of Schramm *et al.*'s turning point at eleven years, only one-half of the boys' favourite programmes were actually true to life – namely, football, news, documentary and children's programmes. As suggested above, problem boys actually did prefer programmes that were true to life (57 per cent of their favourites) while only half the conformists (49 per cent) and even less of the rebels (38 per cent) wanted to see reality on their television screens as well as confront it daily in school.

Problem boys said that 61 per cent of their favourite fantasy programmes (exciting series, family series, films and westerns) were either very true to life or true to life; rebels maintained that half of their favourite fantasy programmes were similarly true to life while one-third of conformists said their favourite fantasy programmes were similarly true to life. Throughout this book we have consistently argued that to confuse reality-fantasy indicates involvement with television programmes, and that isolated boys are most involved, followed in turn by gregarious boys, while boys with an average number of friends are least involved. Results obtained in this study, which were statistically significant, echo and reinforce this pattern, only we can now say with confidence that this is as true of favourite programmes as it is true for the specific programmes cited in Chapter 4. Moreover, we can state with confidence that reality-fantasy confusion results from identity strain.

Central to the arguments in Chapters 1 and 3 is the basic assumption that televiewing does not necessarily involve identity loss, whereas both books and films in the cinema do demand loss of identity. Boys were asked, therefore, 'How often do you forget who you are/where you are, when watching films in the cinema, detective programmes on television, news, family serials and reading a good book?' They were asked to choose either very often, often, not so often, or never. Predictably, at least according to Chapter 1, good books demanded the greatest loss of identity since no less than three-quarters of boys said they lost their identities at some time, and 40 per cent very often and often lost their identities when reading. Films in the cinema demanded the next greatest loss of identity, two-thirds sometimes losing their identities and one-third often losing their identities. Even the most exciting television programmes, detective series, demanded less loss of identity than either books or cinema films; some two-thirds sometimes, and only a quarter often losing their identities. Moreover, even those programmes of which American mass communication researchers most approve, namely the news, demanded greater identity loss than family serials when viewed on television. Boys reported that they sometimes lost their identities when watching the news (45 per cent) but less often did so when watching family serials (41 per cent) and likewise twice as frequently 'often' lost their identities when attending to the news (21 per cent) rather than family serials (11 per cent). Thus, to argue that to attend to television is an escape whereas to read books is non-escapist, as researchers have suggested in Chapter 4, makes no sense if we define escape in terms of identity loss. Moreover, we must recognise the uniqueness of family serials on the television screen; they demand that viewers play opposite recognised characters with their sense of identity intact. We should also explain why the news involves more identity loss than family serials. As previously noted, boys find the greatest number of uses for the news. The very heterogeneity of news content means that the newsreader is the only link between items which the viewer is then left to organise.

These points aside, we have argued that boys suffering from identity strain will more frequently seek relief from the contradictions of an inconsistent identity than boys whose identities are integrated and stable. More than half the conformist boys (55 per cent) reported that they never lost their identities when attending to this selection of mass media, compared to only a third of problem and rebel boys alike (36 per cent). While books induced the greatest identity loss for each type of boy (rebels 82 per cent, problem boys 81 per cent, and conformists 57 per cent), different types of programme prompted different types of boy to lose their identities. Results fell into the now familiar pattern – rebels much more frequently lost their identities when watching the lone hero in cinema films (76 per cent) or detective series (82 per cent) than either problem boys (cinema 69 per cent, detective 62 per cent) or conformist boys (50 per cent of each type). Conversely, problem boys much more frequently lost their identities when watching their favourite fare, regularly appearing communities in family serials (50 per cent) and celebrity news readers (56 per cent), than either rebels (41 and 39 per cent) or conformist boys (31 and 39 per cent). Thus, boys suffering from different types of identity strain lose these identities by attending to different media. Rebels who reject the definition of self imposed by others seek out and pay most attention to those programmes which feature the lone urban man presenting self on a variety of social stages. Problem boys, whose identity is unclear, seek out and pay most attention to regularly appearing communities or personas on the television screen with whom they can predictably interact.

The social context of televiewing

These boys watched television together in a communal room set aside for that purpose in the boarding school. What effect does communal viewing have on these three types of boy? We know that only problem boys have to watch programmes which annoy them; are they disturbed when attending to their family serials by the presence of other boys who possibly will shout at the characters? They are, problem boys report that it is much harder to watch television with other people in the room (69 per cent). Conversely, both rebels (79 per cent) and conformists (60 per cent) say it is much more fun to watch in company. Finally, when asked whether compared to the cinema, films on television are more or less exciting, rebels are indifferent (50 per cent), conformists think films are more exciting on television (60 per cent) while problem boys who find even social televiewing a strain report that films are much less exciting on television (69 per cent).

SUMMARY; THE TELEVIEWING STYLES OF REBEL, CONFORMIST AND PROBLEM BOYS

Let us begin by analysing the televiewing style of conformist boys who are probably best adjusted. These are boys whose self-concept is integrated, who see themselves as they think they are seen by others and whose self-image in the past and projected into the future is congruent with the way they think others see them. These are boys who are integrated within their peer groups and accepted by significant adults. The way they view television reflects both their identity status and their high degree of social anchorage which gives them accurate mirror reflections of self. These boys show a preference for news and comedy programmes and, moreover, these favourite programmes are the ones which they talk about frequently with their parents. The very stability of their identity permits them to also seek out and enjoy programmes which scare them a little, and those programmes which make them happy, since they have less need to relieve tension by seeking out programmes which make them laugh. These are boys who rest easy in the present and thus seek out programmes which show them likely future social roles, programmes which show successful young men and things they might do in the future.

However, there is little evidence amongst these integrated boys of any compulsion to watch either those programmes showing the detective presenting himself on a variety of social stages every week or to watch a regularly appearing community of people in family serials. Nevertheless, these boys are the best predictors of the ways these characters will behave and the fact that they recognise at least two characters indicates that stable boys with integrated identities are most able to predict the way two characters in close relationship will interact. Conformist boys who show the highest degree of self-acceptance show the least need to lose their identities when attending to any media and consequently show the least involvement with television and are not confused about whether their favourite programmes do or do not portray reality. Stable boys enjoy viewing in the company of both parents and teenage friends and can both talk back to recognised characters and lose their identities via identification with the light off when occasion demands.

Rebel boys' televiewing style is no less dependent on both social anchorage and on identity status. These are boys who reject the self-image they see reflected by both peers and family; boys who see themselves as the opposite to the way they were reared in the past and equally oppose the way they think significant others seek to define them in the future. Yet just as much as conformist boys, rebels have a peg on which to base identity, even if they only use that peg to define what they should not be. These are boys who receive mirror images of self yet exploit them perversely. I suspect that a degree of rebellion of this kind between fourteen and fifteen years is very necessary in the types of village community described in Chapter 1, since it is via this dialectic negation of others' opinions that new ideas and change are brought to communities which might be in danger of atrophy. Rebels show a marked preference for westerns and films on television and as we have repeatedly seen they particularly enjoy exciting 'one-off' series programmes. They give their parents a hard time and likewise one suspects that equally, their parents give them a hard time. They don't talk to their families about television and their favourite programmes are most probably regarded by their parents as 'escapist nonsense'. Parents try in vain to persuade rebel boys to watch news and documentary programmes which they attempt to discuss with them. Opposing perceived parental demands, though, is stressful and results in a televiewing style which to a degree shows that private eyes are also rebellious adults, a style which evokes tension relief in the form of laughter and a style whereby a large number of programmes are watched so that they can be used to start conversations with friends. Rebels who have burnt the bridges of the past, and who only have ideas about what not to be both in the present and in the future, seek out programmes which define what an ideal teenager should be and programmes which help to define future roles, especially how to obtain sex. These boys identify least and are as rude to adult personas, especially newsreaders, as they are to adults in real life.

They recognise only one character and he is predictably the lone hero who represents urban man presenting himself on a variety of undefined social stages.

Rejection of parental standards leads to an equal rejection of family serials, but the strain experienced in managing such an identity results not only in a compulsion to view lone heroes, even though each episode is self-contained, but also in fairly frequent loss of identity when attending to a variety of media. Identity loss is most marked though for their favourite programme type, for which they are not only best at predicting outcome but which they also maintain portrays reality. The private eye programmes, the tension of which is only interrupted by the advertisements, uniquely provide rebel boys with an opportunity to see how as loners they might present themselves when in the future they become mobile and move from one undefined situation to another. At the same time, however, these boys particularly seek out 'aggressive' programmes which not only allow them to vicariously work out the hostile feelings pent up inside them, but which also provide models for relational interaction in the form of happy families and co-operation. I refer, of course, to westerns and war films. These boys need the recognition of their peers so much that they think it is much more fun to watch television in the company of other boys.

When you read the questionnaires of problem boys, you immediately begin to feel sorry for them. These are boys who say they watch anything on the television when lonely and to make time pass. These are boys who cannot stand to miss programmes and literally in some instances whose only friends and parents are television characters. When we presented our list of 'problem' boys, based on the self-concept data, to teachers they were immediately able in many cases to disclose horrendous family histories which I am not at liberty to reveal. Suffice it to say, these are boys who have not received consistent images of self in the past from significant adults and who find themselves in the present isolated from their peers in the midst of an acute disintegration of identity, unable to cope with the present, let alone able to project themselves into the future. I sometimes wonder whether this is the price we have to pay for the erosion of the extended kin grouping with its consequent mirror breaks. These are marginal boys who assume different identities in different geographical and social stages and are unable to knit these selves together. Unlike other boys they do not outgrow their identity crisis at sixteen years.

Above all, these boys prefer to see a small regularly appearing group of people on the television screen. Their extended kin are the characters in family serials and they can interact better with personas, even newsreaders, than with their families, with whom they attempt to talk about television and yet fail to do so. Boys who are unsure as to who they are have to watch television programmes which annoy them; use television programmes as a talking point with other boys and have to relieve tension by laughing at those relationships which they have failed to manage in the past. Boys with no adequate mirror reflection of self from any source seek out programmes which act as a substitute mirror – those which show boys like the self. Nevertheless, these boys are concerned with the future, particularly with future relationships. They need to watch on television those happy marriages and happy families many of them have never seen in real life. While identity strain results in compulsive viewing, their compulsion is for family serials – a surrogate extended kin – which necessarily becomes real to them and yet at the same time does help to instruct them in the art of managing relationships which on television, at least, they are learning to predict. Uncertain as to who they are, these boys frequently lose their identities by attending to a variety of media, but most saliently lose them even when watching the newsreaders as well as when watching family serials. These boys recognise at least two characters from the same programme, which suggests a heightened need for instruction in relationships but also need to identify in order to submerge their identities below consciousness. They watch television so intently that even the presence of others in the room is distracting.

11

Tailpiece – excursions from theory

Much of what was said in Chapter 1 was borne out by the data collected and reported in the previous chapter. Televiewing seems to demand less identity loss than either books or cinema films, and it is possible that each succeeding generation of mass media calls for increasing participation from audience members who do not lose their identities. Almost certainly the next development in the media will be to remove the mass audience and either offer cassette recordings of programmes which people can acquire and play back at will, or truly local television stations will emerge. With local television it should become possible for people to see themselves in action on the small screen. Where in the past extended kin members had to tell individuals how they appeared to others, local television can provide this information in unambiguous form simply by showing people themselves. While there is no future in being a prophet, McDowell and Noble (1974) attempted to explore the consequences of such a development by taking video-recording equipment into a particularly depressed area in Dublin.

TELEVISION AS A MIRROR

The area chosen is notorious for its poverty, its density of a shifting population, its crime rate and for its children who are regularly to be seen clinging to the back of passing lorries. We might reasonably expect that many of these children simply do not receive reflections of self from a stable group of kin, and consequently have had little opportunity to acquire a self-concept. Deprived of information about the 'me's they present to others, these children may never acquire a realistic picture of themselves in their own minds. We asked 20 seven-and eight-year-old boys and girls to draw themselves and a man or a woman – the figure opposite shows two self portraits. These drawings were used to assess the mental age of the child by counting the amount of detail included. The drawings you see here are the best and the worst.

Children who think they look physically like drawing 1 cannot be expected to have any clear idea of their psychological makeup, whereas children who think they look like drawing 2 can be expected to have some idea of self. We prompted these children to describe

Two self-portraits by eight-year-olds

1. Mental age three years nine months

2. Mental age eleven years six months

themselves psychologically by saying, 'I am a man', and asking them to keep saying, 'I am a . . .', until they ran out of ideas. We hoped by this question to find out how children expressed their identity in words, but more importantly we wanted to know whether these seven- and eight-year-olds had any ideas about themselves in the future. We prompted children to tell us, 'In ten years' time I will . . .' again until they ran out of self descriptions. Children's answers fell into four main groups. First, they described how they appeared physically – either now, 'I have pierced ears', or in ten years' time, 'I will have orange hair still'. Boys and girls gave us either two or three physical descriptions of themselves now, but were only able to tell us one physical description of self in the future.

Secondly, children gave us descriptions of themselves which implied a fairly formal comparison of themselves with other people, such as, 'I am the middle one in the family', and in the future, 'I will be a mummy and have babies'. Children described themselves now twice in this manner but, more interestingly, described themselves in the future three times in this way. The sight of a stable group of kin, if available, would appear to help children envisage themselves in the future, since then they would be like either their parents or elder brothers and sisters. Thirdly, children described themselves in informal comparison with others both now, 'I do be love killing young flits [I like hitting small boys]', and in the future, 'I would bring my little brother to the pictures then', and media-influenced descriptions such as, 'I would join the army and shoot the baddies in the North'. Children described themselves now in three such ways but could only manage one informal description of themselves in the future. Lastly, children described themselves in essentially abstract ways both now, 'I love God', and, 'In ten years' time I would like to have wings and fly up to the stars and be no-body'. Not surprisingly, only three of the twenty children described themselves in this way.

Half of these children were chosen, by sticking a pin in the list of names, so that we could show them themselves on television. Their play was recorded on videotape on three successive afternoons in each of which they played for an hour at running about, dressing up, acting out weddings and other unstructured play in between watching recordings of themselves. All the twenty children were then again asked to draw themselves and a man or woman, and to think of as many answers as they could to describe, 'I am . . .' and in ten years' time 'I will . . .'. We wanted to see if seeing themselves on television affected not only the way they saw themselves physically but also if it affected the ways children were able to describe themselves psychologically.

Those children who saw themselves on television understandably drew themselves considerably more accurately after viewing than before viewing. In fact the mental age of these children, as reflected in their drawings, increased by one year. There was no change in the mental age of children who did not see themselves on television. While it may appear that we have laboured to prove the obvious, we should not forget that television enables the child to see himself in moving action and when acting in ways that glass mirrors will not permit.

The more important question is whether or not the sight of the self as a social object on the television screen helps children to describe themselves now and the way they will appear in the future more adequately. Predictably, children who had seen themselves on television gave 5 physcial descriptions of self in the 'I am' test, compared with an average of 2·5 descriptions before viewing, and no change was apparent amongst children who had not seen themselves. More importantly, children who had seen themselves on television increased the number of descriptions, which implied formal comparison with other people by one and the number of more informal comparisons by two, where no change was noted in the control group. Children did not, however, alter the number of abstract descriptions of self after televiewing. These results suggest that children who see themselves in action on the television screen, are helped not only to a better understanding of their bodies but also to a better understanding of how they appear to behave when seen by other people. The self becomes something of an object, or a 'me', which can be critically evaluated when it is seen on the television screen.
Moreover, children who had simply seen themselves on television seemed better able to imagine what they would be like in ten years' time. Where before viewing children could only be prompted to five descriptions of themselves in ten years' time, those who had seen themselves on television could be prompted to eight descriptions of themselves in the future, while those who did not see themselves could still only be prompted to five descriptions one week later. Nor was the increase limited to physical descriptions, which indeed increased by one; these children also added one more to those descriptions which implied both formal and informal comparisons with other people. Seeing themselves on television appears to enable relatively 'deprived' children not only to see themselves now as others might see them but also allows children to bring the picture they see of themselves into comparison with the older people they see around them and helps them to envisage the future.
The eight-year-old boy who thinks he looks like Drawing 1, with a mental age of less than four years, chose to fight with the others and to

also attack a teddy-bear by kicking and hitting it. When we sat him down to see the video-recording he repeatedly turned away from the screen and eventually demanded that he go home. On one other occasion he viewed himself through his fingers but soon turned away. He did not change his self-concept but he refused to look at himself. It seems likely that the sight of himself acting aggressively was painful, just as an accurate reflection of such a self would be painful if reflected by people he respects.

Television as a medium of mass communication does not at this time allow for feedback by audience members. If results from this very limited study are in any way valid, it would seem possible that local television could help both individuals and communities towards greater awareness and give some insights about where they fit into the wider society. Possibly one of the most fruitful research strategies would be to attempt to establish such a local station in a deprived area and monitor both community awareness and the self-concepts of individuals who comprise that community.

THE MYTH OF NARCISSUS

Both Freud and McLuhan invoke the Narcissus myth in order to throw light on the human condition. The reader is by now aware that this author takes myths fairly seriously. The myth of Narcissus reflects in metaphoric form one of the essential enigmas which results from being human – an enigma which fascinated both the Ancient Greeks and Freud alike. McLuhan offers a new interpretation of this myth in *Understanding Media*. He argues that Narcissus does not fall in love with himself as Freud supposed, but rather that Narcissus does not know who it is that is reflected in the water. I suggest that the myth in part reflects the basic paradox between the 'I', the aware viewer of the 'me', which is the object image of the 'I' as seen by others. Narcissus I suggest suffered the first acute identity crisis, since he was unable to work out the relationship between the 'I' and the 'me'. We are told that he talked to the image, tried to embrace it, languished for it and pined until he died, when his body mysteriously disappeared. He was unable even to hear words of Echo so intense was his struggle to reconcile the knowing 'I' with the image of self – or the 'me' – as it appeared in the water.

Unlike Narcissus, our aggressive boy can hardly bear to see himself; it is too painful for him to reconcile the 'I' with the aggressive 'me' portrayed on the screen. Television and film, unlike any other media, can provide the individual with images of the self in developmental progression. These media can show each of us how we appear during the seven ages of man. Faced with such data, we are probably forced to ask what is the identity which underpins not only the developmental sequence of our life space, but which also underpins our frantic changes in mood and disposition. As argued in Chapter 1, if such information is available we are once again forced to establish an identity which is the same throughout the visible changes in the 'me's which we present to other people. Where previously the extended kin group forced the individual to so evaluate himself, it seems that local or personal television could fulfil the same function.

If a man were to see himself with his family, to see himself at work, to see himself with friends, might he not begin to question the nature of the self which underpins all these social selves? Similarly, if an alcoholic were to see how he appears in stupor, or a delinquent hitting an old lady – would they be prepared to repeat such acts in the future? Within the village such acts might not be accepted, but neither would privacy be sought. Local television might invade privacy, but privacy and anonymity provide a shield to hide deviance, and are not likely to result in an identity suitable for all occasions, nor a basic respect and tolerance for the way others choose to live their lives publicly. Man, I believe, is essentially a social animal who only achieves an identity within a community grouping of his fellows.

ADVICE TO PARENTS

Bearing in mind what was said in Chapter 1 about experts, I am somewhat reluctant to advise parents about their children's tele-viewing, especially since children vary so considerably. To a degree the book has failed if the reader does not better understand television, and is not in a better position to make up his own mind. However, in a recent survey, I asked middle-aged mothers what programmes they would prefer that younger children did not see. Three main areas seemed to cause the most concern – violence, sexual displays and horror films.

Violence, as we have seen, is a tricky area. In my opinion the effects of violence on the small screen depend, first, on the type of televised violence and, secondly, on whether or not your son is aggressive. Many boys are aggressive, and I would recommend that these boys work out these feelings by watching fantasy aggression where there is a distance between aggressor and victim, such as westerns, war films and historical violence. Where possible I would try to prevent my young child from watching news violence and violence seen in the neo-realistic police and detective programmes. These latter types of violence, I fear, do show that violence is normal and accepted in everyday life and possibly define the targets at whom aggression can be directed. The sight of children in the news throwing stones at soldiers is for me the worst offender. Such violence takes place in streets similar to those in which our children live, the soldiers are recognisably different and thus a uniform target and overall such sights show your child how his counterparts in the wider society do conspicuously behave. There is a danger that by mere exposure we legitimate such acts of violence. I would have no fear, though, about children, whether aggressive or not, watching *Tom and Jerry*, since the violence therein is stylistic, removed from life and even, dare I say it, imaginative.

We should also enter serious dialogues with programme makers to see whether or not they can be made to appreciate parents' points of view and to listen to their reasons about why and how they present violence for our children. I would say to them that the example of Greek tragedy is too rarely exploited in their programmes. In Greek tragedy the violence took place off-stage, the actual acts being left to the audiences' imagination. Television, I fear, completes too many images in our children's minds and then concentrates on the aggressive act rather than on the consequences of aggression. If we leave the narrative at the point where we see the victim antici-pating what is to come we allow children to experience his feelings and thus exploit television as an art form. If we leave such events to the viewer's imagination we can be reasonably sure that the viewer will not conjure up scenes which are likely to overwhelm his capacity to cope with them.

Sexual portrayals are another matter. Here I feel televised pre-sentations do act as a charter for social action. They help to define what is normal and acceptable in the wider society beyond the family. Again dialogue between programme makers and their audiences would be fruitful. Personally I feel the act of sex should not be a taboo area and my reading of the evidence is that sexual displays on television do not prompt our children immediately to experiment with sex but in the long term may accustom children to the idea that it is natural to sleep with the opposite sex both in and out of wedlock. Societies around the world vary enormously in their attitudes to sex, and in many countries such attitudes are con-ventional. Since attitudes to sex in our culture are also moral questions, this is an area where I feel it is the parent's duty to be explicit about their moral values to the child and to explain to them at least before and during puberty, why they object to sexual por-trayals on the television screen and encourage the child not to watch them. Other parents who feel that the act of sex is the culmi-nation of a feeling of love will feel no qualms about their children viewing such acts. In either case, merely to censure and/or make no comment seems an abnegation of parental duty. Just as parents in the village would have commented on the sexual acts of those they saw around them, today's parents should also reasonably comment on those acts which are public displays on our television screens.

Horror programmes are designed to frighten, since horrid means literally bristling with hair or making hair stand on end. Remarkably few television programmes are so potent, but I would have no qualms in recommending that children, especially before seven years, should not see and thus become unduly frightened by televised horror programmes. These are the programmes which invade a child's dreams and I feel overwhelm his imagination. My own view is that only mature and relatively stable individuals can enjoy being horrified; young children are simply too young and many children are simply too immature to be able to cope with horror. Horror can safely be left in the cinema or to the book reader's imagination, or left until late at night on the television screen.

As we have seen, children mature through two relatively distinct televiewing styles until at age eleven they begin to understand television as we adults do. I fear we remain comparatively ignorant about the way the very young child views television. I would recommend that before seven years, the parent and child watch television together, and get into the habit of talking about what they have seen. Once the child is accustomed to this televiewing style, fruitful dialogues are easily established. To a lesser degree, communal viewing is rewarding between seven and eleven years. Between these ages your child will seek, and should not be discouraged from watching, programmes with a standardised format. He will have to see many such programmes before he learns to predict what is going to happen. At eleven-plus you can begin to converse with him, tolerably confident that he understands television as well, if not better, than you. In my view no parent should feel threatened by television. A mature relationship between parent and child should ensure, first that the television set is not used as an indiscriminate baby-sitter just to get the child from under their feet, and, secondly, that parents and children watch and talk about programmes together. If parents are prepared to let their children view society's machinations without comment, they have only themselves to blame when the child accepts the implicit values shown on television rather than parental standards.

Remember above all that your child's televiewing style tells you a fair deal about your child. Children who watch television persistently, or who constantly read books and have to be dragged from them, are most probably signalling distress – a lack of adequate friendship and parenting in the real world. Moreover, if your child persists in believing that fictional television programmes are real after eleven years in particular, that child is probably not enjoying any great social success. The solution to these problems involves solutions in the real world.

I would also be inclined to worry if a child showed anxiety at having to miss an unduly large number of series and serial programmes, which would suggest that he does not encounter a sufficient range of people in real life. I would not worry, though, nor would I ever prevent a child watching something which he knows his friends are watching and which he will need to watch in order to keep in the swim in school tomorrow. Everything said here implies very strongly that you know what your child watches and to a degree what his friends watch – should you fail to know this you are missing a chance to understand, talk to and get close to your child – I would almost dare to suggest that you are failing as a parent. In my view television can give you a chance to get close to children when they go through difficult ages. After all if you can laugh with your young child at *Bugs Bunny*, and enjoy the skill with which private eyes, such as *Rockford*, present themselves with the difficult boy adolescent, or admire David Cassidy's looks and his sister's aplomb with the young girl teenager you are never in danger of atrophying into sedantry middle age before your time.

A NEW SHAPE TO BROADCASTING

It often appears to me that production agencies fill time schedules in a near mechanical way; they seem unduly frightened of repeats and extended open-ended discussion. At the same time viewers do not see enough of the background and build-up to newsworthy and other events. Often news coverage 'hosted' by the impartial man in the middle is so brief that it is rather like asking a jury to decide a man's fate by requesting them merely to listen to the case as presented by a journalist, without hearing the arguments from the prosecution and defence. Exposure to a variety of views concerning events would not only allow more people to gain access into the hallowed media halls but in theory should lead to greater objectivity.

In a study of the 27th October 1968 anti-Vietnam war demonstration, 200 middle-aged evening-class students were simply asked whether or not they had seen the demonstrators hit the policemen and the policemen attack the demonstrators in the newscast. In each case, twice as many viewers said they had seen the demonstrators hit the policemen and that they had seen the policemen attack the demonstrators (respectively 87 and 42 per cent) if they had only seen one newscast, than if they had seen three or four newscasts (42 and 11 per cent). Those who had seen two newscasts fell between the two extremes (56 and 15 per cent). Likewise, before the protest, viewers were asked whether they had talked about the event with friends and what they perceived to be the aim of the demonstration. Predictably adults who had not talked about the event with friends had tacitly accepted the media definition of the event, widely billed as bloody and revolutionary, since half of them said that the event was for 'revolutionary' purposes and half said it was about Vietnam. Of those 40 per cent who had talked about the event with friends, less than a quarter thought the protest was motivated by political unrest and three-quarters said it was to be about Vietnam. With the benefit of hindsight it would seem that, where people either see an event from two perspectives or where a second perspective is afforded by conversation, that greater objectivity results. If we may again draw the analogy between the viewer and the jury, there was less risk of a false conviction when viewers saw events from differing perspectives. I believe we must very seriously question the unassailed right of the media men in the middle to claim objectivity; were more people given access to present their cases on the mass media we would not only enshrine the ideal of free speech but also allow the viewer at home to reach a considered judgement about important issues, both at a national and a local level.

SOCIETY AND COMMUNICATION

Dewey maintains that society exists in and through communication. So often we note that a common language marks the parameter of a culture and a common colloquial language marks the boundary of a subculture. Similarly, the geographic area served by a mass medium marks the limits of a nation. Throughout this book we have argued that television shapes and forms children's conceptions of occupational, social and national roles and helps them to define both situations and what they might do in the future. We may therefore expect the audience for a mass medium to come to accept tacitly the definition of various situations projected by the media institutions. The question of access to the mass media thus assumes critical importance since it is all too easy for production agencies to rely on comparatively few sources of information. The question of who controls the mass media and to whom these individuals are responsible is perhaps one of the most salient issues facing society today. There would appear to be no *a priori* grounds for the comparatively few institutions which control the mass media in various nations unless something akin to national consensus is the tacit goal of governments.

Given that media institutions are so powerful, we must ask: Why are so many television programmes imported from America? Virtually anybody could establish a television station and relay American packaged programmes. If production agencies cannot themselves produce enough home-based material, why do they occupy such an important position in our society? If television makes society visible, and I have yet to experience a national network without its own family serial, why are so many programmes imported from America? The answer to this question I am told is purely economic in that American producers have a sufficiently large home market to pay off production costs, which means that they can sell their products abroad at a price cheaper than these countries could produce a similar product. Unfortunately, this means that while television has the unique power to make society visible, we tend purely for financial reasons to show our children how Americans both live and choose to define various situations. We import programmes which metaphorically express American values from a country not particularly noted for its ethical beliefs. We must question the way our media are financed and ask whether economic criteria are sufficient to control media output.

THE PROSTITUTION OF BROADCASTING?

Whenever we buy a product advertised on television we are in fact paying for the programmes made to surround that advertisement. Not only are we not in a position to present our views openly on the mass media but our conventional power as consumers of advertised products is not directly related to programme content. Indeed the programmes are often conspiratorially different from the advertisements which interrupt them – as one nine-year-old said: 'Advertisements take away the exciting feeling I get when watching the programmes'. I can think of few reasons why broadcasting should be regarded as a profit-making activity and not as a public service. In modern industrial societies where individuals necessarily lead fragmented and discontinuous lives we need information about our fellow men as much as we need water. In the village that information was free and readily available; in industrial societies we must be prepared to spend our affluence on public service broadcasting so that we can once again understand the nature of the society in which we live. I, for one, am not prepared to cost the price of alienation.

Bibliography

ALBERT, R. S. (1957). 'The role of the mass media and the effect of aggressive film content upon children's aggressive responses and identification choices', *Genetic psychology monographs, 55*, 221–85.

ALDISS, B. W. (1962). *Introduction to best fantasy stories*. London: Faber & Faber.

ANCONA, L. (1963). 'Il film come elemento nella dinamica dell'aggressivita', *Revue internationale de filmologie, 13*, 27–32.

BAILYN, L. (1959). 'Mass media and children: a study of exposure habits and cognitive effects', *Psychological monographs, 71*, 1–48.

BANDURA, A. (1963). 'What tv violence can do to your child', *Look*, October, 46–52. [Also in Larsen, O. N. (ed.), *Violence and the mass media*. New York: Harper & Row (1968)].

BANDURA, A. (1972). *Aggression: A social learning analysis*. Englewood Cliffs: Prentice Hall.

BANDURA, A. & MENLOVE, F. L. (1968). 'Factors determining vicarious extinction of avoidance behaviour through symbolic modeling', *Journal of personality and social psychology, 66*, 3–11.

BANDURA, A., ROSS, D. & ROSS, S. A. (1963a). 'Imitation of film-mediated aggressive models', *Journal of abnormal and social psychology, 66*, 601–7.

BANDURA, A., ROSS, D. & ROSS, S. A. (1963b). 'A comparative test of the status envy, social power and secondary reinforcement theories of identificatory learning', *Journal of abnormal and social psychology, 67*, 527–34.

BANDURA, A., ROSS, D. & ROSS, S. A. (1963c). 'Vicarious reinforcement and imitative learning', *Journal of abnormal and social psychology, 67*, 601–7.

BANDURA, A. & WALTERS, R. H. (1963). *Social learning and personality development*. New York: Holt, Rinehart & Winston.

BARKER, R. G. (1968). *Ecological psychology*. Stanford: Stanford University Press.

BARKER, R., DEMBO, T. & LEWIN, K. (1941). *Frustration and regression: An experiment with young children*. University of Iowa, Studies in Child Welfare, 18.

BAXTER, B., BARNES, E. & GILL, R. (1970). *Blue Peter book of television*. London: BBC.

BERKOWITZ, L. (1962). *Aggression: A social psychological analysis*. New York: McGraw-Hill.

BERKOWITZ, L. (1964). 'The effects of observing violence', *Scientific American, 210*, 35–41.

BERKOWITZ, L. & GEEN, R. (1966). 'Film violence and cue properties of available targets', *Journal of personality and social psychology, 3*, 525–30.

BERKOWITZ, L. & RAWLINGS, E. (1963). 'Effects of film violence on inhibitions against subsequent aggression', *Journal of abnormal and social psychology*, *66*, 405–12.

BERNINGHAUSEN, D. K. & FAUNCE, R. K. (1964). 'An exploratory study of juvenile delinquency and the reading of sensational books', *Journal of experimental education*, *33*, 161–8.

BLUMER, H. & HAUSER, P. M. (1933). *Movies, delinquency and crime.* New York: Macmillan.

BOGART, L. (1955). 'Adult talk about newspaper comics', *American journal of sociology*, *61*, 26–30.

BREED, W. (1955). 'Social control in the newsroom', *Social forces*, *33*, 326–35.

BRONFENBRENNER, U. (1974). 'The origins of alienation', *Scientific American*, August, 53–61.

BUTLER, J. M. (1960). 'Self concept change in psychotherapy', *Counseling Center discussion papers*, Chicago, *6*, 13.

CHANDLER, R. (1940). *The lady in the lake.* Harmondsworth: Penguin.

CHAYEFSKY, P. (1955). *Television plays.* New York: Simon and Schuster.

CLARK, K. (1969). *Civilisation.* London: BBC.

COMSTOCK, G. A. & RUBENSTEIN, E. A. (Eds) (1972). *Television and social behavior.* Vols 1–4. Washington: US Government Printing Office.

CRESSEY, P. G. & THRASHER, F. (1933). *Boys, movies and city streets.* New York: Macmillan.

CROCE, M. A. (1963). Controllo dell'effetto mnestico Zeigarnik con materiale filmico tematico. *Revue internationale de filmologie*, *13*, 45–50.

DE FLEUR, M. L. (1964). 'Occupational roles as portrayed on television', *Public opinion quarterly*, *28*, 57–74.

DE FLEUR, M. L. & DE FLEUR, L. B. (1967). 'The relative contribution of television as a learning source for children's occupational knowledge', *American sociological review*, *32*, 777–89.

DEJEAN, A. (1972). 'Structural analysis of some French and American cartoons', Mimeograph Montreal: George Williams University.

DYMOND, R. C. (1954). 'Effects of psychotherapy on self consistency', *Journal of counseling psychology*, *4*, 15–22.

ELKIN, F. (1950). 'The psychological appeal of the Hollywood Western', *Journal of educational sociology*, *24*, 72–86.

ELKIND, D. (1961). 'The development of quantitative thinking: a systematic replication of Piaget's studies', *Journal of genetic psychology*, *98*, 37–46.

ELLIOTT, P. R. C. (1969). 'Television for children and young people', in *Second progress report and recommendations.* Leicester: Leicester University Press.

EMERY, F. E. (1959). 'Psychological effects of the Western film: a study in television viewing', *Human relations*, *12*, 195–214. [Also by EMERY, F. E. & MARTIN, D. (1957), Melbourne: University of Melbourne.]

ERON, L. D. (1963). 'Relationship of tv viewing habits and aggressive behavior in children', *Journal of abnormal and social psychology*, *67*, 193–6.

ERON, L. D., LEFKOWITZ, M. M., WALDER, L. O. & HUESMANN, L. R. (1972). 'Television violence and child aggression: a follow up study', in *Television and social behavior*, Vol. 3 (ed. Comstock, G. A. & Rubinstein, E. A.). Washington: US Government Printing Office.

EYRE-BROOK, E. R. (1972). *Scarecrow.* Munich: Prix Jeunesse.

FEFFER, M. H. (1959). 'The cognitive implications of role taking behavior', *Journal of personality*, *27*, 152–68.

FESHBACH, S. (1961). 'The stimulating versus cathartic effects of a vicarious aggressive activity', *Journal of abnormal and social psychology*, *63*, 381–5.

FESHBACH, S. & SINGER, R. D. (1971). *Television and aggression: An experimental field study*. San Francisco: Jossey-Bass.

FLAPAN, D. P. (1965). 'Children's understanding of social interaction'. Unpublished Ph.D. dissertation, Columbia University.

FOOTE, N. N. (1951). 'Identification as the basis for a theory of motivation', *American sociological review*, *16*, 14–21.

FREUD, S. (1933). *New introductory lectures on psycho-analysis*. New York: Norton.

FRIEDSON, E. (1953). 'The relations of the social situation of contact to the media in mass communication', *Public opinion quarterly*, *17*, 230–8.

GARRY, R. (1969). 'Clown Ferdl', in *Findings and cognition on the television perception of children and young people*. Munich: Prix Jeunesse.

GEEN, R. G. & O'NEAL, E. C. (1969). 'Activation of cue-elicited aggression by general arousal', *Journal of personality and social psychology*, *11*, 289–92.

GEMELLI, A. (1951). 'Cinema e psicologia', *Vitae pensiero*, *34*, 315–21.

GERBNER, G. (1969). 'The television world of violence', in R. K. Baker & S. J. Ball (eds), *Violence and the media*. Washington: US Government Printing Office.

GERBNER, G. (1971). 'Violence in television drama: Trends and symbolic functions', in *Television and social behavior*, Vol. 1 (ed. Comstock, G. A. & Rubenstein, E. A.). Washington: US Government Printing Office.

GERHARTZ-FRANCK, I. (1955). *Neber Geschenogestaltungen in der Auffassung von Filmen durch Kinder*. Leipzig: Barth.

GLASER, D. (1956). 'Criminality theories and behavioral images', *American journal of sociology*, *56*, 433–44.

GLUECK, S. & GLUECK, E. (1943). *Criminal careers in retrospect*. New York: Commonwealth Fund.

GOLLIN, E. S. (1958). 'Organizational characteristics of social judgement: a developmental investigation', *Journal of personality*, *26*, 139–54.

GOMBERG, A. W. (1961). 'The four-year-old child and television: the effects on his play at school'. Unpublished Ed.D. dissertation Columbia University Teachers College.

GORANSON, R. E. (1969). 'A review of recent literature on psychological effects of media portrayals of violence', in *Violence and the media* (eds Baker, R. K. & Ball, S. J.). Washington: US Government Printing Office.

HALLORAN, J. D., BROWN, R. L. & CHANEY, D. (1970). *Television and delinquency*. Leicester: Leicester University Press.

HALLORAN, J. D. & ELLIOTT, P. R. C. (1969). 'Television for children and young people', in *Second progress report and recommendations*. Leicester: Leicester University Press.

HALLORAN, J. D., ELLIOTT, P. R. C. & MURDOCK, G. (1970). *Demonstrations and communications: A case study*. Harmondsworth: Penguin.

HARTMANN, D. P. (1969). 'Influence of symbolically modeled instrumental aggression and pain cues on aggressive behavior', *Journal of abnormal and social psychology*, *11*, 280–8.

HAZARD, W. R. (1967). 'Anxiety and preference for television fantasy', *Journalism quarterly*, *44*, 461–9.

HERZOG, H. (1944). 'What do we really know about day-time serial listeners?', in *Radio research, 1942–43* (eds Lazarsfeld, P. & Stanton, F.). New York: Duell, Sloan & Pearce.

HICKS, D. (1965). 'Imitation and retention of aggressive peer and adult models', *Journal of personality and social psychology*, *2*, 97–100.

HICKS, D. (1968). 'Short and long term retention of affectively varied model behavior'. *Psychonomic science*, *11*, 369–70.

HIMMELWEIT, H. T. (1962). 'Television revisited', *New society*, *5*, 17.

HIMMELWEIT, H. T., OPPENHEIM, A. & VINCE, P. (1958). *Television and the child*. London: Oxford University Press.

HOLADAY, P. W. & STODDARD, G. D. (1933). *Getting ideas from the movies*. New York: MacMillan.

HORTON, D. & WOHL, R. R. (1956). 'Mass communication and para-social interaction', *Psychiatry*, *19*, 215–29.

HOULT, T. F. (1949). 'Comics books and juvenile delinquency', *Sociology and social research*, *33*, 279–84.

HOYT, J. (1967). 'Vengeance and self-defense as justification for filmed aggression'. Unpublished MA dissertation, University of Wisconsin.

HYMAN, H. H. (1973). 'Mass Communication and socialization'. Paper presented to the Arden House Conference on Directions in Mass Communications Research, New York.

JOHNSTONE, J. W. C. (1961). 'Social structure and patterns of mass media consumption'. Unpublished Ph.D. dissertation, Chicago University.

KATZ, E. (1959). 'Mass communication research and the study of culture', *Studies in public communication*, *2*, 1–6.

KATZ, E. & FOULKES, D. (1962). 'On the use of the mass media as "escape": Clarification of a concept', *Public opinion quarterly*, *26*, 377–88.

KEILHACKER, M. & VOGG, G. (1965). *Television experience patterns in children and juveniles*. Munich: Prix Jeunesse.

KNIVETON, B. H. & STEPHENSON, G. M. (1970). 'The effect of pre-experience on imitation of an aggressive film model', *British journal of social and clinical psychology*, *9*, 31–6.

LARSEN, O. N. (1969). 'Posing the problem of effects', in *Violence and the mass media* (eds Baker, R. F. & Ball, S. J.). Washington: US Government Printing Office.

LINNE, O. (1971). 'Reactions of children to violence on television'. Stockholm: Sveriges Radio, Internal Report.

LORENZ, K. (1963). *On aggression*. London: Methuen.

LOVIBOND, S. H. (1967). 'The effect of media stressing crime and violence upon children's attitudes', *Social problems*, *15*, 91–100.

LYLE, J. & HOFFMAN, H. R. (1972). 'Children's use of television and other media', in *U.S. Surgeon-General's report*. Washington: US Government Printing Office.

MACCOBY, E. E. (1951). 'Television: its impact on school children', *Public opinion quarterly*, *15*, 421–44.

MACCOBY, E. E. (1954). 'Why do children watch television?', *Public opinion quarterly*, *18*, 239–44.

MACCOBY, E. E. (1964). 'Effects of mass media', in *Review of child develop-*

ment research (eds Hoffman, M. L. & Hoffman, L. W.). New York: Russell Sage Foundation.

MACCOBY, E. E. & WILSON, W. C. (1957). 'Identification and observational learning from films', *Journal of abnormal and social psychology*, *55*, 76–87.

MCDOWELL, S. & NOBLE, G. (1974). 'The self concept of deprived urban children before and after seeing themselves on television', Dublin: Department of Psychology.

MCLUHAN, M. (1964). *Understanding media*. London: Routledge & Kegan Paul.

MCQUAIL, D. (1969). *Towards a sociology of mass communications*. London: Collier Macmillan.

MASTERS, F. G. & TONG, J. E. (1968). 'The semantic differential test with Borstal subjects', *British journal of criminology*, *8*, 20–31.

MERTON, R. K. (1957). *Social theory and social structure*. New York: Free Press.

MEYERSON, L. (1966). 'The effects of filmed aggression on aggressive responses of high and low aggressive subjects'. Unpublished Ph.D. dissertation, University of Iowa.

MIALERET, G. & MALANDAIN, C. (1962). 'Etude de la reconstitution d'un récit chez l'enfant à partir d'un film fixe', *Enfance*, *2*, 169–90.

MIALERET, G. & MELIES, M. G. (1954). 'Experiences sur la compréhension du langage cinématographique', *Revue internationale de filmologie*, *5*, 221–8.

MILGRAM, S. & SHOTLAND, R. L. (1973). *Television and antisocial behavior: Field experiments*. New York: Academic Press.

MILGRAM, S. (1974). *Obedience to authority: An experimental view*. London: Tavistock.

MUSSEN, P. & RUTHERFORD, E. (1961). 'Effects of aggressive cartoons on children's aggressive play', *Journal of abnormal and social psychology*, *62*, 461–4.

NATIONAL COMMISSION ON THE CAUSES AND PREVENTION OF VIOLENCE (USA), in *Violence and the media* (eds Baker, R. K. & Ball, S. J.) (1969). Washington: Government Printing Office.

NEWCOMB, T. M. (1956). 'The prediction of interpersonal attraction', *American psychologist*, *11*, 575–86.

NEWSON, J. & NEWSON, E. (1963). *Patterns of infant care in an urban community*. London: George Allen & Unwin.

NOBLE, G. (1969a). 'Report and analysis of the "Blue Peter" project', in *Report of the first EBU workshop for producers of children's television programmes* (ed. Taff, P.). Geneva: European Broadcasting Union.

NOBLE, G. (1969b). 'Informal learning from mass media', *New university*, *6*, 16–18.

NOBLE, G. (1969c). 'Patrick and Putrick,' in *Findings and cognition on the television perceptions of children and young people*. Munich: Prix Jeunesse.

NOBLE, G. (1969d). 'Clown Ferdl', in *Findings on the television perception of children and young people*. Munich: Prix Jeunesse.

NOBLE, G. (1969e). 'Identification of the roles of television characters: A process leading to involvement in a television programme', *Bulletin of the British Psychological Society*, *22*, 145.

NOBLE, G. (1970a). 'Film-mediated creative and aggressive play', *British journal of social and clinical psychology*, 9, 1–7.

NOBLE, G. (1970b). 'Concepts of order and balance in a children's tv program', *Journalism quarterly*, 47, 101–8:159.

NOBLE, G. (1971a). 'Discrimination between different forms of filmed aggression by delinquent and non-delinquent boys', *British journal of criminology*, 230–44.

NOBLE, G. (1971b). 'Some comments on the nature of delinquents' identification with television heroes, fathers and best friends', *British journal of social and clinical psychology*, 10, 172–80.

NOBLE, G. (1973). 'Effects of different forms of filmed aggression on children's constructive and destructive play', *Journal of personality and social psychology*, 26, 54–9.

NOBLE, G. & BARNES, D. S. (1972). 'Film and television stars'. Mimeograph Montreal: George Williams University.

NOBLE, G. & MARTIN, C. (1974). 'Sport outcomes and subsequent aggression among aggressive and non-aggressive viewers'. Dublin: Dept. of Psychology.

NOBLE, G. & MULCAHY, J. (1974). 'An experimental attempt to isolate a cathartic response to televised aggression', *Bulletin of the British Psychological Society*, 27, 175.

NOBLE, G. & MURPHY, E. (1974). 'Developmental trends in adolescent identity'. Dublin: Dept. of Psychology.

O'SHAUGHNESSY, R. (1972). 'The Red Indian as seen by Canadian child televiewers'. Mimeograph Montreal: George Williams University.

PATTERSON, G. R., LITTMAN, R. A. & BRICKER, W. (1967). 'Assertive behavior in children: A step towards a theory of aggression', *Monographs of social research in child development*, 32, whole number.

PAULSEN, K. (1957). 'Was bleibt? Kinder besinnen sich auf einem film', *Film-Bild-Ton*, 7, 8–13.

PEARLIN, L. (1959). 'Social and personal stress and escape television viewing', *Public opinion quarterly*, 23, 255–9.

PFUHL, E. H. (1961). 'The relationship of mass media to reported delinquent behavior'. Unpublished Ph.D. dissertation, Washington State University.

PIAGET, J. (1950a). *Introduction à l'épistémologie génétique*. Paris: Presses Universitaires de France.

PIAGET, J. (1950b). *The psychology of intelligence*. New York: Harcourt & Brace.

PIAGET, J. & INHELDER, B. (1958). *The growth of logical thinking from childhood to adolescence* (trans. Parsons, A. & Milgram, S.). New York: Basic Books.

POOL, I. DE SOLA. & SHULMAN, I. (1959). 'Newsmen's fantasies, audiences and newswriting', *Public opinion quarterly*, 23, 145–58.

REES, A. (1950). *Life in a Welsh countryside. Cardiff:* Welsh University Press.

REDL, F. (1961). Cited in *Television in the lives of our children* by Schramm, W., Lyle, J. & Parker, E. B. Stanford: Stanford University Press.

RILEY, M. W. & RILEY, J. W. (1951). 'A sociological approach to communication research', *Public opinion quarterly*, 15, 445–60.

SANFORD, R. N. (1959). 'The genesis of authoritarianism', in *Psychology of personality* (ed. McCary, J. L.). New York: Logos.

SCHRAMM, W. (1964). *The effects of television on children and adolescents.* New York: Unesco.

SCHRAMM, W., LYLE, J. & PARKER, E. (1961). *Television in the lives of our children.* Stanford: Stanford University Press.

SHERIF, M. & SHERIF, C. W. (1956). *An outline of social psychology* (revised ed.). New York: Harper & Row.

SHERIF, M. & SHERIF, C. W. (1964). *Reference groups.* New York: Harper & Row.

SIEGEL, A. E. (1956). 'Film-mediated fantasy aggression and strength of aggressive drive', *Child development, 27,* 365–78.

SIEGEL, A. E. (1958). 'The influence of violence in the mass media upon children's role expectations', *Child development, 29,* 35–56.

SIEGEL, A. E. (1973). 'Can we await a consensus?', *Contemporary psychology, 18,* 60–1.

SMEDSLUND, J. (1961). 'The acquisition of conservation of substance and weight in children', *Scandinavian journal of psychology, 2,* 71–87.

SMYTH, M. M. & FULLER, R. G. C. (1972). 'Effects of group laughter on responses to humorous material', *Psychological reports, 30,* 132–4.

SURGEON-GENERAL'S SCIENTIFIC ADVISORY COMMITTEE ON TELEVISION AND SOCIAL BEHAVIOR (1971). *Television and growing up: The impact of televised violence.* Washington: US Government Printing Office.

TANNENBAUM, P. H. (1972). 'Studies in film- and television-mediated arousal and aggression: A progress report', in *Television and social behavior,* Vol. 5 (eds Comstock, G. A., Rubenstein, E. A. & Murray, J. P.). Washington: US Government Printing Office.

TOLSTOY, L. (1898a). *What is art?* London: Oxford University Press.

TOLSTOY, L. (1898b). 'Modern Science', in *Recollections and essays* (translated by Aylmer Maude). London: Oxford University Press.

TOOHEY, R. (1972). 'Sesame Street: A case study with three and six year olds'. Mimeograph Montreal: George Williams University.

TRENAMAN, J. (1967). *Communication and comprehension.* London: Longmans.

VERNON, M. D. (1953). 'Perception and understanding of instructional television programmes', *British journal of psychology, 44,* 116–26.

WELLS, W. D. (1971). 'Television and aggression: A replication of an experimental field study', cited in *Television and growing up: The impact of televised violence* (Surgeon-General). Washington: US Government Printing Office.

WERNER, N. E. (1964). 'A study of personality factors in children's thematic apperception of their favorite (child-orientated) television programs'. Unpublished Ph.D. dissertation, University of Chicago.

WERTHAM, F. S. (1968). 'School for violence', in *Violence and the mass media* (ed. Larsen, O. N.). New York: Harper & Row.

WHITE, D. M. (1950). 'The gatekeeper: A case study in the selection of news', *Journalism quarterly, 27,* 383–90.

WOLFE, K. M. & FISKE, M. (1949). 'Why they read the comics', in *Communication research, 1948–49* (eds Lazarsfeld, P. & Stanton, F.). New York: Harper.

WRIGHT, M. E. (1943). 'The influence of frustration upon the social relations of young children', *Character and personality*, *12*, 111–22.

ZAJONC, R. (1954). 'Some effects of the "space" serials', *Public opinion quarterly*, *18*, 367–74.

ZAZZO, B. & ZAZZO, R. (1951). 'Une expérience sur la compréhension du film', *Revue internationale de filmologie*, *2*, 159–70.

Index